Children, Teachers and Learning Series:
Series Editor: Cedric Cullingford

Emotional Problems in Children and Young People

Emotional Problems in Children and Young People

Linda Winkley

CASSELL

To David, Kate and Joe

Cassell
Wellington House
125 Strand
London WC2R 0BB

215 Park Avenue South
New York
NY 10003

First published 1996

British Library Cataloguing-in-Publication Data
A catalogue record for this book is available from the British Library.

ISBN   0-304-32571-6 (hardback)
        0-304-32569-4 (paperback)

Typeset by Action Typesetting Ltd, Gloucester
Printed and bound in Great Britain by
Biddles Limited, Guildford and King's Lynn

Contents

Foreword

The books in this series stem from the conviction that all those who are concerned with education should have a deep interest in the nature of children's learning. Teaching and policy decisions ultimately depend on an understanding of individual personalities accumulated through experience, observation and research. Too often in recent years decisions on the management of education have had little to do with the realities of children's lives, and too often the interest shown in the performance of teachers, or in the content of the curriculum, has not been balanced by an interest in how children respond to either. The books in this series are based on the conviction that children are not fundamentally different from adults, and that we understand ourselves better by our insight into the nature of children.

The books are designed to appeal to *all* those who are interested in education and who take it as axiomatic that anyone concerned with human nature, culture or the future of civilization is interested in education – in the individual process of learning, as well as what can be done to help it. While each book draws on recent findings in research and is aware of the latest developments in policy, each is written in a style that is clear, readable and free from jargon that has undermined much scholarly writing, especially in such a relatively new field of study.

Although the audience to be addressed includes all those concerned with education, the most important section of the audience is made up of professional teachers, the teachers who continue to learn and grow and who need both support and stimulation. Teachers are very busy people, whose energies are taken up in coping with difficult circumstances. They deserve material that is stimulating, useful and free of jargon and that is in tune with the practical realities of classrooms.

Each book is based on the principle that the study of education is a discipline in its own right. There was a time when the study of the principles of learning and the individual's response to his or her environment was a collection of parts of other disciplines – history, philosophy, linguistics, sociology and psychology. That time is assumed to be over and the books address those who are interested in the study of children and how they respond to their environment.

Each book is written both to enlighten the readers and to offer practical help to develop their understanding. They therefore not only contain accounts of what we understand about children, but also illuminate these accounts by a series of examples, based on observation of practice. These examples are designed not as a series of rigid steps to be followed, but to show the realities on which the insights are based.

Most people, even educational researchers, agree that research on children's learning has been most disappointing, even when it has not been completely missing. Apart from the general lack of a 'scholarly' education tradition, the inadequacies of such study come about because of the fear of approaching such a complex area as children's inner lives. Instead of answering curiosity with observation, much education research has attempted to reduce the problem to simplistic solutions, by isolating a particular hypothesis and trying to improve it, or by trying to focus on what is easy and 'empirical'. These books try to clarify the real complexities of the problem, and are willing to be speculative.

The real disappointment with educational research, however, is that it is rarely read or used. The people most at home with children are often unaware that helpful insights can be offered to them. The study of children and the understanding that comes from self-knowledge are too important to be left to obscurity. In the broad sense real 'research' is carried out by all those engaged in the task of teaching or bringing up children.

All the books share a conviction that the inner worlds of children repay close attention, and that much subsequent behaviour and attitudes depend upon the early years. They also share the conviction that children's natures are not markedly different from those of adults, even if they are more honest about themselves. The process of learning is reviewed as the individual's close and idiosyncratic involvement in events, rather than the passive reception of, and processing of, information.

Cedric Cullingford

CHAPTER 1

Children's Emotional Needs: An Overview

Introduction

CHILDREN'S MENTAL HEALTH

Children's emotional needs tend to be a neglected area even though mental health problems are relatively common in children and at present are on the increase (Rutter, 1991). Between 10% and 20% of children may require help at some time in their school lives (Department of Health, 1995). A mental health disorder is defined as a disturbance in the area of relationships, mood, behaviour or development of sufficient severity to need specialist help (Department of Health, 1995).

THE IMPORTANCE OF CHILDREN'S MENTAL HEALTH

Children's mental health is important because:

1. untreated mental health problems create distress not only in the children themselves but in all those who care for them;
2. unresolved problems may continue or become worse in adult life;
3. emotional and behavioural problems in children increase the demands on social services, the educational services and the juvenile justice services (Department of Health, 1995);
4 untreated children's mental health problems will affect the health and happiness of the next generation and the stability of their children.

EFFECTS OF CHILDREN'S MENTAL HEALTH PROBLEMS

Such problems affect many or all areas of a child's life. All people and agencies who work with children have a part to play even though the promotion and maintenance of emotional health may not be their main purpose. Parents, carers, teachers, social workers and GPs are all involved.

Mental health problems affect children's ability to concentrate and their readiness and ability to learn.

INCREASE IN PSYCHIATRIC DISORDER IN CHILDREN AND YOUNG PEOPLE

Recent research shows that there is a steady increase in psychiatric disorder among children and young people, particularly in disorders such as attempted suicide, depression, delinquency, anorexia nervosa and alcoholism (Rutter, 1991).

The Mental Health Foundation (1993) published findings that almost one in four children, especially those living in urban areas, suffer from a degree of mental disorder which has serious and adverse effects on their lives. This figure seems rather high, although it includes children with learning difficulties and children with mild disorders.

Rutter (1991) reports that at least one in ten children suffer from emotional and behavioural problems which need professional help beyond that which can be provided by their teachers.

There has been a 25% increase in serious mental illness among children and adolescents over the period from 1986 to 1991. Figures from the Department of Health (*Independent*, 1994) show that the numbers of children and young people admitted to psychiatric hospitals increased from 7000 in 1986 to 8800 in 1991, with the most striking increase in the numbers of children under the age of 10 years.

INCREASED PRESSURE ON CHILDREN'S MENTAL HEALTH SERVICES

Several factors have increased the pressure on these services:

- Demand on the services has increased in volume and type.
- More difficult, complex and longstanding problems are being referred.
- The understanding of the needs of children and young people has become more sophisticated (Department of Health, 1995).
- Emotional and conduct disorders are the most frequent problems seen in children and adolescents, and both are becoming more common.
- Depression is being increasingly recognized as affecting children, even those as young as 4 or 5 years of age. Children from deprived, unhappy homes are particularly at risk, as are very young children who experience poor quality of parenting or depression in their mothers (Tennant, 1988).
- Increased mental health resources are needed to provide appropriate intervention and treatment for physically and sexually abused children as the numbers increase and effective treatment methods become more established (Wolfe, 1991).

FACTORS RELATED TO THE INCREASE IN CHILDREN'S MENTAL HEALTH PROBLEMS

The social factors responsible have not been clearly identified but the following factors are certainly very relevant:

- Unemployment continues at very high levels.
- The poor are poorer in relation to the rich.
- The rate of homelessness has doubled.
- Pre-school provision is among the worst in Europe (Rutter, 1991).

All these factors are known to increase stress within society which will inevitably affect the children.

It could be argued that late twentieth-century society is facing an internal crisis. The integrity of the family is threatened by an ever-increasing incidence of divorce; the changing role of women within society is having effects on men; traditional attitudes towards work are being threatened by record long-term unemployment and a new policy of short-term contracts; the need to move for jobs is threatening the stability of local communities; and religion has declined.

Some of these changes may eventually prove to be beneficial but each greatly increases the levels of anxiety, depression, neurosis and alienation, and together they threaten the cohesion of society (Holmes and Lindley, 1991).

BREAK-UP OF THE FAMILY

We are facing one of the greatest social changes that has taken place in this country over the last fifteen years, and that is the break-up of the family. The Family Policy Study Centre (Kiernan and Wicks, 1990) reports that by the year 2000 half of the next generation of children will not grow up in a conventional family with two parents, and, if present trends continue, one in five children will experience their parents' divorce before the age of 16. The number of one-parent families has doubled in the past 20 years, with 1.3 million single parents caring for 2 million children. These social changes have enormous implications for children's security and emotional health.

IMPORTANCE OF SCHOOLS

In these circumstances schools have an even more important part to play for children made less secure by disruption and discord within the home. At their best, schools function very much like an extension of a well-functioning family, offering structure, thoughtfulness, and an emotionally stable and caring environment combined with encouragement and clear limits. Research has shown that schools have an important influence on children's emotional development as well as on their educational achievements (Rutter *et al.*, 1979).

Thus although teachers may not see themselves as the guardians of children's emotional health, child psychiatrists have long recognized the important and protective influence of teachers and the potential of schools to provide a secure and positive experience (Rutter, 1985).

Children's emotional development: the foundations

Children need a firm emotional foundation on which to build, and Bowlby (1988) has emphasized the central importance of consistent attention, responsiveness and care in the early years. This is hopefully provided by the parents within a dependable and loving home. The basis for this secure emotional foundation is found within the child's relationship with both parents, and if all goes well is built up and established over the first two years of life.

SENSE OF SELF AND ABILITY TO LEARN

Young infants develop a sense of themselves through an adult's responsiveness and understanding of their needs. Children need these experiences in order to develop a sense of trust in others. Part of their stability comes from feeling securely held in the parents' minds and encompassing care and, as the children grow older, through the setting of clear limits and boundaries.

Children grow through these relationships, firstly with their parents and immediate family, and later through wider relationships at nursery and at school. The foundations of learning are laid in the relationship between the mother and her baby. Memory, curiosity, persistence and concentration are all developed within a relationship, first with the mother, and later with other adults. Children need to be remembered, attended to and listened to in order to develop a secure sense of themselves, and an adult has to do this for the child.

The child needs a sense of self in order to be able to be curious and to want to make sense of the world. The process of learning is not just about content, and it is important to be aware of this in terms of the National Curriculum, where there is a danger of subject matter taking over at the expense of an understanding of how children learn. Learning is about taking in attitudes, strategies and ways of thinking (Rutter, 1985).

INTERNALIZATION

If all goes well, the child takes in and internalizes these good experiences to form a secure emotional base on which to build, and is able to go out into the world with an inner sense of a mother who cares and is interested. This leads to 5-year-old children who, on starting school, have the wish and conviction that they can learn and that the teacher is interested.

The sense of an internal supportive parent is fundamental to the concept of a secure emotional base. The task of any parent is to provide experiences which allow the child to take in and internalize good parental qualities and create his or her own tolerant and supportive parental figures in internal psychic reality. This internal parent is someone who can always be counted on whether the external parent is physically present or not.

Increasingly, there are more children who do not have such dependable backgrounds, but many are able to take in good experiences wherever they find them, and use these experiences to build up a secure base. This sense of inner security gives rise to feelings of hope and is the basis of positive self-esteem.

RESILIENCE

Children need to have developed a certain resilience in order to be able to cope in a class of 30 other children. In addition, this capacity to deal with stress is also necessary for children to be able to fulfil their potential. Rutter (1985) found that the ability to cope with stress comes from secure, affectionate relationships, success and achievement and positive experiences. It is these experiences which enable people to have the capacity to process stress within themselves and feel that they can take some control over the situation and can choose to act rather than just react. Interestingly, Rutter found that people's ability to act positively had much more to do with their self-esteem and feelings of self-efficacy than with their range of problem-solving skills.

Role of teachers and school

FOSTERING CHILDREN'S EMOTIONAL DEVELOPMENT AND LEARNING

It is in these areas of fostering security and self-esteem that teachers can take on a very important role. The whole-school ethos can help in terms of making children feel valued and respected, as well as the work of individual teachers in building relationships, understanding the children's needs, fostering achievement, providing success and setting limits. All schools would claim to be setting out to achieve these goals to a lesser or greater extent but they may not be aware of the underlying research in child development which supports and validates their longstanding practice. It is worth emphasizing, for example, the value of positive relationships and experiences in fostering children's learning as well as their healthy emotional development.

Need for attention

Clearly, all children benefit from and need individual attention from their teachers, but often with large classes the teachers feel that they cannot do enough and it is an impossible task to give individual attention to all 30 children every day. However, it is important to acknowledge that teachers can make a very significant contribution and that this is even more important for children who have been deprived of good enough early experiences and have not yet established a secure inner base. Most teachers are very aware and try to give these children extra attention and care.

> A good example here is one 8-year-old boy who was very unhappy and could not relate to other children. He would surreptitiously hit or poke other children and then try to put the blame onto them. Understandably, he had no friends. When he changed class his new teacher was particularly aware of children with difficulties and she set out to make him feel more valued by giving him jobs and responsibility within the class. He responded well to this and his behaviour towards other children changed. He was now being given the attention he needed and no longer had to provoke the other children for some form of attention, albeit negative.

Providing positive experiences

There is no doubt that schools can provide a sense of security for children from deprived or chaotic homes and offer many good experiences through which children grow and learn. Teachers' genuine interest and encouragement can transform children's lives in countless ways. The long-term educational benefits from positive school experiences probably stem much less from what children are specifically taught than from the effects on the children's attitudes to learning, their self-esteem, their task orientation and their work strategies.

Some may question the emphasis on the role of schools in

fostering emotional development and say that primarily 'we are here to teach the children'. In fact, evidence shows that the two processes go hand in hand. Rutter's findings (Rutter, 1985) relate educational achievements to positive attitudes and positive self-esteem; he writes 'the process of learning is not just about content: learning is about taking in attitudes, strategies and ways of thinking' (Rutter, 1985).

RESEARCH EVIDENCE ON THE ATTRIBUTES OF GOOD SCHOOLS

Schools with an intake of children from similar backgrounds have been found to have very different outcomes in terms of the numbers of children with conduct and behavioural disorders and the rates of absence (Rutter *et al.*, 1979). This research shows that children do best in schools where the staff have clear expectations and consistent methods of disciplining the children, and where they work together as a group and support each other.

In addition the teachers need to be firm but also good-natured towards the children themselves, showing respect for the children and involving them in decisions whenever possible. The research was clear that encouragement and praise achieve better results than methods based on punishment. It is important that teachers have the same standards for their own behaviour as they do for the children's behaviour (Cottrell, 1993).

REFERRAL TO SPECIALIST AGENCIES

Clearly, teachers are well placed to recognize those children whose behavioural and emotional development falls outside the range of normal over a period of time. These children need early referral to an appropriate agency. Generally there will be very few such children in any one school, although schools in areas of social deprivation may well have increased numbers. Rutter *et al.* (1970) and Rutter (1973) found that 7% of 10–11-year-old children in a rural community and 10% in an inner city area had actual psychiatric disturbance.

CHILDREN WITH EMOTIONAL AND BEHAVIOURAL PROBLEMS

The most worrying children in terms of their future adjustment are those who cannot relate to others and are described as solitary and having great difficulty making friends; this is a very strong indicator that the child needs help. Children with psychiatric disorders tend to have abnormal patterns of relationships and the majority fall within two broad groups showing either defiant, aggressive, destructive behaviour (conduct disorder) on the one hand, or withdrawn, more anxious and unhappy behaviour on the other (emotional disorder). Many children with conduct disorder are also unhappy but the behavioural problems tend to predominate, leading to a poorer outcome.

There is evidence that some of the important factors leading to psychiatric disturbance are related to poor parenting skills combined with financial hardship and also to broken homes, especially where there is a history of marital discord or violence (Rutter, 1991). In any of these situations, however, there may be moderating and protective factors.

If problems occur mainly within the school, and for learning problems in particular, referral to an educational psychologist may be most appropriate. Alternatively, if the problems are severe or more widespread, needing more intensive work with the child and family, then referral to a child psychiatry service with a multi-disciplinary team of professionals may be indicated.

LONG-TERM OUTCOME

It is sometimes thought that child psychiatric disorders are not important, that they represent a transient phase and the child will 'grow out of it'. While this may be true for the small number of children who react to a particular short-lived stress, it is not true for the majority of child psychiatric disorders. These increasingly tend to be serious, longstanding problems which need urgent attention, particularly because without treatment there is frequently a poor outlook for adult life.

The established facts are that a large number of children and young people with psychiatric problems go on to suffer from mental disorders as adults. This applies across a wide range of disorders and is particularly relevant for early-onset conduct disorders as well as for emotional disorders. Throughout the country, child psychiatric services are working with increasing numbers of children with serious and longstanding problems.

EARLY REFERRAL

Early referral is of crucial importance because the longer the child's abnormal patterns of development and behaviour continue, the more established they become and the more difficult it is to effect any change. It is very painful to have to think about children's suffering and emotional pain and this may be part of the reason why we as a society are very slow in taking seriously and responding to the needs of the increasing numbers of such children who are being disturbed or damaged by their current situation.

> An example of good practice is the referral by a
> school medical officer of Tim, a 6-year-old boy
> whose parents had separated. He was described by
> his teacher as strikingly unhappy, cut off, in a
> dream world at times, a solitary child with no
> friends and great difficulty in learning. She made a
> plea for something to be done urgently.
> The relationship between Tim and his mother
> started badly with him being unplanned and crying
> persistently as a baby. His mother, because of her

own unmet emotional needs, had no awareness of Tim's needs and had become rejecting. Intensive work with mother and Tim did not improve the situation.

It was arranged for Tim to stay with his father for several weeks and the teacher's observations were extremely helpful in planning for his future. She observed that he was a changed child after this stay, coming back smiling, much happier and more outgoing.

Our assessment relied on the teacher's observations, and as a result we felt that he was still able to be helped and was open to change. For Tim there were grounds for hope as he moved to live with his father permanently although still seeing his mother regularly. Tim blossomed; he started to make friends and was also able to learn. In another year it would have probably been too late.

Something can be done to help the majority of children with emotional difficulties, although more can usually be achieved with children who are referred at an earlier age. Teachers may feel reluctant to refer, thinking they are 'labelling' the child, but the teacher, by not referring, may be condemning the child to a life of unfulfilled potential and unhappiness.

EARLY ONSET OF DISORDER

For the most disturbed youngsters one often finds a continuous pattern of behavioural difficulties and problems in relationships starting at nursery and infant school. These children with an early onset of conduct disorder tend to continue with their disturbance and suffer from mental disorders in adult life. This is particularly true for the young men who end up in service units.

John is a good example of how a child showing disturbed behaviour at an early age can be helped by a team approach. He was a large 5-year-old who was both clumsy and aggressive, leading to severe difficulties with other children to the point that the school was thinking of suspending him. At home he was defiant, demanding and aggressive, and the parents were nearing the end of their tether.

John was referred to our service and as a result was diagnosed as having mild cerebral palsy. Our assessment was that John's behavioural problems resulted from his unmet emotional needs, as his sister also had a chronic illness and she had needed a great deal of her parents' attention. In addition, his physical problems had not been addressed.

It was now arranged for John to have physiotherapy as well as occupational therapy to help with his writing skills. We negotiated through social services a scheme of respite care with another family for several evenings during the week after school. The parents were counselled on how to give John more attention and on management strategies. We liaised regularly with his teacher and John's behaviour improved markedly both in school and at home, although there were still some problems.

Environmental influences

FAMILY RELATIONSHIPS

Psychiatric disorders in general are not part of a person's basic constitution and as such totally fixed and unchangeable, but have been found to be responsive to environmental factors and family circumstances. For instance, the outcome of conduct disorders very much depends on family circumstances. If arguments and discord continue, then the outcome is likely to be poor and the disorder will become chronic. Alternatively, if the situation improves, the child's behaviour is also likely to improve.

It is important to recognize, therefore, that whether psychiatric disorder persists into adult life or not depends to a great extent on family relationships. These are considered in greater detail in Chapter 2.

However, it is also true that the wider environment has a significant influence and the peer group and close relationships can have an important effect for good or ill (Rutter and Giller, 1983).

DEPRIVATION, POVERTY AND CRIME

There are pockets of very severe emotional and social deprivation in all outer city areas as well as within the inner city. The nature of the deprivation inevitably leads to children with considerable learning and behavioural problems. At times some schools feel that all they are offering is 'child-minding' because of the sheer numbers of children involved.

The problem is more likely to be overlooked in the outer city, where it is possible to have two schools within one mile of each other with vastly different catchment areas. One school may draw pupils from a relatively wealthy area, have a large number of professional parents and few discipline problems. The neighbouring school may have the majority of children on free school dinners, many single-parent families and large numbers of pupils with learning and behavioural problems and no additional help.

The Elton Report (DES, 1989) recognized that the problems of managing children with behavioural problems was particularly acute in areas of greatest poverty. Birmingham's City Council has commissioned a report on the extent of poverty within the city, poverty here defined as 'the combination of low income, poor and often damp housing, fuel poverty, poor educational and employment opportunities and bad health'. (Birmingham City Council, 1989) It was found that at least 37% of the city's population are on or below the poverty line.

There has in recent years been an increase in both the number of people living in poverty and the depth of poverty experienced. For example, the number of people dependent on welfare benefits has trebled since 1970. Three million people are now reliant on Income Support, including seven out of ten of the 1.3 million one-parent families. According to this report, the best way of helping these families is to remove the barriers which make it financially disadvantageous to work (Burghes, 1993).

Poverty in itself puts additional very severe stresses on family life, especially if it occurs within a relatively affluent society. For instance, it has been found that single parents who are suffering from financial hardship are more likely to have children at risk for mental health problems than single parents who are financially better off.

It has been found that for many environmental influences relative comparisons are more important than absolute levels (Dunn and Plomin, 1990). The effect of the increasing social divisions within society (Northcott, 1991) means that those who are most disadvantaged feel it more acutely than if there were less extreme differences.

Statistics published by the government in *Social Trends* (Central Statistical Office, 1988) show that in 1985, 30% of the poorest households contained children. Many parents living in very deprived areas are young, single mothers who are under considerable stress both financially and emotionally. Other families living in such areas are very unstable, sometimes violent, sometimes with a parent in prison.

Many of the schools in deprived areas find that they have a 40% turnover of children each year. This presents teachers with a severe challenge in terms of trying to provide a meaningful learning experience to children whom they know will be moving on.

Another area of concern is that in 1993, 13,000 families were living in bed and breakfast accommodation; 8000 of these were in London and 5000 in the rest of the country. It has been shown that children living in such accommodation suffer from more accidents, ill-health and emotional problems.

Research studies have consistently shown that the characteristic social background of persistent delinquents involves a high incidence of broken homes, inconsistent discipline and upbringing, neglect, educational failure and a socially deprived neighbourhood.

Educational failure is linked to truancy and in 1992 it was found that 48% of all offenders had played truant and more than half of all 15-year-olds in inner city schools missed lessons. Of the small group of persistent delinquents who tend to come from the most deprived backgrounds and suffer serious educational failure, the majority have anti-social personality disorders and have been damaged by social and family adversities.

This small group of serious, persistent delinquents causes trouble out of all proportion to their numbers. Without early intervention and treatment many of these youngsters are condemned to suffering from life-long personality disorders (West, 1982).

Research evidence quoted in the Elton Report seems to show that the majority of children who are persistently absent from school live in very poor material circumstances. Absentee pupils are more at risk for involvement in criminal activity than those who attend school regularly.

It is important to be clear that social factors such as poverty, unemployment, poor housing and social deprivation generally, which are all outside the remit of the NHS, have a crucial bearing on the mental health of large numbers of children and young people.

The difficulties faced by schools in deprived areas are obvious and the solutions generally very slow in coming. There is a need for all agencies to work together in a planned way. A carefully planned intervention can make a difference when it involves housing, pre-school education, neighbourhood respite care, an increase in resources to the local schools, after-school activities and support for vulnerable families through social services, voluntary agencies and health agencies. In these circumstances the schools can make a central contribution to the emotional and educational development and well-being of deprived children. This can be achieved through a very positive school ethos, firm and consistent limits, work with parents and work with individual pupils to improve their educational chances and enhance their sense of self-worth.

Other studies have shown that the wider environment also has a significant role to play in the outcome. Good experiences at school are able to protect the child from developing disturbance. The peer group and other close relationships do have an influence. It has been shown that a move from the inner city to an area outside London resulted in a significant reduction in delinquency (West, 1982).

It is clear that good experiences even after childhood can have a positive effect. For example, Quinton and Rutter (1988) found that marriage to a stable partner proved to have a beneficial and protective effect on a group of children brought up in institutions who were showing conduct disorder when young. They also found that good school experiences were protective. The most interesting aspect of these findings is that those who had the ability to plan and felt they had some control over what happened in their lives were the ones who made the happiest marriages. Indeed, any success in school, crafts, sport, responsibility and relationships as well as on the academic side increased the chances that the youngsters would develop these planning abilities.

The important point to emerge is that interventions can actually influence outcome. They influence outcome through their effect on psychological processes involving coping strategies and the sense of agency, competence and capacity to take action when under stress.

Emotionally disturbed and damaged children

Children can be psychologically damaged by early experiences to varying degrees. Children with more minor degrees of disturbance can often be helped through mobilizing a network of professional workers together with support and counselling for the family. Teachers have a central place in this network because they are in daily contact with the child.

It is often helpful to call a meeting of all relevant professionals to agree a plan of action. Several schools are now setting this up on a regular basis, with the schools themselves co-ordinating the meetings. Problematic children are discussed with the educational psychologist and educational social workers as central members of the group. The local child psychiatrist may very well be willing to join such a meeting to contribute to the discussion and help with the thinking.

THE CHILD PSYCHIATRIC SERVICE

Children with moderate degrees of disturbance often attend a child psychiatric or child and family consultation service on a regular basis. These services usually consist of a highly trained multi-disciplinary team made up of a combination of child psychiatrists, specialist social workers, community nurses, child psychotherapists, psychologists and occupational therapists (see Appendix 2). An assessment is made and various combinations of treatment may be offered, including individual psychotherapeutic work with the child, counselling for the parents, work with the whole family, behavioural methods or, rarely, drug treatment.

It is most helpful if the service can offer a multi-disciplinary approach as is recommended by all recent reports on child mental health services (Kurtz, 1992; Hill, 1994; Department of Health, 1995). The treatment recommended in each case would be offered by the most appropriate professional and would depend on the nature of the problem as well as the child's and parents' wishes.

> Philip, for example, was an 11-year-old boy
> referred at the point when he transferred to
> secondary school. He was terrified of the thought of

the new school and had shown previous symptoms of school refusal in his junior school. However, he had overcome these with help from the staff.

At assessment he was full of anxieties which stemmed originally from difficulties in the very early mother – child relationship. Philip was offered individual psychotherapeutic work on a weekly basis because of the longstanding and ingrained nature of his difficulties, whilst his parents were counselled by the clinic social worker. He responded well and managed to attend his secondary school on a regular basis.

LOSS OF MENTAL HEALTH RESOURCES

The situation throughout the country varies but in some areas previous resources are being lost; some child guidance and psychiatric teams are being cut, particularly through the loss of social workers, leading to longer waiting lists and the loss of the vitally important team approach (Hankin, 1993). Therapeutic community schools, who work with the most damaged children, are also at risk through changes in many LEAs' policies related to funding 'out of district placements'. This is a result of cuts in government funding to LEAs.

HOW TO REFER FOR PSYCHIATRIC ASSESSMENT AND TREATMENT

If teachers are in doubt whether to refer or where to refer, they can always discuss this by phone with the local child psychiatrist or other members of the team. Many child psychiatrists will accept direct referrals from a school, although some ask for the referral to come via the child's GP.

SERIOUS FAILURES OF PARENTING

Children with more severe problems are those who have experienced serious failures of parenting which may be caused by neglect, rejection, deprivation or abuse. When all attempts at helping the parents to meet the children's needs fail, then as a last resort the children need to be taken away from the situation which is damaging them. Occasionally there is no other way but to find an alternative home, either a foster or adoptive home, for these children. If at all possible, an adoptive home is preferable as it offers more of a sense of commitment and security to the child.

One commonly seen effect of emotional deprivation on children is to make them more destructive of relationships and of belongings, both their own and others'. This may make it particularly difficult to find suitable adoptive homes for these children. Other children who may pose difficult problems for foster or adoptive parents are those who have been physically or sexually abused. Such children may cope by identifying with the aggressor and go on to abuse others. In fact, about 50% of boys who have been sexually abused go on to sexually abuse other children, and girls are also showing this pattern of response.

SEVERELY DAMAGED CHILDREN

Some children may be so damaged by their earlier experiences that they need long-term specialist help before they are able to live in a family. These children have often had to defend themselves from the emotional pain of feeling rejected and unloved and have erected psychological barriers around themselves like armour. It can be very difficult to reach these children emotionally, as understandably they have had to cut off from their feelings in order to survive. They often develop a hard, tough exterior and may react in a mechanical way or become more like robots without feelings.

Such seriously deprived children can be very aggressive

and destructive within a family, despite being given all the necessary love and care. The psychological barriers built up over years allow no space for the love to reach them. Specialist help is needed to find a way to reach the often very small and vulnerable child within. In some cases a child psychotherapist can work on this while the child remains within the family. Other children are so damaged and their behaviour is so unacceptable and demanding that they cannot be managed within a family setting.

THERAPEUTIC COMMUNITY SCHOOLS

Therapeutic community schools were set up to help severely damaged children and they provide commitment and consistency within a clear philosophical framework. The framework includes an understanding of the deep-seated nature of the children's problems and an understanding of their very disruptive and frequently violent behaviour (Rollinson, 1993).

Some very damaged children are often described as unintegrated. The state of unintegration is seen in the way such children cannot stay with one occupation for long but move from one activity to another, and similarly in their talk they may jump from subject to subject without any obvious links. In school they cannot concentrate or settle but tend to wander out of their seats and disrupt other children. Using a consistent and professional approach, the staff aim to reach the small, vulnerable and often frightened child within who hopefully still has the potential to grow. Other children, despite their surface toughness, are felt to have an emptiness inside.

The staff aim to develop the child's capacity for trust and dependence which the lack of early nurturing has impaired. This is a long and painstaking task. Through their training, the staff are confident in managing the aggression and often violent temper outbursts and at the same time they offer the understanding and emotional security which gradually enables the child to relax some of his or her defences. As a

21

result of such processes, the children gradually take in good parenting experiences which then enable them to integrate themselves around a more secure internal structure, based on good and caring internal parental figures. The majority of these children have never known ordinary good enough parenting.

This approach does work but it may take at least two to three years for the child to become integrated and ready to learn. The process of integration is very much linked to building a secure emotional base. The work is clearly very emotionally demanding for the staff, who commit themselves to be available day and night over a period of several years.

One therapeutic community school was previously an approved school where 80% of the young people re-offended after leaving, whereas now it is a therapeutic community, 80% of the school leavers do not re-offend (Tonkin, 1987). Fortunately, only very few children will need such specialist provision. However, it is useful for teachers to have an understanding of such severely damaged children. It enables them to recognize such a child's need for a particular kind of specialist resource so that they can then join with other professionals and fight for the right provision.

These therapeutic community schools may seem costly at first sight but taking into account the potential savings in the future in terms of secure accommodation, prison or psychiatric hospital costs they offer very good value. They are a preventative, cost-effective resource and need protection as they are becoming increasingly scarce.

Conclusion

Clearly, the subject of children's emotional needs is a painful one and as a society we are very slow in thinking about children's suffering and emotional pain. The situation is worsening, with Rutter's findings (Rutter, 1991) that at least one in ten children is now suffering from a degree of psychiatric disorder which is adversely affecting his life.

The majority of these emotionally disturbed children can be helped by a professional team approach consisting of specialist workers from education, health and social services. At the time of writing it is therefore important to make clear that many of these specialist services are in a serious situation because of continuing under-funding and perhaps from a more general lack of national commitment to children's emotional needs.

Relatively simple changes could make a great difference to many children. For example, the UK has one of the poorest records on nursery provision and yet there is evidence that children who attend nurseries have better educational outcomes, are more likely to have a job and show less delinquency than children who did not have that opportunity (Sylva, 1986).

The very valuable contributions made by teachers appear to be easily overlooked, with the emphasis being on deficits rather than on achievements. This can lead to low morale of staff with consequent effects on the children. It is important to recognize that teachers as professionals are engaged in one of the most difficult, demanding and seemingly unappreciated jobs, that of shaping and educating the next generation.

Summary

1. Children's emotional needs tend to be a neglected area.
2. The numbers of emotionally disturbed children have been increasing throughout the 1980s and 1990s, with an increase in the numbers of seriously disturbed children.
3. Teachers can have an important and protective influence on children's emotional development by providing emotional security and positive experiences: good experiences at school are able to protect children from developing emotional disturbance.

4. The foundations for learning are laid down in the relationship between a mother and her baby.
5. Learning difficulties are often a result of emotional and behavioural disorders and treatment of these underlying disorders leads to improvement.
6. Children thrive on positive experiences, and any success within school, whether in art, sport, responsibility, relationships or on the academic side, increases the chances of children developing good self-esteem, resilience and constructive planning abilities.
7. Educational achievements are related to positive attitudes and positive self-esteem.
8. The majority of child psychiatric disorders increasingly tend to be serious, longstanding problems which, untreated, have a poor outlook for adult life.
9. Early referral is crucial, before maladaptive patterns of behaviour become too entrenched.
10. The majority of children with emotional and behavioural disorders can be helped by a specialist child psychiatric approach, working together with teachers and other professionals within the community.
11. Teachers in their role as educators and as guardians of children's emotional health are engaged in one of the most important, difficult and demanding jobs, which is that of shaping and educating the next generation.

References

Birmingham City Council Urban Policy Team (1989) *Document on poverty: A Profile*. Birmingham: City Council.

Bowlby, J. (1988) *A Secure Base*. London: Routledge.

Burghes, L. (1993) *One Parent Families: Policy Options for the 1990s*. London: Family Policy Studies Centre.

Central Statistical Office (1988), *Social Trends*, No. 18, T. Griffin (ed.) London: HMSO.

Cottrell, D. (1993) Causes of disorder, II. In D. Black and D.

Cottrell (eds) *Seminars in Child and Adolescent Psychiatry*. London: Gaskell, pp. 39–53.

Department of Health (1995) *A Handbook on Child and Adolescent Mental Health*. Oldham, Lancs: HMSO Manchester Print.

DES (Department of Education and Science) (1989) *Discipline in Schools: The Elton Report*. London: HMSO.

Dunn, J. and Plomin, R. (eds) (1990) *Separate Lives: Why Siblings are so Different*. New York: Basic Books.

Hankin, J. (1993) Child and family mental health services: the struggle continues. *Young Minds Newsletter*, No. 16, 2–4.

Hill, P. (1994) *Purchasing Psychiatric Care: Contribution of the Child and Adolescent Psychiatry Section*. London: Royal College of Psychiatrists.

Holmes, J. and Lindley, R. (1991) *The Values of Psychotherapy*. Oxford: Oxford University Press.

Independent (1994) Mental Illness among Children, 23 May.

Kiernan, K. and Wicks, M. (1990) *Family Change and Future Policy*. London: Family Policy Studies Centre.

Kurtz, Z. (1992) *With Health in Mind: Mental Health Care for Children and Young People*. London: Action for Sick Children.

Mental Health Foundation (1993) Mental Illness, The Fundamental Facts. *The Observer*, 19 September.

Northcott, J. (1991) *Britain in 2010*. London: Policy Studies Institute.

Quinton, D. and Rutter, M. (eds) (1988) *Parenting Breakdown: The Making and Breaking of Intergenerational Links*. Aldershot: Avebury.

Rollinson, R. (1993) By my violence you will know me and I will know that I exist. *Young Minds Newsletter*, No. 16, 11–12.

Rutter, M. (1973) Why are London children so disturbed? *Proceedings of the Royal Society of Medicine*, **66**, 1221.

Rutter, M. (1985) Resilience in the face of adversity; protective factors and resistance to psychiatric disorder. *British Journal of Psychiatry*, **147**, 598.

Rutter, M. (1991) Services for children with emotional disorders: needs, accomplishments and future developments. *Young Minds Newsletter*, No. 7, 3.

Rutter, M. and Giller, H. (eds) (1983) *Juvenile Delinquency: Trends and Perspectives*. New York: Penguin Books.

Rutter, M., Maughan, B., Mortimore, P. *et al.* (1979) *Fifteen Thou-

sand Hours: Secondary Schools and their Effects on Children. London: Open Books.

Rutter, M., Tizard, J. and Whitmore, K. (1970) *Education, Health and Behaviour*. London: Longman.

Sylva, K. (1986) Hard choices in the nursery. *Association for Child Psychology and Psychiatry Newsletter*, **8** (4), 16.

Tennant, G. (1988) Parental loss in childhood: its effects in adult life. *Archives of General Psychiatry*, **45**, 1045–9.

Tonkin, B. (1987) Order out of chaos. *Community Care*, 27 Aug.

West, D. J. (1982) *Delinquency: Its Roots, Careers and Prospects*. London: Heinemann Educational.

Wolfe, D. (1991) *Preventing Physical and Emotional Abuse of Children*. London: The Guilford Press.

CHAPTER 2

Psychiatric Disorders in Childhood: Prevalence and Causal Factors

The majority of psychiatric disorders found in childhood and adolescence present as abnormal patterns of behaviour which may be found to a lesser degree in normal children. For instance, a conduct disorder may be said to exist if a child shows continuing aggressive, defiant and destructive behaviour of sufficient severity as to cause ongoing suffering to others.

A working definition is that psychiatric disorder consists of an abnormality of behaviour, emotions or relationships which is sufficiently marked to cause persistent suffering to the child, parents or community and to need specialist help.

The classification of psychiatric disorders tends to concentrate more on external behaviour than on understanding how the child is feeling or what is happening inside the child's mind. Such a classification is useful in giving a broad overview but does not contribute to understanding the individual child and how he or she experiences the world.

Prevalence of psychiatric disorder

This is the proportion of a child population who have psychiatric disorder at a point in time.

PREVALENCE ACCORDING TO AGE

Pre-school children
Richman *et al.* (1982) studied the total population of 3-year-olds in a London borough and found that 1% suffered severe psychiatric problems, 6% moderate problems and an

additional 15% mild problems. Although equal numbers of boys and girls showed disturbance, boys were more likely to be overactive and have difficulties with bladder or bowel control and girls to show nervousness.

Primary school age

The prevalence of psychiatric disorder is higher in urban areas, 25% as compared to 12% in rural areas (Rutter *et al.*, 1975). Overall, between 10% and 20% of children suffer from some psychiatric disorder in the course of their school lives and require specialist help.

Adolescence

There is a definite increase in psychiatric disturbance during adolescence. Rutter *et al.* (1975) in a study of 14-year-olds on the Isle of Wight reported a prevalence rate of 20%.

PREVALENCE ACCORDING TO SEX

Almost all psychiatric disorders in childhood are commoner in boys and this is largely because of the higher rates of conduct disorder and developmental delay. Emotional disorders occur equally in boys and girls.

There is evidence that boys are more vulnerable to adversity in that they mature more slowly than girls and are more susceptible to environmental stress. However, during adolescence the ratio changes, with more girls showing psychiatric disturbance; this is much closer to the adult pattern of illness.

MOST COMMON DISORDERS

The two most common psychiatric disorders in childhood and adolescence are conduct and emotional disorder. These are broad behavioural descriptions and cover a wide range of underlying problems.

Conduct disorder is by far the most common psychiatric disorder found in primary schoolchildren and includes defiant, disruptive, aggressive, destructive behaviour as well as lying, stealing and delinquency. It particularly affects boys, and untreated can have a poor outcome.

Emotional disorders form the second largest group of disorders found in pre-adolescent and adolescent children. Among younger children there are roughly equal numbers of girls and boys affected but during adolescence emotional disorder becomes more common in girls. The main symptoms are related to either abnormal levels of anxiety or to abnormal sadness.

PREVALENCE OF SPECIFIC DISORDERS

1. *Conduct disorder*: 6–11% among 10-year-olds; higher in urban areas. In an inner London borough the figure was 12% (Rutter *et al.*, 1975).
2. *Emotional disorder* (with onset in childhood): 4.5–10% of 10-year-olds (Department of Health, 1995).
3. *Psychotic disorders* (these involve altered contact with reality): schizophrenia and manic-depressive psychosis are extremely rare before puberty, but have a prevalence of 0.1%, or 1 in every 1000 young people at middle adolescence. Schizophrenia in childhood has a suggested prevalence of 0.02% (2 in every 10,000 children).
4. *Anorexia nervosa*: recently, the condition has been found to be becoming more common, with a prevalence of 0.5–1% of 12–19-year-old girls (Department of Health, 1995).
5. *Bulimia*: 1% of adolescent girls and young women.
6. *Encopresis* (faecal soiling): the Isle of Wight study (Rutter *et al.*, 1970) found prevalence rates of 1.3% for boys and 0.3% for girls aged 11–12 years, based on soiling occurring at least once a month.

7. *Enuresis* (bedwetting): prevalence varies according to the population studied and the criteria used. A general approximation is that 10% of 5-year-olds and 5% of 10-year-olds wet the bed at least once a month. Only 1–2% continue into adolescence.

8. *Hyperkinetic disorder* (hyperactivity): recent studies give a prevalence of 1.7% in primary age boys (Department of Health, 1995).

9. *Autism*: a prevalence rate of about 0.04% or 4 per 10,000 children has been found (Wing, 1980). Recently, the numbers of children with autistic spectrum disorders have been increasing.

10. *Educational difficulty*: specific reading retardation – 3.9% (Isle of Wight) and 9.9% (London) of 10-year-olds. General reading backwardness – 8.3% (Isle of Wight) and 19% (London) of 10-year-olds (Department of Health, 1995).

Continuities between child and adult disorder

The question is sometimes asked, 'won't they just grow out of it?' The answer is usually 'no', although with experience we are getting better at predicting who is likely to overcome their symptoms and which groups are less likely to have a good outcome. The work of Robins (1978) has confirmed that there are broad continuities between child and adult disorder. In general, conduct disorders, psychoses and emotional disorders in childhood tend to take the same form, either continuing into or recurring in adult life. Of these emotional disorders, undue anxiety and fears have the best outlook and psychotic disorder the worst.

Factors affecting the outcome of a mental health disorder

1. *The severity*: the severity of the symptoms and natural history of the disorder; the degree of distress caused; the level of care the child needs.
2. *The complexity*: the number of agencies involved; the presence of more than one illness or disorder; the presence of poor parenting, social and emotional deprivation and family disadvantage.
3. *The persistence*: the length of time the disorder has persisted or is likely to continue.
4. *The presence of protective factors*: good-quality early parenting experiences with good attachment relationships.
5. *The presence of risk factors*: marital discord, parental separation or divorce with persisting conflict.
6. *Stressful social circumstances*: poverty; unemployment; financial stress; poor housing and poor environments (Department of Health 1995).

Causal factors

There are factors within the child, the family, society and the child's environment which all have an effect on children's mental health. Factors within the child and family can be summarized as follows:

Family factors:

- marital discord or separation;
- parental mental illness/alcoholism;
- poor parenting skills;
- social and emotional disadvantage;
- violence within the family.

Factors within the child:

- physical, sexual or emotional abuse;
- chronic physical illness;
- extremely traumatic experiences;
- bereavement;
- language or communication difficulties;
- genetic factors;
- brain damage;
- learning difficulties;
- chromosomal or other genetic problems;
- difficult/vulnerable temperament.

Many of these factors interrelate to produce a particular disorder in any one child. The most significant influences are discussed below in greater detail.

FAMILY FACTORS

The care that a child receives from the earliest days has a direct and lasting effect on development. Some of the most important and obvious areas of difficulty are outlined but there are many subtle ways in which early relationships can be damaging to a child, for example a mother who is emotionally unavailable or one who transmits her own problems to the child. It is very rare that a parent deliberately sets out to harm the child, and in the majority of cases it is clear that the parents are doing their best but that they have not had their own emotional needs met and therefore cannot fully meet the child's needs.

Lack of a father figure
The effect seems most obvious on boys. The best situation for children is to be brought up in a loving home by a mother and a father. However, this is not possible for all children for many different reasons and many mothers are able to bring children up successfully on their own.

Biller (1970) found that aggressive and impulsive behaviour was common, learning difficulties occurred and there was difficulty in making friendships among boys who lacked a father figure. Other researchers have shown a relationship between absent fathers and delinquency (Biller and Solomon, 1986). Part of the problem seems to be related to inadequate discipline which is compounded by the effects of poverty, lack of a role model and attempts to assert masculinity.

There is increasing evidence of the very important role that fathers play in bringing up children. Minerva (1991) quotes a study of 128 young offenders who were convicted between the ages of 10 and 13, where it was found that the leading predictive factor for offending was the rare participation of the father in leisure activities. It was also a key factor in those aged 21–32 years who persisted in criminal activity.

Other difficulties may arise relating to the mother's relationship to her son. In some cases the mother may treat the child as a husband, imposing unhelpful burdens and expectations upon him. Sometimes, especially where he has been spoilt, this results in the boy becoming overconfident, arrogant and aggressive. In other instances he has to grow up too quickly and take on responsibilities beyond his years. In both situations there are difficulties for the boy in having his own needs met and establishing a secure sense of identity.

Effects of divorce

Divorce always has effects on the children. Clearly, where there has been serious violence between the parents it may well have beneficial effects on the children's sense of security and mental health. However, in the vast majority of cases there are likely to be some adverse effects on the children, although with sensitive handling these can be minimized.

A recent study by Kathleen Kiernan of the Family Policy Studies Centre (Kiernan, 1991) shows that in addition to the potential for emotional damage caused by divorce, the remarriage of the parent fails to repair that damage. The research shows that although children brought up by a single parent do worse in general than children brought up by both their natural parents, children brought up by a parent and a step-parent often do the worst of all. This research can only suggest broad trends and does not apply to individual cases.

It clearly demonstrates that the harmful effects on the children do not simply result from poverty. Poverty is an almost inevitable problem for single mothers, often a desperate problem. Yet after remarriage the economic position of the family improves but the outcomes for the children do not improve (Hetherington *et al.*, 1992) and frequently become worse.

Divorce has many psychological consequences for children which may show outwardly as behavioural problems and difficulties in learning. There is the disruption to their daily life that a separation brings, but more importantly is the lasting pain and grief involved in losing one parent. Children tend to blame themselves for the break-up and can be left with unresolved feelings of grief and guilt. Paul's story exemplifies this.

> Paul experienced his parents' divorce when aged 4 and did not understand what was happening. He remembers his terrible fear of losing both parents at the time and years later he found he could not get upsetting thoughts about the divorce out of his mind. The pain and continuing upset seriously interfered with his life, affecting his friendships, his learning and his mood.
>
> Paul welcomed sessions with a psychotherapist who was able to take in some of the overwhelming sadness and pain which he conveyed. Alone he had found the pain unbearable but with her skilled help he was able to process and work through the unresolved grief. The process can be likened to enabling a longstanding wound to heal, but recognizing that there will always be a scar.

Divorce can have serious effects on a child's self-esteem, as the parent who leaves has chosen to separate from the child as well as from the partner. It can be felt as a rejection and unless the parents are very aware they can further damage the child's self-esteem by undermining the absent parent, blaming him or her and making out that the other parent is all bad. The impact of inter-parental conflict is a major factor in producing psychological disturbance (Hill, 1993).

Divorce often means loss of contact with other relatives of the partner who leaves, leading to less rather than more support for the child. The greatest wish for the majority of these children is that their parents will get together again, and this again serves to emphasize how important it is to support parents and try to preserve the relationship between mother, father and child.

Hetherington *et al.* (1992) found that young adolescents from divorced families showed more delinquency and behavioural problems and were seen as less competent than a comparable group from intact families.

Divorce from the child's perspective

Parents represent the child's protection against the world. If they separate, the child needs to mourn the loss of the previous family unit as well as the loss of the parent who leaves. Mourning involves anger, guilt and sadness. Children's anxieties may make them hide feelings of anger against the parents and their feelings of insecurity may lead them to become clinging and more attention-seeking.

Children's understanding and reaction to divorce

Obviously this depends on the age of the child. Younger children often have difficulty in understanding and become very anxious and insecure, afraid of being abandoned altogether.

In middle childhood anger can lead children to become sullen and withdrawn or aggressive and defiant. They understand but have difficulty in accepting, almost always wanting their parents to stay together. Divorce, particularly when associated with inter-parental conflict, is commonly a risk factor for adolescent mental health (Hill, 1993).

Adolescents may show their anger and pain by cutting off from their parents and turning to their friends. Divorce seems to have an adverse impact of its own on adolescent psychological functioning (Hill, 1993).

Ways of lessening children's pain and distress

- Children need clear, truthful information, being told in terms that make sense and are appropriate to their age.
- Children need to maintain the best possible relationships with both parents and to be protected from any conflict between them.
- Children need to be able to express their feelings and talk about their fears and anxieties. It is important to listen to the children's point of view and recognize that they may feel that their parents have chosen to do the one thing that they fear the most.
- Children need continuity, which means that it is best not to move the child's house or school, if at all possible. It is important to tell the teacher what is happening so that he or she is in a position to understand and support the child.
- It is important to establish a regular pattern of contact with the non-resident parent.

Depressed mothers

Depressed mothers are less emotionally available to their children. Observational studies of depressed mothers have shown that they tended to talk less to their 3-month-old infants, were more critical of them and were more preoccupied with themselves than a group of mothers who were not depressed (Murray, 1991). The babies were less alert and less engaged with the mother.

The human infant is born prepared for social interaction and very quickly begins to elicit and respond to peculiarly human attributes (Schaffer, 1984). The development of a responsive two-way relationship is clearly disrupted by the experience of an unresponsive mother. At three to six months the babies had adapted to their mother's depressed state and tended to turn away from her and were less responsive. This maladaptive behaviour continued into other social relationships and in this way influenced later development in terms of the acquisition of language and the ability to make close relationships.

Long-term effects on the children of depressed mothers have been described in terms of cognitive deficits, an increased incidence of depression, difficulties with concentration and anti-social disorders of behaviour (conduct disorder). The depressed mothers were more critical and their negative attitude tended to undermine the children's self-esteem and ability to cope with life events.

In these studies the adverse effects on the mother-child relationship and on the children's emotional and cognitive development were found in spite of the mother's depression mostly remitting within a few months (Coghill *et al.*, 1986; Stein *et al.*, 1991). These findings provide a strong argument for the early detection and treatment of postnatal depression.

Children at risk from depression

Jaenicke *et al.* (1987) found that children at risk from depression had more negative self-concepts and more negative attitudes and these seemed related to the degree of blame and criticism they met from their mothers. In addition, it was found that this negative way of thinking influenced how these children experienced the impact of stressful events, which had the effect of making the situation seem worse than it really was.

It seems likely that there is a genetic component to depression and these children may have their ability to cope with stressful situations undermined by their mother's depression in the ways described, as well as inheriting some genetic vulnerability. Certainly, depressed parents have children who are more at risk from depression (Angold *et al.*, 1987).

Psychiatric disorder in parents

There is no doubt that there are links between psychiatric disorder in children and parents. Some of the underlying mechanisms involved have already been discussed in relation to depression in mothers. There are two general ways in which this may happen. Firstly, there is the increased genetic risk for children whose parents have a serious mental illness, such as schizophrenia or manic-depressive illness. However, the majority of psychiatric disorder consists of conditions involving depression and anxiety with or without some degree of personality disorder and there is much less certainty about the importance of genetic factors here.

The second mechanism is the direct environmental impact of living with mentally disordered parents. Rutter (1966) found that the association between psychiatric disorder in the parent and in the child was strongest when the parent's symptoms impinged on or involved the child in some way. Children seemed at most risk if they were victims of aggressive acts or hostile behaviour, were involved in parental delusions, were neglected because of the illness or were part of the parent's symptoms.

Some of the harmful effects may result indirectly from the illness. For instance, Rice *et al.* (1971) showed that the illness itself led to the break-up of the family, with children being placed outside the home either in foster care or with friends or relatives. Other studies of depressed (Cox and Mills, 1983) or schizophrenic (Rodnick and Goldstein, 1974) women have found that the illness may interfere with the abilities needed to parent children successfully. This can occur through the parents being less involved, less able to keep the child in mind and empathize, and less able to sustain positive interactions, and being more frequently involved in unsuccessful attempts to discipline their children.

It is possible that some of the harmful effects are caused by the marital discord which is so frequently associated with mental disorder (Birtchnell and Kennard, 1983). It has been firmly established that marital discord carries a substantially increased risk for psychiatric disorder in children (Emery, 1982).

Rutter and Quinton (1984) set up a four-year study to investigate the links in more detail and they found that, compared to a control group in the general population, the patients' families showed a higher rate of psychiatric disorder in the spouses and a much higher level of family discord. Both of these tended to persist over the four-year period, although the persistence of both was much more marked if the parent had a personality disorder. The psychiatric risk to children was greatest where the parent had a personality disorder which involved the children being exposed to high levels of hostile behaviour. Overall, the children of psychiatric patients had an increased rate of persistent psychiatric disturbance, usually in the form of a continuing conduct disorder.

FACTORS WITHIN THE CHILD

Genetic
Both personality and temperament are to some extent genetically determined. Many personality traits are influenced by genetic factors (Simonoff *et al.*, 1994). The role of heredity is, however, very far from being fully understood.

Genetic factors are not wholly responsible for any childhood psychiatric disorder but play a part in schizophrenia and manic-depressive illness in young people.

Genetic traits are often modified by social and psychological influences and this certainly occurs with the trait known as intelligence. Twin and adoption studies have shown that although intelligence is largely determined by genetic factors, heredity alone is not enough and a responsive and facilitating family background is necessary for the full development of the child's genetic potential.

Evidence has been put forward to show that genetic factors contribute to bedwetting, reading difficulties, travel sickness, nail-biting and thumb-sucking (McGuffin and Gottesman, 1985).

Temperamental factors

The extent to which temperament is inherited is still a matter for debate as the relationships established within the family have a crucial effect on personality development. It has been found that babies show significant temperamental differences from birth and that some babies are very much more placid and easily satisfied than others. The babies with the more difficult temperaments tend to show more behavioural problems as they grow up and the initial temperamental traits tend to persist over time (Thomas and Chess, 1982).

Physical factors/chronic illness

Children with any kind of disability are at greater risk of psychiatric disorder. Those with epilepsy or organic brain damage are at five times the normal risk because of the effects on brain function as well as the psychological effects of chronic illness and disability.

Chronic illness in itself increases the risk by two to three times as a result of the increased stress on the family causing difficulties in family life, neglect of other children, marital disharmony and even breakdown. Parents who are trying to bring up a child with a disability or a chronic illness may become overprotective or experience difficulties in relating to their young child because of the continuing grief, guilt and disappointment associated with the loss of their hoped-for normal child.

ENVIRONMENTAL FACTORS

These include the quality of the neighbourhoods where the children live, housing and schools. The impact of each of these has been discussed in Chapter 1.

References

Angold, A., Weissman, M., John, K. *et al.* (1987) Parent and child reports of depressive symptoms in children at low and high risk of depression. *Journal of Child Psychology and Psychiatry*, **28**, 901–15.

Biller, H. B. (1970) Father absence and personality development in the male child. *Developmental Psychology*, **2**. (2), 181–201.

Biller, H. B. and Solomon, R. S. (1986) *Child Maltreatment and Paternal Deprivation: A Manifesto for Research, Prevention and Treatment.* Lexington, MA: Lexington Books.

Birtchnell, J. and Kennard, J. (1983) Marriage and mental illness. *British Journal of Psychiatry*, **142**, 193–8.

Coghill, S., Caplan, H., Alexandra, H., Robson, K. and Kumar, R. (1986) Impact of postnatal depression on cognitive development in young children. *British Medical Journal*, **292**, 1165–7.

Cox, A. D. and Mills, M. (1983) Paper given to British Psychological Society, Developmental Section, Annual Conference, Oxford.

Department of Health (1995) *A Handbook on Child and Adolescent Mental Health.* Oldham, Lancs: HMSO Manchester Print.

Emery, R. E. (1982) Interparental conflict and the children of discord and divorce, *Psychological Bulletin*, **92**, 310–30.

Hetherington, E., Clingempeel, W., Anderson, E. *et al.* (1992) Coping with marital transitions. *Monographs of the Society for Research in Child Development*, **57** (2–3, Serial No. 227).

Hill, P. (1993) Recent advances in selected aspects of adolescent development. *Journal of Child Psychology and Psychiatry*, **34**. (1), 69–99.

Jaenicke, C., Hammen, C., Zupan, B. *et al.* (1987) Cognitive vulnerability in children at risk for depression. *Journal of Abnormal Child Psychology*, **15,** 572–99.

Kiernan, K. (1991) *The Effects of Divorce on Children.* London: Family Policy Studies Centre.

McGuffin, P. and Gottesman, I. (1985) Genetic influences on normal and abnormal development. In M. Rutter and L. Hersov (eds) *Child and Adolescent Psychiatry: Modern Approaches*, 2nd edn. Oxford: Blackwell, pp. 17–33.

Minerva (1991) Views. *British Medical Journal*, **302**, 1476.

Murray, L. (1991) Postnatal depression and infant development. *British Medical Journal*, **302**, 978–9.

Rice, E. P., Ekdahl, M. and Miller, L. (1971) *Children of Mentally Ill Parents: Problems in Child Care*. New York: Behavioural Publications.

Richman, N., Stevenson, J. and Graham, P. (1982) *Pre-school to School: a Behavioural Study*. London: Academic Press.

Robins, L. (1978) Sturdy predictors of adult antisocial behaviour. Replication of longitudinal studies. *Psychological Medicine*, **8**, 611.

Rodnick, E. H. and Goldstein, M. J. (1974) Premorbid adjustment and the recovery of mothering function in acute schizophrenic women. *Journal of Abnormal Psychology*, **83**, 623–8.

Rutter, M. (1966) *Children of Sick Parents: An Environmental and Psychiatric Study*. Institute of Psychiatry Maudsley Monographs, No. 16. London: Oxford University Press.

Rutter, M. (1991) Services for children with emotional disorders: needs, accomplishments and future developments. *Young Minds Newsletter*, No. 7, 3.

Rutter, M. and Quinton, D. (1984) Parental psychiatric disorder; effects on children. *Psychological Medicine*, **14**, 853–80.

Rutter, M., Tizard, J. and Whitmore, K. (1970) *Education, Health and Behaviour*. London: Longmans.

Rutter, M., Cox, A., Tupling, C., Berger, M. and Yule, W. (1975) Attainment and adjustment in two geographical areas II. The prevalence of psychiatric disorder. *British Journal of Psychiatry*, **126**, 493–509.

Schaffer, H. R. (1984) *The Child's Entry Within A Social World*. London: Academic Press.

Simonoff, E., McGuffin, P. and Gottesman, I. (1994) Genetic influences in normal and abnormal development. In M. Rutter, E. Taylor and L. Hersov (eds) *Child and Adolescent Psychiatry: Modern Approaches*. Oxford: Blackwell, pp. 129–51.

Stein, A., Gath, D., Bucher, J., Bond, A. and Cooper, P. (1991) The relationship between postnatal depression and mother child interaction. *British Journal of Psychiatry*, **158**, 46–52.

Thomas, A. and Chess S. (1982) Temperament and follow-up to adulthood. In R. Porter and G. Collins (eds) *Temperamental Differences in Infants and Young Children*. London: Pitman, pp. 168–72.

Wing, L. (1980) *Autistic Children: A Guide for Parents*. London: Constable.

CHAPTER 3
Psychological Development: Early Childhood

Psychiatric disorders in children need to be seen within the framework of normal child development. The first two years of life are particularly important as they lay the foundation for all future growth. There are two main models of child development which hopefully can be brought together to provide a fuller and more integrated picture of children's very early emotional and cognitive development.

The models being used here are taken from developmental psychology and psychoanalysis. Both of these disciplines rely on detailed observations as well as, in the case of psychoanalysis, some reconstruction from clinical material provided by patients of all ages, including work with very young children. Early childhood experiences have a special significance, as they impinge on the child's developing mind and may set in train patterns of response which are difficult to modify or change.

Pregnancy

Pregnancy is a time of preparation, both emotionally and physically, for motherhood. For many women it is a rewarding and fulfilling experience and a time of special contentment. The first task for the new mother is to accept the young life growing inside her, and in these early stages to be able to experience the baby as a benign part of herself.

Unconscious identifications

The next event is linked to the first movements, when the mother begins to recognize the stirrings of a separate being. At this stage she may unconsciously identify with her baby, and many of her fantasies and feelings may stem from her earlier relationship to her own mother. If all goes well she will be able to identify with both the mother and the baby. The experience of pregnancy at an unconscious level can facilitate a re-working of unresolved conflicts to do with her own dependency needs through these identifications.

Pines (1981) describes how the mother, through the mediation of her unborn child, can re-experience the rewarding aspects of her early relationship with her own mother and in this way revitalize herself and make progress in her own development as a separate individual. This facility to feel in contact with a good mother inside herself increases the new mother's confidence and becomes a source of inner strength. It is very similar to the process whereby toddlers learn to progressively separate from the mother by being able to run back and re-establish contact with her whenever they feel the need.

As the pregnancy progresses and all goes well, the mother has space in her mind for the growing baby as well as for her established family. One very young mother I saw during pregnancy was clearly focusing her attention inwards while with me, and a recurrent theme in our work centred on her deep-seated feelings about protecting the unborn baby and keeping the baby safe. I felt she was identifying both with the baby who needed protection and with a caring and concerned mother, in touch with her baby's needs. It seemed important to keep both her and the baby in my mind to support her while she consolidated this work of identification, especially as her external circumstances were difficult. However, I was reassured by her deep-seated caring and nurturing feelings towards the baby which continued after the baby's birth.

Mothers under stress

If a mother has particularly strong unmet needs, the arrival of a new baby may stir these up in an unmanageable way and a child part of the mother may feel in competition with her child for nurturing and attention. If this dynamic continues in a consistent way, the baby's needs may not be recognized or adequately met.

Women who have had their early emotional needs met to a large extent during their own childhoods will generally find it easier to accommodate the new baby and make space in their minds for the baby as well as for their existing family, including their other children.

Sadly, not all mothers and babies have a good start. The mother may not want the baby or there may be severe stress through illness, poverty or marital tensions. These difficulties can be overcome if the mother and baby are sufficiently robust. Sometimes specialist intervention is necessary and child psychotherapists are increasingly working with mothers, fathers and their young babies.

Mothers are especially vulnerable during and in the early days after the birth. A difficult or traumatic delivery can have repercussions for both mother and child, which means that nurses and doctors need to be very aware of the emotional impact of the experience. Some premature baby units are particularly aware and encourage mothers to put the premature babies to the breast regularly and encourage parents to be very involved with all aspects of the baby's care, including holding and cuddling. The staff need to hold in mind the experience from both the mother's and child's point of view. The staff may well need support as this can be extremely painful.

Early development

STATE OF 'AT ONENESS'

Psychoanalytic writers such as Winnicott postulate that during the first weeks of life there is a continuation of the emotional state of 'at oneness' with the mother which began within the womb. Many mothers feel this consciously, as, for example, one mother who said, 'the baby is an extension of me'. Winnicott (1975) believes that it is important for the child's future development to feel that he or she is able to create the mother when she is needed and in this way the baby has some control. He feels this stage is necessary in order to counteract the reality of the baby's total dependence. The mother fosters this illusion by being almost totally available to meet the baby's needs at the beginning of life, and she gradually allows the illusion to fade as the baby becomes able to cope with some frustration.

Harris (1975) describes how the very early experience of feeling at one with an ideal mother is important for future development. It lays the foundation for states of total happiness and fulfilment. In addition, such states of mind create a memory of a totally blissful experience, an experience of what we might call heaven. The memory remains within the mind as something to strive for and of infinite value. This is one factor which enables people to hold on to feelings of hope in times of despair.

MATERNAL REVERIE AND CONTAINMENT

Bion (1962) describes this very early experience slightly differently, focusing primarily on the mother's state of receptiveness to her baby, which he calls maternal reverie. This involves the mother monitoring her baby in a very intuitive manner and lasts for the first few months of the baby's life. At this time the mother's mind is uniquely focused and open to that of her child in such a way as to make her available to take in any sudden anxieties or fears.

Very young babies try to hold themselves together when the mother is absent through sucking their thumb or fingers or attaching their gaze to a light or toy. However, if the mother is away too long the baby may start to experience feelings of falling apart or disintegration (these words are being used as the nearest available to describe feeling states before the baby has words). It is during the time immediately after birth that the baby's primitive anxieties are likely to be at their height. The mother takes these anxieties into her own mind intuitively, filters them of their distress and returns them to her baby in a far less threatening form. This process, described by Bion (1962) as 'containment', enables the baby's mind to start to work on the experience for itself.

The mother's focused state of mind continues for some months, being gradually phased out as the baby slowly learns to process the components of emotional experience on his or her own. This ability is based on an internalization of and an identification with a thinking, containing mother and at this stage (about 6 months of age) the baby becomes able to hold on to an experience and memory of the mother. This helps the baby cope with separation: when the mother leaves, the baby now has the memory and assurance within that she will return. Processes of integration centre round this internalized reliable parental figure.

Of necessity the baby is at the centre of the mother's attention during this phase of gradual processing and learning. The intuitive mental processes are seen outwardly in the way a mother responds to her baby's distress, picking the baby up, and trying to understand and offer comfort.

The mother, through her protection and care of her newborn baby, enables the baby to gradually build up the confidence to reach out to new experiences. She carefully controls and moderates experiences so that the baby is not overwhelmed and can take these in and assimilate them.

ORGANIZATION OF THE BABY'S EXPERIENCE INTO GOOD AND BAD

At the beginning the mother fulfils two main needs for her baby. First, she supplies the love, security and understanding together with the milk and a loving feeding experience. Secondly, she takes away the bad experiences, the pain, the frustration and the physical discomforts such as urine, faeces and wind. The baby, from the repeated experiences of needs being met, gradually organizes them into a picture of the mother, a good mother who offers comfort, thoughtfulness, liveliness, company and playfulness (Harris, 1975).

Similarly the baby organizes the bad experiences, the failures of understanding or when the mother is not there, leaving the baby in a state of anxiety, fear or terror, and makes these into a picture of something bad and frightening. In this way internal representations of both a good and a bad mother are created. These are thought to form the basis for images of good and bad figures such as beautiful fairy godmothers and wicked witches.

However, when the mothering is 'good enough' the good mother is much stronger and the baby holds on to her as a part of himself or herself, the very centre of his or her being (Harris, 1975). As the baby matures and gradually realizes that the good mother is the same person as the bad mother who inevitably frustrates sometimes, the baby becomes able to integrate the good and the bad, the loving and the hating feelings through a central awareness of the mother as good and loving and based on love for her. This new capacity for integration, which occurs around the age of 6–7 months, allows for more complex perceptions of the world, including more awareness of self and others.

Stern (1985) recognizes this new capacity, which he calls 'intersubjective relatedness', occurring at about 7–9 months when he feels the baby has a qualitatively different sense of self and others, in that the baby is able for the first time to hold other people in mind and is aware that others hold him or her in mind. The baby is now able to attribute motives and intentions to others and to correctly identify feeling states in other people. The latter ability has recently been found to be missing in autistic children (Hobson, 1989).

In order to be able to organize experience the baby needs the mother to be available as a focus for development. Being with a young baby for significant periods of time has its own particular stresses. The mother needs to be able to identify with her baby in order to be in touch with the baby's needs. This means that she has to identify with the helpless baby, which is extremely painful at times. There is also the danger that she may lose her adult self, and here the support of her family and friends is essential. The mother needs adult company to keep her in touch with the adult world and to help her to hold on to confidence in her adult self.

Sense of self/identity

It is important for anyone working with children to have some understanding of how children develop a secure sense of self (which is the same as a sense of identity), as this is at the heart of thinking about children's emotional development and needs. Stern (1985) postulates that it is the sense of self which forms the organizing focus for development. Although difficult to define, he places the sense of self at the very centre of any thinking about the baby's early experiences of life. The way that each individual processes experience and information in a unique and subjective manner through his or her own individual organizational process is what Stern would call the sense of self.

Despite the difficulties in definition, there is no doubt that people generally do have a very real sense of self which permeates all areas of their lives. Psychoanalysts would say that the sense of self is based on the equally individual and unique internalization of parental figures and grows out of relationships with others, in particular, during the early months, from a central relationship with the mother. This relationship provides the fixed point around which the baby organizes experience. A baby's sense of self grows out of seeing himself or herself reflected in the mother's eyes and face, her loving handling and, in the early days especially, being at the centre of her mind.

Bowlby (1988) supports this view, stating that the sensitivity of the mother to the infant's needs is the most important determinant of healthy emotional development. Indeed, experimental work by Ainsworth *et al.* (1978) has repeatedly confirmed the powerful correlation between maternal sensitivity and an infant's later feelings of security and well-being as shown by social competence and higher self-esteem.

These different perspectives on development are not incompatible. The sense of self, which derives from the baby's relationship with the mother as the fixed point, may then be seen as the organizing focus for development.

Both psychoanalysts and developmental psychologists postulate that babies begin to experience a sense of emerging self from birth. From 2 to 6 months of age, if all goes well, babies consolidate the sense of a core self as a separate, cohesive and bounded unit.

It is important to maintain a sense of continuity for the baby from life inside the mother to life outside. Too many changes are likely to disrupt the process whereby the baby starts to recognize and anticipate events and so begins to build up a sense of self and the mother (Shuttleworth, 1989).

This links with Bion's work on maternal reverie and how the mother protects the baby from undue emotional impingements. The amount of frustration that a very young baby can bear without serious consequences for future mental development is limited and mothers need to intuitively modulate their babies' experience.

EFFECTS OF TRAUMA

With the above in mind, it is important to recognize that it is not always possible to protect the baby. Traumatic events occurring during the baby's birth can seriously effect emotional development.

Autistic states of mind
In the most extreme case a baby who nearly dies at birth can be so affected by overwhelming feelings (terror and fear of annihilation) that the immature mind reacts to such a massive impingement by various degrees of cutting off from the world. It seems likely that some more innately vulnerable babies may cut themselves off into autistic states of mind as a result. Not all cases of autism can be related to psychological trauma in this way but certainly some can.

Psychotic states of mind
Traumatic events or severe lack of receptivity to the infant's emotional needs over time, or a particularly vulnerable temperament, may also contribute to the development of abnormal mental states. The more psychotic type of defences lead to a child who has difficulty in distinguishing between reality and fantasy and who shows changeable mood states for no external reason. Some of these children are later described as showing a 'Jekyll and Hyde' type of personality because of unpredictable changes from being a pleasant, responsive child to someone totally ruthless and unscrupulous. Clearly this is an extremely serious condition and the child needs expert help from the child psychiatric team, preferably with input from a child psychotherapist as early as possible.

Barrier between parents and baby
In other cases painful and difficult births may not have been talked about and processed by the parents, who are left

feeling traumatized by the experience. The baby has also experienced hurt and fear and, without anyone realizing it, the trauma can cause a barrier to come between the parents and the baby. The result may be a baby who screams for hours, refuses to feed and fails to develop any affection for the parents. In these cases early intervention is crucial. The child psychotherapist is trained in understanding feelings which cannot be expressed in words, and works on building up the trust and relationship between the parents and baby.

In many cases it takes only a few months of such specialist work before the problems are overcome. The parents may need help in coming to terms with the totally unexpected trauma, and encouragement in understanding the baby's reactions and feelings. The baby may feel very isolated, frightened and hurt and may need a lot of reassurance in order to start to trust and turn to the parents for comfort. Parents may blame themselves when in reality no one is to blame for the traumatic start of the relationship with their baby.

INTEGRATION

Assuming that all goes well, Stern (1985) describes how an internal change takes place at around 2–3 months of age, reflected in the quality of relationships; young babies begin to make eye-to-eye contact, smile more frequently and start to coo. There is a growing sense of the baby as a person with a sense of self as well as of others. It is well known that development occurs in leaps and bounds and there are times of relative quiet to allow for consolidation between periods of rapid change. This social change at 3 months is also seen in observational studies of babies.

ASPECTS OF THE SENSE OF SELF

Stern (1985) describes one important form of organization, which is a stable and unchanging pattern of awareness. He believes that this forms the basis for the developing sense of self, particularly as it may exist before the child has words. It includes the sense of having control over actions, of physical cohesion, of continuity in time and of having intentions in mind.

It is important to add that these different aspects of the sense of self which form the foundation for individual and social development grow through the relationship with a loving and responsive mother or other care-giver. Dividing the sense of self into some of its component parts is helpful in understanding how disturbed children have difficulties in functioning. For instance, some very disturbed children do not have a stable pattern of awareness and this may link with more psychotic ways of functioning. These children suffer inexplicable mood and personality changes which are not related to external events but are regulated by internal shifts in mental state. In short, they have not developed a secure sense of self with continuity over time. Many of these children have suffered from severe emotional deprivation and have not been given the necessary early loving relationships.

There are two main ways in which such a distortion of normal functioning can occur. The first is through very adverse environmental factors and the second is as a result of being born with a particularly envious and destructive temperament.

> One child, Simon, who understandably was unable to integrate his early experiences of love and hate and consequently the good and bad sides of himself, had had the terrible experience of being hated by his mother during the earliest months of his life.
>
> Although he received more caring experiences later on, his sense of self had been damaged and he was unable to bring the feelings of love and hate together in a way that allowed the love to modify the hate. This was because he had actually experienced more hate than love at a very crucial developmental stage, leaving him full of unconscious hate and rage which could be triggered by

> very minor events. Simon developed two sides to his personality, a kinder and more caring side, and an angry, destructive and ruthless side. He could change between these two quite suddenly and had no conscious control.

Children like this are often described as having a 'Jekyll and Hyde' personality and have not established a secure sense of identity. In my experience temperamental factors on their own are much rarer as a cause, but Gary is an example of this.

> Gary developed the same condition despite being given a sufficiently good start in life. In his case he was unfortunate enough to be born with a particularly envious and destructive side to his personality. This prevented him from taking in the love that he was given and left him feeling deprived and hating his mother for this. Again because of the strength of the hatred he was unable to integrate inside himself the loving and the hating feelings so that he also developed these two very separate sides to his personality.

Genetic unfolding

Some aspects of development are innate and follow a genetic unfolding, a biological process. It has been suggested that smiling which starts at 6–8 weeks is part of a genetic unfolding and this may be so, but for the baby's responsiveness to continue there must be a warm and encouraging mother to respond to these overtures.

Two-way relationship

Developmental psychologists have described the 'interactional synchrony' between a mother and her baby which takes place unconsciously (Trevarthen, 1993). Microanalysis of videotapes have shown that babies on the first day after birth move in precise synchrony with adult speech. Babies of 2 months are frequently found to imitate the mothers' mouth and tongue movements as she speaks, and the mothers frequently mimic the babies' facial expressions. The significance of the turn-taking shown by mothers and babies from the earliest months is central to the development of later mutually responsive relationships. They use what Trevarthen calls 'protoconversation' for their reciprocal exchanges with each other.

The total dependence of the very young baby soon changes, and by the 3–5 month stage the baby is progressively taking control of the relationship. The baby begins and ends the social engagement through the use of direct eye contact. In gazing, smiling and vocalizing the baby is a very potent social partner and these are all powerful forms of social communication. From the very earliest days the baby influences the parents as well as being influenced by them.

Attachment

Bowlby's work (Bowlby, 1988) on the central importance of attachment to a responsive and dependable mother or caregiver can be integrated into the findings of developmental psychologists and of psychoanalysts. The patterns of attachment which change and develop to maintain attachment at different ages form part of the overall process of development, both as seen in external behaviour and as reflected in internal relationships.

Attachment theory can now be used to describe a set of infant behaviours, a relationship between a mother and her baby, a theoretical construct and a subjective experience for the baby in terms of 'internal working models' or 'representations'.

Internal working models

The concept of internal working models is describing something very similar to the idea of internalized parental figures. Klein (1975) describes how young children internalize mother and father figures based both on their real experiences of their parents and also on internal factors relating to their own temperament; for instance, a child with a naturally loving temperament is more likely to take in experiences of loving parents and vice versa. These internalized figures can be modified by new experiences throughout life, and that awareness forms the basis of much analytical work. Analysts through their training set out to provide an experience of sensitive parenting which may have been missing originally, blocked off or otherwise attacked by a child with a particularly difficult and vulnerable temperament. In all these cases the analyst is aware of mental processes which may prevent the taking in of a good experience.

These internal working models based on parental figures, if good, form the basis for feelings of internal security and well-being. If they are less well established or bad, in terms of being, for instance, unfeeling, harsh or cruel, they may leave the individual exposed to feelings of low self-esteem, insecurity and self-criticism as well as causing difficulties in establishing trusting and mature relationships.

All child health practitioners now agree on the central importance of parenting and in particular on the importance of being sensitive and responsive to the child's needs. A child needs to be wanted, listened to, thought about, remembered in absence, empathized with and understood; in short, to be loved (Holmes, 1980). In addition, a child needs structure to his or her life, with regular routines and, later on, clear rules and limits for unacceptable behaviour.

The concept of internal working models or internal parental figures provides a way of understanding how experiences of parenting affect our emotional development, tend to be passed on from one generation to another, and deeply influence how we experience the world.

Memory

Moore (1993) describes how research work is being under-taken based on the idea that human beings have memories related to different senses or modalities as well as having multiple layers of memory. It is postulated that from birth or perhaps even earlier the infant has available two types of memory. The first is a memory for content, events and objects which is called declarative memory and is primarily based on words. The second is a totally separate system, known as non-declarative or procedural memory. It relates to how people interact, what occurs between two people, habits, gestures and learnt skills such as bicycle riding or swimming.

Procedural memory is not always accessible to declarative memory (Squire, 1992). One example is trying to describe how to ride a bicycle. Any verbal description misses out on the body memory of what it means to pedal and keep one's balance. All physical skills, which once learnt are never forgotten, form part of procedural memory. In certain disturbed mental states or following a brain lesion, memory can be severely affected. However, a patient with such a brain lesion still knows how to ride a bicycle because the lesion only affects declarative memory (Cohen and Squire, 1980).

Moore postulates that babies from the first days after birth begin to anticipate interactive processes with the mother and begin to organize their experience around these. At 6 months of age the baby has no way of talking but the memories are there, built on the verbal interactions with the mother. The timing of the turn-taking in 'conversations' between baby and mother is exactly the same as that between two adults.

This is a development of Trevarthen's work (Trevarthen, 1993) on 'interactive synchrony' which demonstrates the features of basic emotional communication between a mother and her baby, involving adjustments to the timing, form and energy of their expressions in order to obtain synchrony and harmonious transitions in their emotional relationship. The infant develops, as the adult has developed, an interactive knowledge about give and take within relationships and uses this knowledge without being consciously aware. This is a typical procedural memory.

Effect of disturbed relationships

When relationships between mothers and their babies are disturbed, these patterns of disturbance are also built into procedural memory. Moore describes two characteristic responses by young children to mothers who are preoccupied with their own internal problems and are unable to respond to their children as separate individuals.

First, there are the children who remain engaged with the mother for every second she is in the room, noticing mother's mental state and settling her down. These children seem to use constant care-giving towards their mother in order to keep themselves alive in her mind. The second broad group are known as the 'punitive controlling' children. They respond with anger and reject their mothers. At 5–6 years of age these children are still angry and talk to their mothers in negative ways, for example 'I'm not talking to you'. Here again the motive is the same, which is to keep the mother engaged with them and to stay alive in her mind.

Both of these responses are related to procedural memory. The children unconsciously try to fit the model which mother wants and which fits most closely with her inner world. These mothers' early life experiences are so unresolved that they unconsciously re-live them with their babies. A pattern is set up before there is any thinking about meaning in a relationship, and procedures are established in a very unconscious way. These ways of relating, based on relationships with internal parental figures, are thought to be transmitted from generation to generation through procedural memories. Moore has used the work of Bowlby and the more recent research on memory to expand our understanding of how pathological ways of relating are passed on from parent to child.

Resilience and empowerment

From the age of 3–9 months the attachment to a care-giver becomes a means by which the infant can overcome and weather stresses. A mother or father can now calm an upset or frightened baby with the help of an established and familiar style of response. Such an experience of being repeatedly calmed will help the infant to develop a sense of confidence and trust in the world and establish a sense of inner security and a feeling that he or she is safe. It is through repeated experiences of things being made all right, of finding out that the world can be made safe, that the baby eventually builds up a capacity for resilience.

Where parents have been emotionally deprived themselves it is extremely difficult for them to be fully responsive to their baby's needs but despite some difficulties the majority do develop a strong and mutual attachment. Problems arise where there is a major mismatch between the needs of the infant and the care-taking abilities of the parents. Research has shown that children who were insecurely attached to their mothers in infancy and showed this by repeated turning away and not greeting their mother after a short absence were significantly less resourceful and showed less resilience at 6 years of age.

Most parents will automatically echo or mirror the infant in play, which fosters the infant's sense of value as an individual as well as fostering the ability to become involved in a two-way relationship. Babies experience of how they can affect changes in the environment gradually brings about an awareness of causality and the power they have to influence things. This sense of empowerment is one of the very important sources of a child's self-esteem.

An environment which is unable to read the infant's signals and to respond to them is very likely to inhibit the development of a sense of internal security, inhibit normal emotional growth and compromise the development of later coping strategies. The majority of babies and young children are reasonably adaptable and many can recover from adverse early experiences if given the chance.

Autonomy and independence

Independence grows out of secure attachment (Bowlby, 1988). This is seen as early as 3 months in the way securely attached infants regulate their engagement with others; they can end an interaction by looking away and start it again through gazing, smiling and vocalization. Similarly, at the age of 1 year infants will move away from their mother but need to know she is still there and that they can choose when to return. Many of these developmental tasks are in fact issues which need to be struggled with throughout the whole of life. Certainly the capacity for independence and the development of individuality both come into this category.

Self-esteem and self-confidence

These two concepts seem inevitably linked but it is useful to consider them separately. Self-esteem has been broken down into six different aspects which are helpful in thinking about how to take care of children.

1. The sense of being safe, of physical and emotional security; this is the first and core aspect which is crucial and yet may not immediately spring to mind. This sense is compromised in any child who has been physically, sexually or emotionally abused and can be used to emphasize to professionals the central importance of ensuring that the child is safe. Jones (1994) and his

researchers found that 43% of children who had been investigated for sexual abuse were not felt to be safe from further abuse and were offered no follow-up service by social services, presumably due to lack of resources. This is extremely worrying.

2. The sense of intrinsic worth and of being valued for oneself.

3. A sense of identity; the feeling of having a sense of self in relation to other people and to the activities of daily living.

4. A sense of affiliation, the feeling of belonging and being linked to others; this provides an anchor to the wider community, together with a sense of belonging to the human family.

5. A sense of competence; a feeling of empowerment and of being able to cope with life.

6. A sense of mission; having a sense of what one wants to achieve.

Self-confidence is clearly closely related to self-esteem. Trevarthen (1994) has developed a new concept, 'the infant as hero'. He is referring to the child's wish to be admired and to be at the centre of the stage. Young children enjoy showing what they can do. Trevarthen is drawing our attention to the importance of allowing the child to 'perform' for adults and to experience this sense of admiration in order to build up self-confidence. Both self-esteem and self-confidence need to be built up by adults over the first 16 years of life.

Development of intimacy

While separation may be proceeding in some areas, it is interesting to realize that the infant from 9 to 18 months is also engaged in finding new ways of being with another person which have only just become possible. These include learning that one's subjective life, one's thoughts and feelings, can be shared with another.

Stern (1985) describes how infants at 9 months of age seem to sense that they have an inner, subjective life of their own and that others do also. From 15 months of age the sense of intimacy with others broadens through the use of words and through shared meanings. These developments are very early precursors of an emerging capacity for empathy.

Separation

The baby gradually has to recognize that he or she is not the same as the mother and that she has a life of her own. It can be hard for the babies to realize that they cannot control her and make her do what they want. Harris (1975) describes how children try to cope by holding on to reminders of their experience of a comforting mother through cuddling a teddy or by using memories and imagination. Some children find it more difficult than others to let their mother go with love. Those who find it easier to separate are able to let their mother go at the same time as being able to hold on to a good experience of her in their minds.

Weaning, which means giving up the breast or the bottle, usually occurs at about 9–11 months of age. It involves separation and both the baby and the mother have to work on this. As Harris says, it is a psychological as well as a physical process and involves a little mourning. It means giving up something known and valued for the sake of growth. Here it represents a move away from dependence and allows for the introduction of new foods, new experiences.

All future changes or developments will involve similar processes of loss as well as gain. If parents are emotionally in touch, each stage of their child's development may re-awaken their own memories and experiences at that age. However, it is important for parents to recognize that their children may feel differently and have different experiences from themselves.

Dealing with frustration

Parents often need to use their intuition to decide whether a child can cope with the anxiety and frustrations of a given situation of whether they need to intervene to protect the child from being overwhelmed. Children need to be allowed to test themselves within the safety of a framework where a trusted person is available to step in and help. Everyday situations provide many opportunities for growth, for instance learning to feed themselves, manipulating a toy, or, later on, dressing themselves, coping with separations and mixing with other children. These all represent moves away from dependence and towards independence.

However, it is important to move at the child's pace. Some children are pushed to grow up too quickly, and others to conform too much, with the result that they suppress parts of themselves. The effects of trauma and deprivation have been discussed earlier in this chapter.

Any experience which is too much for the child to manage runs the risk of damaging the child's mental functioning. It may be a one-off severe trauma or more regular repeated experiences over time. As Harris writes, if anxiety becomes too strong the child is tempted to turn away and avoid the frustration, thereby shutting out and limiting what he or she experiences. As a result, the child does not learn how to cope with the frustration in a way which builds up coping strategies and resilience.

Children can also achieve the same result by splitting off impulses and feelings within themselves that give rise to pain. If these processes become habitual and part of their normal way of responding to the world, children become cut off and fail to connect experiences of seeing and feeling. Such mental processes also tend to limit and fragment children's experience of other people.

In extreme cases this cutting off can give rise to autistic states of mind or to withdrawn daydreaming. It can also cause more psychotic states of mind and result in a child who easily becomes confused and may make inconsequential jumps in thinking. Many normal people may have the experience of using these mechanisms on occasion to protect themselves from something which feels too much or too unbearable.

Conclusion

The major task for the young child over the first two years of life is to move from total dependence to the beginnings of independence. If all goes well the child will have embarked on the long process of separation. For stable development the moves towards separation and independence which take place in the outer world are dependent upon parallel changes within the inner world, related to the internalization of parental figures and the development of a stable sense of self. In analytical terms the young child becomes increasingly able to rely on and turn to these internalized figures for confidence and support and therefore needs the actual presence of the mother less.

During these early years the child is developing a growing sense of self and others. At the same time the mother is finding her own way of learning to know her baby and of coping as best she can with the rewarding but demanding task of bringing the baby up and fostering the normal processes of development.

Summary

1. The first two years of life are particularly important as they lay the foundation for all future development.
2. The mother's focused state of mind known as reverie continues for some months after the baby's birth, being gradually phased out as the baby learns to process the components of emotional experience on his or her own.
3. The ability to process and work through his or her own

feelings is based on the child's internalization and identification with a thinking and 'containing' mother. Children who miss out on this experience tend to cut off from or otherwise avoid emotional experiences and are not fully in touch with their own feelings.

4. It is thought that young babies organize experiences into good and bad, initially based on their relationship with their mothers: the good mother is the one who offers comfort, love and understanding whereas the bad mother is formed from experiences when the mother is absent or inevitably frustrates. In this way internal representations of both a good and bad mother are created and these may form the basis for images of good fairy godmothers and wicked witches.

5. When the mothering is 'good enough', the good mother is much stronger than the bad and the babies holds on to her as a part of themselves, the very centre of their being.

6. The baby's sense of self derives from the relationship with the mother as the central fixed point around which the baby organizes experience, which leads to a sense of physical cohesion, of continuity in time, a stable pattern of awareness and a sense of having intentions in mind.

7. The turn-taking shown by babies and their mothers in 'protoconversations' lay the foundation for later reciprocal relationships.

8. Any experience which causes more anxiety than the child can manage runs the risk of damaging the child's mental functioning: it may be a one-off traumatic event or more regular, repeated harmful experiences over time.

9. The sense of safety, self-worth, belonging and empowerment are important factors in developing a child's positive self-esteem.

10. Independence grows out of secure attachment, a strong and stable relationship with the mother which is consolidated over the first two years of life.

References and further reading

Ainsworth, M., Blehar, M., Waters, E. and Walls, S. (1978) *Patterns of Attachment*. New Jersey: Erlbaum.

Bion, W. R. (1962) *Learning from Experience*. London: Heinemann.

Bowlby, J. (1988) *A Secure Base*. London: Routledge.

Cohen, N. J. and Squire, L. (1980) Preserved learning and retention of pattern-analysing skill in amnesia: dissociation of knowing how and knowing that. *Science*, **201**, 207–9.

Harris, M. (1975) *Thinking about Infants and Young Children*. Perthshire: Clunie Press.

Hobson, P. (1989) Beyond cognition: a theory of autism. In G. Dawson (ed.) *Autism: Nature, Diagnosis and Treatment*. New York: Guilford.

Holmes, E. (1980) Assessing parental relationships. *Fostering and Adoption*, No. 102.

Jones, D. (1994) The Consequences of Professional Intervention when Child Sexual Abuse is Referred for Investigation. Lecture to Royal College of Psychiatrists, 18 March.

Klein, M. (1975) Envy and gratitude. In M. Khan (ed.) In *Envy and Gratitude, Collected Works*, Vol. III. London: The Hogarth Press, pp. 176–235.

Moore, M. S. (1993) Disturbances in attachment. Lecture to Autism Workshop, Tavistock Clinic, London, 1 December.

Pines, D. (1981) In the beginning: contributions of a psychoanalytic developmental psychobiology. *International Journal of Psychoanalysis*, **8**, 15–33.

Shuttleworth, J. (1989) Psychoanalytic theory and infant development. In L. Miller, M. Rustin, M. Rustin and J. Shuttleworth (eds) *Closely Observed Infants*. London: Duckworth, pp. 22–51.

Squire, L. (1992) Declarative and non-declarative memory: multiple brain systems supporting learning and memory. *Journal of Cognitive Neuroscience*, **4** (3), 232–43.

Stern, D. N. (1985) *The Interpersonal World of the Infant*. New York: Basic Books.

Trevarthen, C. (1993) The self born in intersubjectivity: the psychology of an infant communicating. In U. Neisser (ed.)

Ecological and Interpersonal Knowledge of the Self. New York: Cambridge University Press.

Trevarthen, C. (1994) To the infant hero: A bright, daring and melodramatic companion, whom indifference betrays. Lecture to the Squiggle Foundation, 20 March.

Winnicott, D. (1965) *The Family and Individual Development.* London: Tavistock Publications.

Winnicott, D. (1975) Transitional objects and transitional phenomena. In M. Khan (ed.) *Through Paediatrics to Psychoanalysis.* London: The Hogarth Press, pp. 229–42.

CHAPTER 4

Psychological Development: Childhood, Healthy Families and Adolescence

This chapter continues with the theme of development but of necessity is only able to cover some of the important developmental tasks of childhood and adolescence. At the centre is the 'healthy family research' which outlines the attitudes and relationships resulting in the most mature and balanced family functioning. These findings add another dimension to the already complex field of healthy child development.

As might be expected the protective effects of good, trusting relationships with parents, teachers or other family members are carried through into adolescence (Alsop and McCaffrey, 1993). This is important, as adolescence and starting at a new school are two particularly stressful events in a child's life.

CHILDHOOD STRESS

Children generally do not talk about feeling under stress but show there is something wrong through changes in their behaviour. These are frequently accompanied by poor motivation and lack of self-esteem which result from feelings of powerlessness. Children are particularly vulnerable, as they have less control over their own lives than do adults. However, where children feel that they do have some control they actually experience less stress.

It has been found that boys respond to stress with destructive behaviour, as do girls who have no competent role model (Masten, 1988). A mother's competence helps her daughter to cope effectively with high levels of stress. Similarly, babies with strong attachments to their mothers cope much better with separation than babies with less secure attachments.

Junior schoolchildren were ranked in order of events which they found stressful, including both major life events and the less evident daily stresses (Alsop and McCaffrey, 1993). The resulting order was:

1. loss of parent through death or divorce;
2. wetting in class;
3. getting lost; being left alone;
4. being bullied by other children;
5. being chosen last for the team;
6. being ridiculed in class;
7. arguments between parents;
8. moving to a new class or school;
9. going to the dentist or hospital;
10. tests and examinations;
11. taking home a bad report;
12. breaking or losing things;
13. being different (accent or clothes);
14. a new baby in the family;
15. performing in public;
16. being late for school.

These results are interesting, as they show that children find loss and feeling lost most stressful, followed by being made to feel humiliated in front of other children; being bullied and feeling not wanted also rank highly. Many of these stressful situations are related to school, which means that teachers do have some opportunities to relieve the stress on children. It is clear that children often feel under increased stress while at school, as the attempted suicide rate increases during school term times and reduces significantly during school holidays (McGibbon et al., 1992). Although teachers are in no way responsible for coping with all the stressful events in a child's life, their attitude and understanding can have a positive effect and greatly reduce the child's distress.

GENDER IDENTITY

The child's awareness of being a girl or boy is usually formed around the age of ten months and is known as gender identity. It is based partly on the parents' expectations, partly on biological factors, and partly on the child's observations of the difference between the sexes.

Rarely, some boys in early or middle childhood (4–9 years) show feminine behaviour and a wish to dress in girl's clothes. This is called transsexualism and is extremely difficult to treat. The evidence so far suggests that an overly tolerant attitude by the parents to the feminine behaviour, a tendency to treat the boy more like a girl out of frustrated wishes for a girl and the failure of the father to act as a role model may all contribute to the problem with gender identity (Green, 1985). Gender identity problems in girls are less obvious and probably less frequent.

Once children feel clear about which sex they belong to, the question arises of their position relative to the parents. Freud (1953) first described the Oedipus complex, which postulates that deep in the unconscious mind there is a sense of rivalry with the parent of the same sex and a wish to marry the parent of the opposite sex. This is often never made explicit but young children may show such desires through dreams or play. This conflict is normally resolved by the little girl identifying with her mother and the boy with his father.

It is common for children between the ages of 2 and 5 to show curiosity about the differences between girls and boys. Play involving undressing and interest in the genitalia of other children is normal.

Masturbation frequently occurs as part of normal development but if it becomes compulsive further investigation is needed, particularly as to the possibility of sexual abuse. The majority of sexually abused children fall into the under-5 age group. In normal circumstances, if dealt with sensibly, by distracting the child for instance, the masturbation generally lessens and eventually stops.

DEVELOPMENT OF CONSCIENCE

A sense of conscience is gradually built up through the child's identification with the parents' attitudes and values. The child internalizes these and generally does not question their validity until adolescence. Through this identification the child comes to feel that certain actions and attitudes are right and others are wrong. Thus children do have a clear sense of right and wrong from a young age.

The child is more likely to incorporate parental values if there is a loving relationship and the parents convey that what the child does matters because the child matters. The behaviours which the parents encourage and those they either ignore or punish will influence the child's sense of values. If parents do not value honesty it is very likely that the child will not either (Rutter, 1975).

Winnicott (1964) writes that it is no use trying to instil moral values or cultural patterns in a 4-year-old child. The important factor is the parent, the parent's behaviour and the relationship between the two parents as perceived by the child. The child takes this in and imitates or reacts against the parents' attitudes, behaviour and relationships and continues to use these in the complicated process of personal development.

Naturally the process is likely to be impaired if the child does not have a stable and caring relationship with the parents. This was clearly demonstrated in the past through observations of children brought up in large institutions (Lowrey, 1940; Wolkind, 1974). These children developed an affectionless, aggressive personality with a relative absence of conscience and a lack of guilt. Similarly, in today's society children from very unstable, emotionally deprived or disturbed homes do not have the full opportunities to develop a conscience or a sense of guilt.

> Joshua was the seventh in a family of nine children. The family was chaotic, with a culture of aggression and violence, extending from the father to the older brothers and now affecting Joshua. His older brother regularly hit Joshua and he would come to

school with bruises on his face and arms. Social services felt unable to take any action because Joshua and the family denied that he was being hit. However, Joshua became more aggressive and would lash out if other children touched him accidentally. He viciously attacked one little girl who had tapped him playfully on the head with a book and could not see that this was wrong. From his perspective, living in a culture where he is frequently beaten up, he interpreted the tap as an assault and felt she deserved his violent retaliation. Despite the teacher's attempts to explain and help him see it from the girl's point of view, Joshua was convinced he was in the right and he felt no remorse or sense of guilt.

In Joshua's case it is easy to see how his values have been distorted by the violence within his home environment. There was a very loving side to Joshua and he clearly wanted to please his teacher but at this stage he still felt that his violent outbursts were justified.

TRANSITIONAL OBJECT

Winnicott (1964) first used this term to mean an object, a toy or a piece of blanket which helped the child to separate from the mother in a graduated and safe way. It has special value for the child, and acts as a source of comfort and reassurance and as a receptacle for aggression. In many ways the transitional object stands for the mother and is often taken everywhere with the child. It is important for parents and teachers to recognize its unique significance and not undermine the child's attachment. The use of the transitional object often represents a step in the direction of increasing independence and in establishing internal security. Children need to be allowed to decide for themselves when they are ready to give it up.

THE IMPORTANCE OF PLAY AND FANTASY

Play occupies a space between inner and outer reality. Kenrick (1991) gives as an example a little girl bathing and hitting her doll while mother baths the new baby. Here play provides a space for the child's powerful feelings about the external reality of the new baby and preoccupied mother. Her feelings are able to be faced and worked through in a symbolic way. The nursery and school can provide an environment where the child can continue to find ways to process her many experiences and feelings through play, which serves to develop and widen the depth and range of relationships (Kenrick, 1991).

A lively and varied fantasy life is normal in young children and is particularly seen through their imaginative play. From the ages of 2 to 8 children create imaginative worlds, often based in their experience of the real world of home and school, as a way of working through and mastering different experiences. Children's stories, fairy tales and adventures among others have a very important place in helping children to articulate and come to terms with ideas of good and bad. Stories allow children to think about frightening things, represented by giants, witches and monsters, in a safe setting and realize that in the end good will triumph. Other stories can help children work through different experiences such as separation or bereavement (Rustin and Rustin, 1987).

Although young children appear very absorbed in their fantasy worlds, they usually have no difficulty in distinguishing fantasy from reality. As children grow older, fantasy tends to become less important as they engage more with the outside world. However, research has indicated that the most creative people in terms of new discoveries and new ideas are those who have retained some of their childishness and an ability to play for the sake of play itself without any aim in mind (Skynner and Cleese, 1989).

TEMPER TANTRUMS

From the age of 18 months and into the second year young children are faced with having their wishes thwarted at times and being told 'no'. At first they may be overcome by the force of their rage, leading to temper outbursts. Temper tantrums are uncontrolled outbursts of anger when the child is overwhelmed by powerful feelings. It can be quite upsetting for an inexperienced mother to find her child responding by shouting, screaming and kicking on the floor, clearly out of control. In normal circumstances toddlers soon learn to control their anger so that temper tantrums tend to occur over a relatively short period of time. Children are more able to modify their feelings in the context of a loving and stable home.

Older children from disturbed and disrupted backgrounds may continue to have violent temper tantrums as a response to frustration. These children have not been given the necessary parenting to help them modify and control their feelings. Many of these children have to be excluded from ordinary school, as they can be a danger to other children. Because of often serious emotional problems they tend to need specialist school provision.

TOILET TRAINING

This may well start during the second year of life but is often not finished until the third year. Children mature at different rates but the majority are able to inhibit reflex voiding by 2½ to 3 years and are clean by 4 years. Parents rely on the child's wish to please, and reinforce the desired behaviour with praise. A good relationship with the mother facilitates toilet training.

LATENCY (AGES 5–11 YEARS)

The primary school years represent a time of relative stability in terms of psychological and sexual development. In general this is not a time of great turbulence and children tend to mix with and identify with children of the same sex.

A stable family remains crucially important in terms of building upon the emotional security already established in the very early years. The importance of fathers is being increasingly recognized, especially for boys (McCord *et al.*, 1962; Biller, 1970). It is during the latency years that boys enjoy becoming involved with their father in his interests and pursuits. The boy needs father's support in order to loosen his attachment to his mother as part of normal development. At this time the father acts as a role model and a figure with whom the boy can identify. Similar processes of identification with their mothers take place for girls. A close relationship with one or both parents is important for the ability to make close and intimate relationships as an adult.

Healthy families research

Skynner and Cleese (1989) describe the 'healthy family research' carried out by Timberlawn and written up by Lewis *et al.* (1976). The researchers divided families into three main groups for the sake of simplicity, with the most healthy at one end and the least healthy at the other, leaving the majority in the middle.

They used simple measures in order to place the families, such as whether anyone had symptoms or problems, whether anyone needed treatment or whether the children had ever been in trouble with the law or attended court. The researchers then looked at various aspects of how these families functioned, and organized their findings around what seemed to be the most important dimensions. The results are interesting and thought-provoking:

1. *Power structure* (a) Least well functioning: there was a chaotic situation with very little order, structure or hierarchy within the family. Frequently there was a coalition

between the mother and the index patient, leaving the father ineffective and excluded. (b) Mid-range: there was a sense of rigid control with little negotiation within the family. The parents either competed for dominance, which tended to produce behavioural problems in the children, or there was a dominant – submissive parental relationship which predisposed towards a neurotic pattern in the children. (c) Healthy: there was a strong, equally powered parental coalition with no hierarchy between them. There was, however, a clear hierarchy between parents and children. The children had to do what they were told but within a relationship based on mutual respect. Clearly it was the parents who made the final decisions but only after large amounts of consultation and discussion with the children, and in these circumstances the children were willing to accept this.

2. *Identity and differentiation.* (a) Least well functioning: the family members had blurred boundaries, unclear identities and shifting roles. (b) Mid-range: the identities were clearly defined but at the cost of emotional closeness. There was a reduction of potential and spontaneity. Roles were more stereotyped between male and female, with less possibility of intimate relationships. (c) Healthy: the family members' identities were more highly defined and secure, which permitted high levels of closeness and intimacy together with greater degrees of independence and separateness. This was felt to be one of the most important findings which was relevant for individuals as well as families. The healthiest people are those capable of both great intimacy and great independence.

3. *Communication.* (a) Least well functioning: communication was generally vague, confused, evasive and contradictory. It included mystification and use of the 'double bind', a device for saying one thing and meaning another. (b) Mid-range: communication was clear. (c) Healthy: communication was open, direct, frank, lively and spontaneous.

4. *Openness to new ideas.* (a) Least well functioning: these

families were impervious to new ideas. (b) Mid-range: they tended to be rather hesitant and unsure of new ideas. (c) Healthy: these families were receptive and responsive.

5. *Relationships*. (a) Least well functioning: relationships tended to be characterized by distrust, an expectation of evil, betrayal and desertion. (b) Mid-range: relationships tended to be coloured by relative distrust. Human nature was seen as basically evil and there was rigid control of the self and others. (c) Healthy: these families had a basic expectation of a positive response to a positive approach. They showed warmth, caring, mutual regard, awareness of others and a reaching out to other people. Such families were characterized by good relationships within the family and extended family as well as being involved in community activities, being generally popular and well regarded.

6. *Reality sense*. (a) Least well functioning: here reality tended to be denied, with a readily used escape into fantasy satisfaction. (b) Mid-range: there was an adequate enough reality sense in order to function effectively but with some distortion of the facts at times. (c) Healthy: the image of self and family was more or less congruent with reality.

7. *Attitude to change and loss*. (a) Least well functioning: these families were unable to cope with change and loss. There was a timeless repetitive quality to their thinking, with an inability to face death and an escape into fantasy. (b) Mid-range: here change and loss was faced but with great difficulty. Separation and death were often not fully worked through. In these circumstances substitutes for the lost person were often found and the previous feelings were transferred on to them, rather than there being an internalization of the lost person. (c) Healthy: these families were able to cope with change, growth, separation and death. They accepted the changes realistically and the losses were worked through. One of the main reasons for this seemed to be a strong parental coalition in relation to both the

younger and older generation, so that whatever happened the parents could not be split but always stood together. The healthy families also had strong, supportive relationships outside the family.

Their capacity to cope seemed to be made possible by the support from within and outside the family as well as through a sense of meaning and purpose which came from what the researchers called a 'transcendental value system'. This could be a religious dimension or a humanitarian philosophy which gave meaning to life through the commitment to some greater cause. They had a perspective which recognized that things outside themselves are more important and saw themselves as part of something greater, as part of the world community for instance.

The capacity to deal with change and loss is extremely important for both individuals and families. It is based on an inner strength and a capacity to bear the painful feelings and work through them. Individuals who survive best in situations of great privation and stress have also been found to have a 'transcendental value system', a belief in something outside themselves, which does seem to confer an additional resilience and strength.

The belief in something greater than ourselves is related to the sense of mission as described in the building of good self-esteem. Not surprisingly, many of the qualities which form the basis of self-esteem (sense of affiliation, identity and mission) are also found in the most healthy families.

The positive features can be summarized as follows. The most healthy families showed an affiliative attitude which is seen in their warm and affectionate relationships and in the positive way they reach out to others. However, this capacity for closeness and involvement was balanced by a respect for individuality and difference. Communication could be frank and open because of the acceptance of the negative as well as the positive features of human nature.

The children felt free to be themselves, secure in the knowledge that they were accepted. They did not have to hide or repress aspects which felt unacceptable to their parents, such as anger, jealousy or depression. There was a high degree of fun, spontaneity and enjoyment as well as a fair balance between order and freedom. The parents were clearly in charge but the children were consulted. Lastly, these families showed a great capacity to cope with loss and change.

Successful institutions

While thinking about what makes for healthy functioning it seems important to include the institutions in which teachers work. Skynner and Cleese (1993) also turned their attention to organizations and found that similar principles applied to successful businesses, schools, hospitals and companies. An affiliative attitude and sense of responsibility towards the staff led to enjoyment, loyalty and commitment. The most successful companies encouraged independence and delegated responsibility to the staff.

Successful large organizations found a creative balance between the authority of central management and the freedom of operation for smaller teams. Communication was of the greatest importance, covering immediate matters as well as present performance and longer-term planning. Openness and realistic feedback were encouraged. Mistakes and other negative comments were welcomed by the management and seen as essential if there was to be an effective response.

Within institutions it can be difficult to persuade people to accept decisions. However, as with families, it is crucial to listen very carefully and take in what is said before making the final decision. Afterwards, it is important to explain the reasons for the particular decision and give people the chance to criticize and question. It does help people to accept unpopular decisions if they feel that they have been listened to; they are then more likely to say, 'I don't agree but I'll go along with it.'

The companies who are most successful over time also have their equivalent of a transcendental value system. Their general concern for staff goes beyond rational considerations. There are often apocryphal stories about the lengths to which the founders went in order to satisfy a customer. In the same way as healthy families reach out, so also successful companies show a positive reaching out and a trusting attitude towards others. It is heartening to find that the most caring companies tend to be the most successful ones. This research on institutions is also relevant to schools and is supported by much of the research on effective schools.

Adolescence

The developmental period which we call adolescence extends broadly from the ages of 12 to 21 years. It is a time of opportunities and hazards. Interestingly, it has only recently been recognized as a specific developmental phase, dating from the turn of the century when legislation relating to education and health prolonged the time of children's physical and emotional dependence upon parents.

The contention that adolescence is a time of universal unhappiness and confusion has not been confirmed. Rutter *et al.* (1976) found that about 20% of adolescents were significantly unhappy. It is a time of turbulence and change but most adolescents take it within their stride and maintain good relationships with their families.

Parents also need to be adaptable and move forward with their children. In a sense, if they are psychologically in touch, parents may also go through the different stages with their children, providing an opportunity to re-negotiate adolescence to some extent for themselves. A survey of well-functioning families found that parents report an average of two rows per week with their adolescent children and that they consider this to be normal. The rows are over practical matters such as the untidiness of the bedroom, going out or staying out late. These arguments are often an essential part of adolescence, as young adolescents need a chance to rebel (Skynner and Cleese, 1993).

Puberty refers to the physical changes which take place as a result of the rise in the blood levels of the sex hormones. The adolescent process refers more to the psychological challenges and adaptations which the young person has to take on and negotiate as a result of these biological changes. The increased levels of circulating hormones cause an increase in sexual and aggressive drives at adolescence together with their accompanying impulses and fantasies. The search for excitement may lead some young people into delinquency. This is exemplified by the way that the majority of young men grow out of their attraction to crime by the age of 30: a rather slow and prolonged maturation out of adolescence.

It is useful to simplify adolescence into three overlapping and flexible phases. Blos (1962) describes three phases, each covering a major aspect of adolescent development:

1. Early adolescence (12–15 years) – the period of adolescent turmoil.
2. Mid-adolescence (15–18 years) – the period of identification.
3. Late adolescence (17–21 years) – the period of identity and role consolidation.

EARLY ADOLESCENCE: (12–15 YEARS)

This phase is a direct result of and reaction to the physical and hormonal changes. The relative stability of childhood is overturned. There is a sense of unpredictability associated with relatively sudden physical changes such as the changes in genitalia, growth of underarm and public hair and spurt in height. These physical changes may be associated with feelings of inner chaos and loss of control which account for

Blos's description of this phase as the period of turmoil.

Bird (1989) describes how the increase in sexual drive at this stage is diffuse and is experienced as a growing sense of tension. This, combined with the increased sensitivity of the genitalia, can result in a wide range of situations being sexually arousing, for instance sudden or regular movement, shock, fear or states of general excitement.

Masturbation in this context is often seen as an attempt to explore and master the new excitement and tension. It occurs more commonly in boys and can be associated with severe guilt and depression, particularly if the masturbation becomes compulsive. At the same time there may also be an increase in aggression caused by the same sexual hormones and resulting in unaccustomed outbursts of temper or even impulsive attacks on others. These unexpected surges of aggression can be very distressing for the youngster involved.

At this stage the temptation to turn to delinquency can be especially strong as a way of discharging these instinctual tensions and finding excitement and relief. Some more disturbed youngsters carry out their delinquent acts alone. Others become part of a delinquent group with the sense of identity and belonging that this provides. Fortunately, many of these young men will eventually mature out of their delinquency.

Bird (1989) is clear that this inner state of change, turmoil and conflict is largely caused by the unfamiliar feelings and impulses and the attempts to control them. It can be a confusing time. Outwardly there may be inconsistent and contradictory behaviour which often fluctuates between extremes as adolescents struggle with themselves and have not yet found a satisfactory middle point. Arrogance and certainty may alternate with self-effacement and uncertainty; rudeness and lack of concern may alternate with politeness and concern for others; cynicism may alternate with idealism and secrecy with outspokenness. These are all part of the underlying conflicts of early adolescence centred on the conflict between dependence and independence, and need sensitive handling by parents and teachers.

MID-ADOLESCENCE: 15–18 YEARS

In addition to adapting to their changing bodies and feelings, as young people move on to the next stage they take on three further developmental tasks: (1) psychological separation from their parents; (2) the development of their own individual identity; and (3) the development of sexual identity.

Mid-adolescence brings about one of the most central psychological changes, a gradual loosening of the ties to the parents, both internally and externally. As dependence on the external parents lessens, there is a parallel process taking place internally and weakening the bonds to the internal parental figures. This process opens up new possibilities; young people are now free to decide for themselves, whereas as children they were much more likely to unquestioningly identify with parental attitudes and values. In addition, the psychological opening up allows for new possibilities, new people who can act as models for identification and a potential enrichment of the personality.

Opportunities of mid-adolescence
Mid-adolescence represents a turning point. The loosening of the old ties to parents and their values has become essential in order to allow young people to develop a sense of themselves as separate from parents and as individuals in their own right. The strong identification with parents and parental attitudes which was crucial to the child's stable development in early childhood has now become a limiting factor and needs to be relinquished.

New role models can be tried, new identities experimented with on the basis of identification with important adults in their lives. These may be admired teachers or youth leaders, sports people, film stars or pop stars. Through new identifications there is the possibility of enlarging young people's experience, widening their views and enriching their inner worlds.

The hazards of mid-adolescence

This psychological opening at mid-adolescence explains why it is so destructive to place adolescents of this age group in custodial institutions with harsh, punitive atmospheres and with more hardened criminals. As Bird says, they will tend to absorb the coarsest features and develop cold and degrading attitudes towards others. In these circumstances their natural role models will inevitably be the hardened criminals and their time in custody, far from helping, will have served to damage them even further. Home Office statistics only serve to confirm this prediction.

Travis (1994) reports Home Office research which shows that reconviction rates among former prisoners are much higher than previously thought and reach an all-time high of 92% among teenagers. Clearly, the experience of imprisonment for very young offenders has in no way changed their behaviour. The results demonstrate that a startling 92% of 15–16-year-olds who have served their sentence in Youth Custody have then been reconvicted within two years. In addition 71% of those imprisoned under the age of 21 years were also reconvicted within two years, the figure rising to 82% after four years.

A different kind of danger arises if the struggle for independence from parents becomes fraught with arguments and aggression on both sides, as the young person may come to experience both internal and external parents as unduly harsh. This may leave the young person feeling very exposed, with feelings of inner emptiness and loss.

Young people may show they are not coping by using increasingly disturbed behaviour as a cry for help or alternatively by withdrawing from the struggle and withdrawing from friends and outer life. In both cases there is a need to respond; in the first case more support and control from parents and teachers is indicated and in the second a gentle drawing out and encouragement is necessary, moderating the pressures as far as is possible.

If the young person does not recover reasonably quickly the withdrawn behaviour may indicate a breakdown into mental illness. In emotionally vulnerable young people or where there is a genetic predisposition, the demands of establishing their own identity may precipitate an illness such as depression, anorexia. schizophrenia or obsessional disorder.

Establishment of identity

As part of their search for identity, both boys and girls turn away from their families and towards their friends for support. The adolescent group becomes particularly important at this stage, when many young people lack self-confidence. The support of a peer group provides individuals with a range of possibilities for projecting out unwanted parts of themselves and for identifying with different characteristics. It also enables young people to accomplish tasks and ventures that they could not undertake on their own. Adolescents are helped by the group to develop their own social attitudes and moral values, away from the family. Unfortunately, as already described, some vulnerable adolescents may become drawn into delinquent groups.

Erikson (1968) defines identity as a conscious sense of individual uniqueness. Normally, adolescents gradually work through the different phases and eventually find and become identified with their roles as adult people, no longer dependent upon parents. However, this is not the end of the matter as the search for individuality continues throughout life.

In addition to turning to friends, young people often also become more self-absorbed for a time. There is frequently a rich fantasy life and an increased preoccupation with daydreaming; these often serve as a preparation for the next stage, which is the search for a sexual relationship with someone.

Sexual identity

The individual's final sexual identity is established during this phase. The question of gender identity, whether one feels male or female, is settled in the second half of the first year of life. Sexual identity is part of one's overall identity and includes whether one is sexually attracted to men or women; whether one is heterosexual or homosexual.

The biologically fuelled wish for a sexual partner facilitates the process of separation from parents. Many young people find it is easier to make the transition through becoming part of a mixed-sex group before moving on to the later stage of pairing and having their first boyfriend or girlfriend.

Sexual attitudes

There has been a dramatic change in attitudes towards sexual relationships over the last 30 years. Timmins (1994) quotes two surveys. The first, undertaken in 1990, found that 30% of 16–19-year-old girls admitted to having had sexual intercourse before the age of 16, as opposed to only 2% in 1964. A large part of the change can be attributed to the availability of the oral contraceptive pill.

The second survey, which was carried out by Mori and published in 1994, found that 40% of 16–19-year-olds felt that it was morally wrong to have a sexual relationship before the age of 16, although equally a further 40% believed that it was not morally wrong. The survey also found that young people valued sex education in school, with 45% expressing the view that it was being taught at the right time and 37% that it was beginning too late.

LATE ADOLESCENCE: 17–21 YEARS

This last phase is one of building on and consolidating the new role and identity. These are very arbitrary phases and many of us know people who are still working on some adolescent aspect of themselves. Hopefully, however, young people will be well on the way to having established a personal repertoire of skills, values, interests and abilities, and a sense of themselves with a sexual identity, and be able to build stable relationships with others. Maturity is manifested in its most important aspects as the capacity to show concern for others, the ability to wait for emotional satisfaction and the ability to control impulses.

From this position of relative stability the young person is now ready to re-establish good relationships with the internal parental figures as well as with the external parents. The internal parents remain as a source of strength and support but the relationship with the external parents will have changed as the young person is now an adult relating to other adults.

Not surprisingly, how a young person copes with the anxieties and stress of adolescence depends to a great extent on earlier relationships established within the family. The more stable and secure the foundation, the easier the transition into adult life and individual maturity.

Summary

1. Children under stress show a change in behaviour, unhappiness, low self-esteem and poor motivation: boys often respond by developing more destructive behaviour, as do girls who lack a competent role model.

2. The most stressful events for one group of junior school children in order of importance are losing a parent by death or divorce, wetting in class, getting lost and being bullied.

3. Although teachers cannot influence much of the stress in children's lives, their attitude and understanding can have a positive effect and significantly reduced the level of distress.

4. A child's awareness of being a girl or a boy (gender identity) is usually formed around the age of ten months and depends partly on the parent's expectations and partly on biological factors.

5. A child's sense of conscience is gradually built up

through identification with the parents' attitudes and values.

6. The most creative people in terms of new discoveries and ideas are those who have retained some of their childishness and an ability to play for its own sake.

7. Temper tantrums are uncontrolled outbursts of anger when the child is overwhelmed by powerful feelings. They are usually fairly short-lived, with the child being more able to control the anger in the context of a loving home.

8. Fathers are particularly important for boys as role models and for identification. The boy needs his father's support in order to loosen his attachment to his mother as part of normal development.

9. The most healthy families are outward-going, warm and friendly to others; their capacity for closeness is balanced by a respect for individuality and difference. The children feel that both their positive and negative sides are accepted; they are consulted over decisions but the parents are clearly in charge. There is a sense of fun and enjoyment which is accompanied by a great capacity to cope with loss and change.

10. There are three overlapping phases within the developmental period which we call adolescence. These are: (a) the period of adolescent turmoil, resulting from physical and hormonal changes; (b) the period of separation from parents and the development of individual identity; and (c) the period of consolidation of the more adult role and identity.

11. How a young person copes with the stresses and strains of adolescence depends to a great extent upon earlier relationships: the more stable and secure the foundation, the easier the transition into adult life.

References

Alsop, P. and McCaffrey, T. (eds) (1993) *How to Cope with Childhood Stress: A Practical Guide for Teachers*. Harlow: Longman.

Biller, H. B. (1970) Father absence and personality development in the male child. *Developmental Psychology*, **2** (2), 181–201.

Bird, D. (1989) Adolescents and negotiating treatment. Paper given to Birmingham Trust for Psychoanalytic Psychotherapy.

Blos, P. (1962) *On Adolescence: A Psychoanalytic Interpretation*. New York: The Free Press of Glencoe, Inc.

Erikson, E. (1968) *Identity, Youth and Crisis*. London: Faber.

Freud, S. (1953) Three essays on the theory of sexuality. In *The Standard Edition of the Complete Works of Sigmund Freud*, **7**, 125–245.

Green, R. (1985) Atypical sexual development. In M. Rutter and L. Hersov (eds) *Child and Adolescent Psychiatry: Modern Approaches*. Oxford: Blackwell Scientific, pp. 638–49.

Kenrick, J. (1991) Thinking about the problems of young children in nursery classes and primary schools. In Hancock, R. and Winkley, D. (eds), *Special Issues in Primary Education*. Oxford: National Primary Centre, pp. 8–10.

Lewis, J. M., Beavers, W. R., Gossett, J. T. *et al.* (1976) *No Single Thread: Psychological Health in Family Systems*. New York: Bruner/Mazel.

Lowrey, L. G. (1940) Personality distortion and early institutional care. *American Journal of Orthopsychiatry*, **10**, 576–85.

Masten, A. S. (1988) Competence and stress in school children: the moderating effect of individual and family qualities. *Journal of Child Psychology and Psychiatry*, **29**, 6.

McCord, J., McCord, W. and Thurber, E. (1962) Some effects of paternal absence on male children. *Journal of Abnormal Social Psychology*, **64**, 361–9.

McGibbon, L., Ballard, C., Handy, S. and Silveira, W. R. (1992) School attendance as a factor in deliberate self-poisoning by 12–15 year old adolescents. *British Medical Journal*, **304**, 28.

Rustin, M. and Rustin, M. (1987) *Narratives of Love and Loss: Studies in Modern Children's Fiction*. London: Verso.

Rutter, M. (1975) *Helping Troubled Children*. Harmondsworth: Penguin Books.

Rutter, M., Graham, P. and Chadwick, O. (1976) Adolescent turmoil: fact or fiction. *Journal of Child Psychology and Psychiatry*, **17**, 35–56.

Skynner, R. and Cleese, J. (1983) *Families and How to Survive Them*. London: Methuen.

Skynner, R. and Cleese, J. (1989) Families and how to survive them. Public Lecture at The Tavistock Clinic, London.

Skynner, R. and Cleese, J. (1993) *Life and How to Survive It*. London: Methuen.

Timmins, N. (1994) Teenagers divided over the morality of under-age sex. *Independent*, 10 January.

Travis, A. (1994) Study puts lie to claim that prison works. *The Guardian*, 24 June.

Winnicott, D. W. (1964) *The Child, The Family and The Outside World*. Harmondsworth: Penguin Books, pp. 168–70.

Wolkind, S. N. (1974) The components of 'affectionless psychopathy' in institutionalised children. *Journal of Child Psychology and Psychiatry*, **15**, 215–20.

CHAPTER 5
Conduct Disorders

Children with conduct disorders frequently cause major problems for teachers because of aggressive, disruptive and defiant behaviour. These also constitute the commonest type of psychiatric disorders found among primary schoolchildren and young adolescents; inevitably, boys predominate.

Children with conduct disorders represent a major problem for urban society today and unfortunately, as factors within society leading to the problem increase, the numbers of professionals with the expertise to help are tending to be cut back due to financial pressures (*Young Minds*, 1991). Several child psychiatry and child guidance units have been under threat and services have been eroded through specialist social workers being withdrawn from the teams. There is evidence that teachers are often not being given the necessary support and resources required to meet the needs of these young people with serious behavioural problems. Consequently, when schools find themselves without the resources to help disruptive pupils they are increasingly resorting to suspensions or expulsions.

Increase in referrals

Numbers of referrals to all helping agencies of children with conduct disorders have been steadily increasing (Bennathan, 1991). The average age at referral has also decreased, with boys as young as 4 or 5 years being virtually beyond parental control. These problems are invariably greater in inner city areas, linked to poor housing and social environments and compounded by increasing poverty and unemployment. Analysis of those living below half-average

91

income shows that 74% of lone parents were below this poverty line in 1991–1992 compared to 28% in 1979 (HMSO, 1994). Unless remedial action is taken in terms of effective financial and emotional support for the families at risk, we will create long-term social problems of crime and violence.

These issues need to be seen not merely as single issues such as poor educational progress, suicide attempts or delinquency, but as symptoms of more pervasive, underlying problems related to the failure in meeting children's emotional needs and providing good parenting from birth onwards.

Origins of conduct disorder

The main underlying cause in the majority of cases is the lack of basic, stable and secure family relationships. Something has gone wrong over time and these children have failed to develop a sense of inner security and trust, based on consistent, stable and permanent parent figures with whom they can identify. Children from families where the mother has never had a partner are particularly at risk. Children with conduct disorders may have parents who show unconsciously hostile or rejecting attitudes. Behind the rejection there is often evidence of a personality disorder in the parent, and these attitudes can be transmitted from generation to generation.

Much less commonly, other parental attitudes may contribute: for example, an over-anxious or over-valuing attitude may lead to a lack of effective discipline and order. This can result in spoilt children who always expect to get their own way, unable to accept any limitations on their behaviour.

A second group of less damaged children comes from families who stand out from society in general but who live in communities where certain forms of delinquent behaviour are acceptable and culturally ingrained. These children

have identified with their parents and their rather anti-
social way of life but are reasonably well adjusted
emotionally, feeling secure and able to make close, intimate
relationships.

Factors within the child are also important. For instance,
some children are easier to bring up than others, being
more placid and conforming. Others are temperamentally
difficult and more resistant to behaving in socially acceptable ways.

The pattern of family life is, however, much the most
important factor. The more stable, accepting and consistent
the parents, the more stable and accommodating the children.

Children with conduct disorders generally come from
disrupted, disorganized families characterized by absence of
the parents, especially the father, by divorced or separated
parents, by lack of affection within the family, by poor iden-
tificatory figures or by inconsistent management.

However, when relationships are already difficult the
additional stresses caused by poor housing conditions,
poverty and unemployment can lead to increasingly fraught
and hostile parental interchanges which inevitably affect the
children and destabilize the whole atmosphere of the home.

Early symptoms

The early symptoms of a conduct disorder are most
frequently seen within the family and may start with behaviour such as disobedience, lying, stealing, and verbal or
physical aggression towards other family members. If the
condition worsens, these symptoms tend to spread outside
the home and affect the child's behaviour in school and
within the neighbourhood. Many children show transient
episodes of socially unacceptable behaviour but it is the
persistence of such behaviour which leads to the diagnosis of
conduct disorder.

Children with conduct disorders also have difficulties in

making close and stable personal relationships. There is a small number of children with serious and persistent behavioural problems which are obvious from an early age and can be recognized at nursery and infant school. These children need urgent referral to specialist agencies, as otherwise the outlook for adult life is poor. The histories, for example, of a high proportion of boys in borstals showed evidence of disturbed behaviour and relationships in their primary school.

Impact on the community

As the children grow older these behavioural problems may impact on the outer world through truancy from school and staying out late, creating increased opportunities for delinquency. Delinquency is usually defined as behaviour which is against the law, and includes such acts as house-breaking, mugging, shoplifting, stealing from cars, joyriding, fire-setting and vandalism.

Characteristics of children with conduct disorder

This disorder usually arises from a lack of adequate parenting where the child's basic emotional needs have not been met. An impoverishment of personality organization occurs with a weak ego, i.e. poor capacity for making judgements, taking charge or responsibility, or ordering or planning. Similarly, there is often a poorly developed superego with little awareness or concern for others. The capacity for thinking has not been properly developed and behaviour is often impulsive without thought for consequences. These youngsters find it difficult to learn from experience.

Children with conduct disorder frequently display an outward appearance of toughness, hiding low self-esteem, and often appear resentful, with a feeling that they have been unfairly treated. Typically, they blame others for their difficulties and have little self-awareness, tending to be impulsive, reckless and immature. They are often self-centred and have a low toleration of frustration, leading to frequent outbursts of temper. In the more serious cases the youngsters can completely lose control and endanger themselves or others. This is particularly difficult to handle in a school setting, where other children are at risk.

As may be expected, academic achievement tends to be considerably below the child's natural ability. Many factors are involved, including poor school attendance, difficulties with concentration, other specific learning difficulties and the child's often hostile attitude to the adult world.

Glue-sniffing and alcohol and drug abuse are quite common among older children and adolescents. In girls especially, sexual promiscuity and prostitution may form part of the picture of generalized disturbance which lies behind all the varying manifestations of a conduct disorder.

Conduct disorders lie on a spectrum from mild to severe. Mild cases involve behaviour problems either only at school or only at home. In more severe cases there are problems in both settings and the most severe show a progression into delinquency. In general, the outlook relates to the degree of severity.

Crime and unemployment

It has been suggested that there is a link between crime and unemployment and a recent study from Cambridge tends to confirm this (Dickinson, 1994). The findings of the report show an exact relationship between the numbers of burglaries committed by young men under the age of 25 and the rate of unemployment for these young men during the 1980s. Dickinson (1994) writes, 'by allowing mass unemployment to continue and letting young men shoulder a disproportionate burden of this, we condemn ourselves to rising crime now, and create criminals for the future.'

Fire-setting

This represents a particularly rare but dangerous delinquent activity which causes great anxiety and needs to be taken very seriously. It has been described as a severe conduct disorder which occurs predominantly in boys, the majority being in a relatively young age group and showing a high degree of psychosocial difficulties. In comparison with a matched group of other conduct-disordered children, the fire-setters were more destructive, more anti-social and aggressive and had greater relationship difficulties (Jacobson, 1985).

There are two main groups of fire-setters: younger boys, under the age of 10 years, who generally start fires alone within the home, and older boys who work in gangs, setting fires outside the home and showing other, often serious, behavioural problems. Yarnell (1940), in a good early study, found that the younger children often showed latent hostility towards their parents. This was confirmed by Strachan's study (Strachan, 1981), which found a small number of children who started fire-setting at a very early age (4 years) and seemed intent on injuring members of the family. In both groups there tends to be a disturbed family background of parental arguments and separations, including a pattern of anti-social problems and alcoholism.

The younger children may start fires in their bedrooms or the living room, and they frequently appear rejected and neglected, often coming from unstable and violent homes. The fire-setting here may convey both hostility and a cry for help. In contrast, the older boys become drawn to fire-setting for the excitement. They start a fire and wait to watch the effects, only running off when the police arrive.

As with conduct disorder generally, treatment is based on the assessment of the underlying causes. However, because of the frightening nature of the main symptom, an urgent response is often needed. Understandably, residential facilities such as children's homes or residential schools are often very reluctant to take in such children.

Brian, a 9-year-old, set fire to the living room curtains and then fortunately put the fire out. He lived with his mother and stepfather but had missed out on parental attention as his mother was very preoccupied with her own problems. The stepfather was very critical and rejecting and refused to take part in the treatment plan.

The assessment was that Brian had become trapped in a downward spiral of increasingly disruptive behaviour at home and school which was fuelled by the increasingly negative feelings from parents and staff.

A treatment plan was set up which aimed to reverse the spiral. Mother was offered her own individual sessions to focus on her problems and needs while Brian was also offered individual sessions in order to provide a space to think and attention for himself. The psychiatrist liaised regularly with Brian's teacher and explained how Brian was feeling rejected and bad, with very low self-esteem, and how he needed to experience success and praise in order to start to feel better about himself, which would then hopefully lead to an improvement in his behaviour.

This combined approach worked. Brian appeared much happier and his disruptive behaviour settled down. It seemed that the original fire-setting episode had been a very potent cry for help.

Persistent stealing

Stealing is not uncommon in young children. Many children steal once or twice, mainly through impulsiveness, naughtiness or greed, but this does not have any serious implications. Such children are cured by disapproval and a firm response. Where stealing persists, however, there is a much more serious problem.

There are three main groups of children who steal persistently. A younger group often steals from home and sometimes school as part of comfort stealing. The stealing here represents their need for love but sadly often results in more critical and rejecting behaviour from the parents. Without help these children may enter a downward spiral of increasing unhappiness and more serious behavioural problems.

A second group of young adolescents becomes involved in stealing as part of a delinquent behaviour pattern. The majority of these will eventually mature out of delinquency. A relatively new phenomenon is the number of juvenile shoplifters who steal while playing truant; in one large city 150 children are arrested for shoplifting each month and of these 100 are first-time offenders (Foster, 1993). Many of these are influenced by peer pressure and once caught are unlikely to offend again.

The third group consists of a very small number of persistent delinquents who can cause enormous suffering to a community through recurrent house-breaking and damage to property. These young people seem destined for a life of crime.

Running away

Around 43,000 children ran away from home in 1990, many of them repeatedly. The majority of the children were aged between 14 and 16 years, with nearly as many girls as boys. A new survey shows that although only 11% of the children are in care, such children accounted for 30% of the runaways and 96% of these were from residential homes (Annis, 1992). Children who run away from their own homes tend to come from disadvantaged backgrounds and their behaviour gives a strong message that something is wrong. All children who run away need to be listened to and taken seriously.

Juvenile delinquency

Delinquency is a more severe form of conduct disorder. Many forms of delinquency can be seen as aggressive reactions to a hostile or depriving environment. The central problem relates to disturbed relationships between parents and children.

Where unemployment is high, disturbed relationships between young people and society become more likely. The relation between markers of deprivation and admission to psychiatric hospital is well established and now there is evidence that unemployment rates, as currently measured, accurately reflect underlying deprivation (Kammerling and O'Connor, 1993).

Juvenile delinquency is a self-limiting condition with a peak of convictions in the late teenage years and a rapid decrease between the ages of 20 and 25. Only a minority of young offenders continue to be convicted as adults. Disadvantaged youngsters may become involved in breaking the law for the excitement and to relieve boredom. However, young people from more affluent homes also break the law but are much more likely to avoid conviction (West, 1982).

Both convicted and self-reported delinquents tend to come from large-sized, low-income families, to have criminal parents or brothers, to have below-average school attainments and to have experienced unsatisfactory parenting (West and Farrington, 1973).

As might be expected, troublesome youngsters at school are at risk for future delinquency. Teachers' ratings of aggressive, disruptive behaviour in school are highly predictive (Douglas *et al.*, 1968). In general, the worse the behaviour at school and the worse the home background, the more likely it is that the young person will not only turn to delinquency but will have a persistently criminal career (West, 1982).

Delayed reading and anti-social behaviour

It has been definitely established that there is a relationship between psychiatric disorder and difficulty in learning to read. This is particularly strong in the case of conduct disorder. Rutter *et al.* (1976) found in their Isle of Wight study that one-third of children with conduct disorders had delayed reading as compared to 4% of children generally.

Children showing both conditions were found to have a family history of reading problems, delayed speech development, poor concentration and large family size. Douglas (1966) found that a large family size, more than four children, was associated with anti-social behaviour.

In a small minority of cases, behavioural problems arise as a direct result of educational failure. Some children with specific reading difficulties experience intense frustration and feelings of failure. It seems self-evident that struggling alone within a class of children who can read would have a profound effect on a child's self-esteem as well as causing frustration, boredom and in some cases disruptive behaviour. In my experience the behaviour is usually situation-specific, and once the child is being taught in a way which recognizes his or her difficulties the behavioural problems disappear.

Assessment and treatment

It is useful to assess the developmental maturity of the child, and the social maturity scale devised by Erikson (1959) provides a helpful framework. There are seven levels: (1) totally dependent on others; (2) primarily egocentric with other people seen as being there solely to minister to their needs; (3) other people felt to be available for manipulation but with no awareness of their needs; (4) the development of a primitive conscience with a black and white sense of good and bad; (5) an ability to be aware of the needs of others and to empathize; (6) a more sophisticated awareness of right and wrong; and (7) the level of mature adult functioning with sensitivity to others, an efficient but benign conscience and accurate empathy.

These levels can be linked to Klein's (Klein, 1975) different mental states, which she called the paranoid-schizoid (the more early primitive ways of thinking) and the depressive (the mature level of concern for others). The paranoid-schizoid is characterized by splitting people or things into good or bad in a crude way, tending to always blame someone else, never taking responsibility and tending to very easily feel that people are against you. Many adults will fluctuate between these two levels, tending to regress to the more primitive thinking when under stress or tired. Some children, however, become stuck at the primitive level, feeling people are against them and blaming others. These are more likely to react aggressively and are therefore at risk for conduct disorder.

The assessment will include looking at factors within the child such as personality and social maturity, physical health and intellectual ability, resilience and the capacity to tolerate frustration and deal with stress; factors within the family, such as loss of the father through family break-up, intergenerational problems such as continuing cycles of emotional deprivation or cultural acceptance of petty crime; and factors within the environment, such as poor housing, unemployment and poverty. In general, many of these factors interact to give rise to the child's problematic behaviour.

Once the assessment has been made, a treatment plan can be set up involving the parents and child with the relevant professionals. A daily diary which is completed by both parents and teachers (often called a report book), recording both problems and successes in school and at home, can be a very effective way of making the child feel 'thought about' and more secure emotionally. With everyone working together there is a stronger and safer network around the child.

The psychiatrist or psychologist may start a behavioural

programme to try to modify behaviour at home and help with the management of anger. Rewarding good behaviour is more effective than punishment, though a careful management of sanctions may be required. Children need consistent limits and boundaries in order to feel safe.

Clinic social workers may be involved in work with the parents to improve their parenting skills and their overall functioning. In other cases, the child may need more intensive work from a child psychotherapist. Ultimately, it is the multi-disciplinary team in consultation with the parents who set out the overall treatment plan, which may also involve help with benefits and support for a change in housing.

A treatment approach called 'parent training' which is based on behavioural methods is widely used in the USA (Patterson, 1982). Studies show that parents of anti-social children fail to tell such children how they are expected to behave, fail to monitor their behaviour and fail to enforce rules with appropriate rewards and penalties. Parent training aims to address these issues in a structured way.

Sam is a good example of how a child showing disturbed behaviour, a conduct disorder, at an early age can be helped.

> Sam, a 7-year-old, was referred for aggressive behaviour which was causing particular problems in school. He had spent his first three years in an unhappy, unstable home environment where he regularly witnessed his father's violence towards his mother. (His father had been abused by his step-father.) Mother then left the home with Sam but the early years had taken their toll in terms of stirring up Sam's aggression and insecurity.
>
> There were similar problems at home and at school in that although Sam was a loving child he could be very difficult, shouting, lashing out and storming off in a temper over something very minor. He would then block the episode out of his mind and find it very hard to listen when corrected. He generally justified his behaviour, always wanting

to have the last word and keep control of the situation.

Sam was functioning at quite an immature level for much of the time and particularly when he was in trouble. He very easily felt that everyone was against him and found it difficult to empathize with other people or see the situation from someone else's point of view. Sam easily became set in quite rigid, inflexible ways of thinking.

It was felt that Sam's difficulties all stemmed from a basic insecurity and that he had not managed to establish a secure emotional base for his development. This resulted in his changeable, impulsive behaviour, rigid thinking and need to feel in control. On Erikson's social maturity scale he would have reached level 3. The immaturity meant that Sam tended to think in more primitive ways, often convinced that others were against him.

A treatment plan was set up to strengthen Sam's sense of internal security by providing a caring, consistent network around him. This involved keeping a daily diary filled in by the teacher and Sam's mother which recorded both good and bad behaviour, together with sessions for both Sam and his mother with the psychiatrist.

The psychiatrist gave Sam attention and a space to think, often focusing on situations where Sam had lashed out inappropriately and trying to help Sam see these from different points of view. Sam was able to describe his outbursts in concrete terms as a dangerous lion escaping from his cage. He described how the bars of the cage became stronger or weaker depending on his mood but there was no conscious control; it just happened.

As Sam improved he found the bars of the cage felt strong for most of the time and his awareness of the lion grew less and less. Over the next year Sam's aggressive outbursts gradually decreased, although under stress he still reverted to more primitive ways of thinking. The diary was discontinued after one year but Sam continued his sessions with the psychiatrist, although reduced in frequency, for a further year.

The role of teachers

Teachers have a central and crucial role in the treatment of children with conduct disorders. For minor problems they are often the only agency involved in providing consistent limits for the child and counselling for the parents.

Increasingly, schools are taking a leading preventative role in setting up supportive schemes for parents to provide basic information about parenting. At present this particularly involves nursery and infant schools.

In more serious cases the teacher will be part of the treatment network, providing clear limits, rewards and sanctions within the classroom. The teacher's help is also needed in thinking of ways of preventing aggressive outbursts during the much less structured breaks and lunchtimes. An important part of the treatment involves monitoring and assessing the child's behaviour and progress. Clearly, the teacher has to take on this task within the school setting and report back to other members of the treatment team through meetings and phone calls.

If the child continues to show persistently disturbed and disruptive behaviour in school, which is not sufficiently modified by the professional input, the treatment plan may have to be changed in order to provide more intensive support and individual attention. I have been extremely impressed by how many teachers show a commitment to a disturbed child within their class, well beyond the call of duty. This willingness to hold on to the child allows time for the network to find suitable alternative provision.

There are various possibilities, depending upon the severity of the problem. These range from providing additional individual help within the school through the use of an integration assistant, or temporary or part-time placement in a more specialized unit to a permanent placement in a special school. The teacher's observations are very important in making such decisions and in instigating the statementing process if this proves to be necessary. Support from the educational psychologist as part of the team is important from an early stage and is essential for placement in a special school.

Outcome

Many minor conduct disorders will improve following treatment, much depending on the child's emotional development and capacity to make relationships as well as the parents' ability to adapt. If they cannot be successfully treated, children with more severe disorders grow up to become adults with personality disorders, showing continuing difficulty in making relationships, aggressive attitudes and inability to tolerate frustration. Where they have shown delinquent behaviour this will often continue. Robins (1966) found that almost one-third of boys with conduct disorder became delinquent as adults. It has also been shown that parents with personality disorder often have serious difficulties with parenting and thus put the next generation at risk.

Children who have engaged in delinquent behaviour out of school, such as stealing, and whose parents will not support the school in their attempts to deal with this, have a very poor outlook. Lack of parental support is the crucial factor. Where parents are supportive a caution by the police for a first offence has been found to be very effective and the majority of young people do not offend again.

Long-term studies have shown that continuing delinquency during childhood carries a poor outlook for adult life. One study of children referred to child guidance showed that 28% of those manifesting stealing and aggression developed personality disorder as adults as compared to only 4% of those presenting with other problems and 2% of a control group (Robins, 1966).

Prevention

Conduct disorders and delinquency clearly have serious long-term consequences for the future generation. Prevention involves several different agencies and it is interesting to note that smaller, affluent countries, such as Sweden and Finland, with no poverty, have very little delinquency. However, national initiatives such as Home-Start, using trained volunteers working alongside families, are effective and cost £490 per year as compared to up to £150,000 per year to place a child in a secure training centre; the savings to be made in terms of human suffering are even greater (Wilson, 1994).

The importance of communications in the form of civic journalism, networking and encouraging local participation in the revitalizing and rebuilding of communities has been highlighted by the Millennium Report, commissioned by the Rockefeller Foundation (Sharp and Beaudry, 1994). In addition there are large social areas which have an important influence. Preventative approaches would include major political initiatives working towards eliminating poverty, combating unemployment and improving housing. Other measures include:

- Providing extra attention and resources for the under-privileged child. Programmes such as Head Start in the USA have proved to be effective in the long-term. Nurture groups for very young children in school have facilitated learning in London. Evaluation by Enfield Education Psychology Service (1992) of local nurture groups indicates that they constitute a very effective preventative resource, particularly for those families who do not find it easy to attend clinic appointments.
- Supporting schools in providing schemes for parents which offer support and guidance in basic parenting skills.
- Working to keep families together and setting up support systems. These include the provision of adequate numbers of nursery places; supporting volun-

tary agencies such as Home-Start, Newpin and Parents' Network; and financing social services initiatives such as respite neighbourhood care using local foster parents on a flexible basis.

- Resourcing schools and special educational facilities to help meet the needs of children who require additional provision before maladaptive behaviour patterns become entrenched.
- Improving the environment, housing and facilities in impoverished inner city areas.

Summary

1. Numbers of referrals of children with conduct disorders have been steadily increasing, with boys as young as 5 years being permanently suspended from school and virtually out of parental control.

2. The early symptoms of a conduct disorder are frequently seen within the family and include behaviour such as disobedience, lying, stealing and verbal or physical aggression.

3. Delinquency is defined as behaviour which is against the law. A small number of young people show persistent delinquency and cause major problems within a community.

4. The child with a conduct disorder frequently displays an outward appearance of toughness, hiding low self-esteem. Academic achievement tends to be considerably below the child's natural ability.

5. The main cause of conduct disorder is related to the lack of stable, secure family relationships and permanent, reliable parental figures with whom the children can identify.

6. Delinquent children tend to come from homes characterized by marital discord, poor parental supervision, absence of the father, inconsistent management and erratic child-rearing practices.

7. There is a strong association between conduct disorder and difficulty in learning to read.
8. Unless the present increase in serious conduct disorder is faced and remedial action taken in terms of effective emotional and financial support for the families at risk, we are laying up long-term social problems of crime and violence.
9. In addition to the much needed support for families, preventative approaches would include major political initiatives working towards eliminating poverty, combating unemployment and improving housing.

References

Annis, J. (1992) The reasons why children run away. *British Medical Journal*, **304**, 797.

Bennathan, M. (1991) A time for decisions. *Young Minds Newsletter*, No. 7, 1.

Dickinson, D. (1994) Study links crime to rise in jobless. *Guardian*, 7 January.

Douglas, J. W. B. (1966) The school progress of nervous and troublesome children. *British Journal of Psychiatry*, **112**, 1115–6.

Douglas, J. W. B., Ross, J. M. and Simpson, H. R. (1968) *All Our Future*. London: Peter Davies.

Enfield Education Psychology Service (1992) *Report of Nurture Groups in Enfield*. London: EEPS.

Erikson, E. H. (1959) *Identity and the Life Cycle*. Psychological Issues, Monograph 1. New York: International Universities Press.

Foster, J. (1993) Fresh bid to stop thefts by truants. *Metronews*, 26 August.

HMSO (1994) Official figures show one-third of children living in poverty. *Guardian*, 15 July.

Jacobson, R. R. (1985) Child firesetters: a clinical investigation. *Journal of Child Psychology and Psychiatry*. **26**, 759–68.

Kammerling, R. and O'Connor, D. (1993) Unemployment rate predicts psychiatric admissions. *British Medical Journal*, **307**, 1536.

Klein, M. (1975) Notes on some schizoid mechanisms. In *Collected Works*, Vol. III. London: Hogarth Press.

Patterson, G. R. (1982) *Coercive Family Process*. Eugene: Castalia.

Robins, L. (1966) *Deviant Children Grow Up*. Baltimore: Williams and Wilkins.

Rutter, M., Tizard, J., Yule, W., Graham, P. and Whitmore, K. (1976) Isle of Wight studies 1964–1974. *Psychological Medicine*, **6**, 313–32.

Sharp, M. and Beaudry, A. (1994) *Communications as Engagement*. Washington DC: Millennium Communications Group Inc.

Strachan, J. G. (1981) Conspicuous firesetting in children. *British Journal of Psychiatry*, **138**, 26–9.

West, D. J. (1982) *Delinquency: Its Roots, Careers and Prospects*. London: Heinemann Educational.

West, D. J. and Farrington, D. P. (1973) *Who Becomes Delinquent?* London: Heinemann Educational.

Wilson, P. (1994) Start early: end well. *Young Minds Newsletter*, No. 17, 1.

Yarnell, H. (1940) Firesetting in children. *American Journal of Orthopsychiatry*, **10**, 272–82.

Young Minds (1991) Charity urges more help for disturbed youngsters. No. 7, 10.

CHAPTER 6
Aggression, Destructiveness and Bullying: Strategies for Intervention

Descriptions such as 'aggressive' and 'destructive' figure prominently in many of the discussions set up to think about emotionally troubled and disturbed children. It is important to understand as much as possible about the causes of such behaviour, which is not the same as condoning it, in order to be able to plan effective treatments. The aim of treatment is to encourage children to take responsibility for their acts and learn to control their behaviour.

Aggression and anger

Aggression has been described as a non-specific drive behind feelings such as anger, envy, jealousy and greed, which means that it is not a specific emotion in itself. In the majority of cases aggressive behaviour is fired by anger. Anger is generally seen as a positive emotion related to survival. It is a positive response to injustice and unfairness, both of which at a fundamental level represent attacks on our secure sense of self. One central function of anger is to overcome fear and allow us to stand up to people who threaten us either physically or psychologically.

The problem with anger is that it can become explosive, overwhelming and out of control. This is seen typically in the more primitive forms of anger such as the rages of very young children. Toddlers who have temper tantrums are overwhelmed by their anger, as they have not yet developed the emotional equipment to deal with it.

Within the school setting it is very helpful if the teacher can find sufficient time and resources to understand and cope with the children's anger and aggression. If the teacher is unable to tolerate the expression of negative feelings, the child will be forced to store up such feelings and may express them elsewhere. Wittenberg *et al.* (1983) describe how if there is no one available in the child's life to tolerate negative feelings, it increases the child's fear that all aggression is so destructive and powerful that it cannot be dealt with by anyone. As a result the child may inhibit it, leading to an interference with spontaneity and achievements, or become increasingly violent in the hope that someone will help by setting limits.

Destructiveness

Destructive behaviour is closely allied to aggression and may be a result of anger or may be more related to a wish to destroy. Klein (1975), one of the pioneers of child analysis, believes that there is evidence for primary innate destructiveness; a destructive element in us all which we have to keep under control. As the potential for love is innate, it seems likely that the potential for destructiveness is also innate. Undoubtedly there is a very destructive side to human nature which often is not sufficiently acknowledged or controlled.

As part of early development it is crucial that destructive impulses are separated off from more constructive ones. Once having been separated, the two need to be brought together again so that processes of integration can take place. This means that the destructive impulses are modified by kinder, loving feelings and are brought under their control. If something goes wrong and the destructive impulses remain permanently separated off, they are then felt to be unbearable and are likely to be suppressed or disowned. In this state of mind, people are likely to see their own destructive qualities in others and attack them there, treating others very harshly. They are also likely to act in destructive ways without being aware of what they are doing.

Children who act aggressively and who are then treated harshly are not being helped to overcome such tendencies in themselves. These children need to feel that an adult can cope with and understand their behaviour, providing kind but firm limits. This helps them to take responsibility for their behaviour, to feel that it is manageable and to struggle to control it themselves.

It is more difficult to understand the cold destructiveness of the very small group of people previously known as psychopaths and who would now come into the diagnostic category of antisocial personality disorder. These people may show irresponsible behaviour, recklessness, antisocial acts and aggression (Hill and Rutter, 1994), but only a very small minority are violent in a cold, calculating way.

One headteacher reports knowing only one such boy over a period of 15 years. He was charming on the surface but seemed empty inside, attacking other children with a chilling ruthlessness. Consequently, he was a very frightening, unpredictable child with no sense of remorse or guilt. There was no history of deprivation and other children in the family were normal. Despite predictions that he would cause either serious injury or death, no action could be taken as he had not broken the law and he did not want to help himself. However, several years later he ended up in prison committed for grievous bodily harm.

Aggression within the school setting

As a child psychiatrist I tend to see children with problems of aggression where things have gone seriously wrong.

> For instance, a head referred Eddie, a large 5-year-old, urgently when he had to be permanently suspended. All attempts to manage him within school had failed. He was having frequent violent outbursts, lasting for up to an hour, where he completely lost control. Eddie was easily overcome by rage; he couldn't manage even minor frustra-

tions because of the serious deficits in his psychological development, related to a lack of capacity to process feelings.

His mother had experienced a deprived childhood herself. She was depressed after Eddie was born and as a result she was emotionally unavailable to him. Eddie's father had been violent towards his mother, leaving her terrified, and Eddie had witnessed this. He had been exposed to violent experiences which he could neither deal with nor comprehend and as a consequence he was left with enormous inner confusion and had identified with the aggressor, the violent father. Eddie now frightened others, including his mother, particularly when he had an outburst. He was successfully placed at a school for children with emotional and behavioural problems following therapeutic input for both Eddie and his mother.

When he was a young child there was no one available to take in Eddie's feelings, understand them and process them to make them bearable. He had missed out on these normal mothering functions. Bion, as described in Chapter 2, calls this process 'containment'. It is a central concept in all therapeutic work and is something we all do intuitively when responding to others in distress.

Learning to manage violent feelings

A good example of how such moderating experiences repeated over time are eventually internalized and become part of the child's coping processes is seen in the following brief observation.

Marion, a $1\frac{1}{2}$-year-old, was enjoying herself in the garden. It was time to go inside but Marion made it very clear that she did not want to leave. Mother insisted, despite her screams of rage. Mother held onto her, talking to her gently, saying, 'you didn't want to come in, I know, it is hard'. Eventually Marion buried herself against her mother's chest, sobbing. Mother comforted her and she soon recovered.

Here we see a mother helping a child with primitive feelings of rage; holding her both mentally and physically, understanding and conveying that she is safe, mother can tolerate the feelings, and everything will be all right. The overwhelming feelings can be held and thought about until gradually through many repetitions of this process the child will internalize mother's holding ability and will be able to manage her feelings for herself.

In practice, children like Eddie who are too easily overwhelmed by violent feelings need to be made to feel safe and to feel that the violence is containable; this means holding them physically until they calm down and reassuring them that they are safe. Unfortunately, they may need holding for anything from 30 minutes to over one hour. Clearly, it is not possible to manage children who have uncontrollable outbursts like this within an ordinary school, and a more specialized placement is needed. At mother's request Eddie was placed in a day school, but a small minority of emotionally damaged children will require the intensity of 24-hour therapeutic provision within a therapeutic community school if they are to be helped sufficiently.

Causes of aggression

Several factors may give rise to aggressive behaviour, although the first three are relatively rare.

1. Aggression can arise as a result of organic brain dysfunction leading to poor impulse control. Affected children may have a history of difficulties or resuscitation at birth, slow development and immature, impulsive behaviour. They respond to frustration with aggressive outbursts.

2.   Some psychotic children (children with severe disturb-
      ance, out of touch with reality) may have aggressive
      outbursts.
3.   There is a small group of children born with a more
      vulnerable temperament who when under stress very
      easily become aggressive and destructive.
4.   Undoubtedly, however, the most common factor in
      overt aggression in children and adolescents is related
      to negative experiences in early life. Olweus (1980)
      specifically attributes this to negative attitudes and
      rejection by the mother. Similarly, McCord *et al.* (1961)
      found a relationship between aggression in urban, non-
      delinquent   boys   from   lower   socio-economic
      backgrounds aged between 9 and 15 years and early
      experiences of parental rejection, inconsistency, punit-
      iveness and threats.

Patterson (1982) has identified specific problems which can
lead to aggressive conduct disorders. These are related to
difficulties in parenting, such as failures to set rules, to
monitor the child's behaviour, to set out non-aggressive
rewards and punishments, to negotiate compromises and
cope with crises. In these circumstances it is important not
to blame parents but to be aware that they too have difficulties, not of their own making, as a result of either their
temperament or failures in their own parenting.

Wittenberg *et al.* (1983) describe some unhelpful unconscious attitudes towards parents of which the teacher may be
unaware. First, there is hostility towards parents, which may
lead the teacher to very quickly join the child in blaming the
parents and thus avoid looking at the child's contribution to
the situation. This does not help the child to see different
points of view and take on some responsibility. Another possibility is that teachers may be unaware of some unresolved
rivalry with their own parents which may predispose them to
become competitive with parents in an unhelpful way. It is
important, therefore, that teachers and parents see themselves as carrying a joint responsibility for the child's
development and as helping each other in this task.

Outcome for aggressive children

Regardless of the cause, children who are overactive and restless at 3 years of age have an increased likelihood of developing aggressive, defiant behaviour of a severity sufficient to warrant a diagnosis of conduct disorder at 8 years of age (Richman *et al.*, 1982). Conduct disorders in pre-school children may manifest with fighting, defiance and aggression but are typically accompanied by developmental delays, overactivity and emotional disorders, particularly anxiety. Many of these children will need early referral to specialist agencies.

Aggression as rated in secondary schools was found to predict a poor outlook, as it was likely to persist into later life and was associated with other anti-social behaviour (West, 1969). Without help, 50% of aggressive youngsters are at risk of developing an anti-social personality disorder (Robins, 1978). Thus the outcome for children with persistently aggressive behaviour is not good. However, many children can be helped by parents and teachers working together to help children modify and control their aggressive responses.

When to refer for specialist help

Teachers generally know when a child's aggressive behaviour is outside the range of their expertise. For instance, a headteacher explained how she felt the teachers could cope with the majority of children who are aggressive in school but that the boy she was referring was different. He was like a Jekyll and Hyde, changing for no reason from a friendly, pleasant child to someone who was cold, ruthless and destructive. We agreed to see him urgently as this description was worrying and likely to be indicative of a serious disturbance in personality development, when the child has not developed a secure sense of self. Daniel provides a clear illustration of this disturbance and the link between insecurity and destructiveness.

> Daniel, a 5-year-old, had been born with a vulnerable, negative temperament. He managed well until the birth of his brother when he was aged 3 years. Daniel was unable to cope with his jealousy and feelings of being pushed out and it brought out a very destructive side. At times Daniel would viciously attack his brother and could not be left alone with him. Daniel's adjustment and sense of security had been so fragile that his brother's birth had proved too much for him to cope with and left him feeling insecure. As a result his personality changed, with the destructive side frequently taking over and making him cruel and unfeeling.
>
> In school Daniel was usually pleasant but extremely anxious, continually asking for reassurance. However, when the teacher tried to make him more independent, he became very vicious towards other children, hitting them and sneering at the less able children. At home he became unbearable, making his parents' life a misery through his defiant, uncooperative behaviour, and, very worryingly, he had actually tried to harm his brother.
>
> The increased pressure from school had brought out the destructive side even more. Once the pressure was taken off, his attitude and mood improved. Despite normal loving care from his parents, Daniel had not been able to take this in to build up a secure emotional base. This insecurity combined with his more vulnerable and negative temperament made him extremely sensitive to any stressful situation and immediately brought out more destructiveness which then served to protect him from experiencing his own vulnerability. Both Daniel and his mother were offered treatment and this was supported by close liaison with the school. Daniel gradually improved but remained vulnerable.

Aggression and destructiveness as a defence

Most of the children will have experienced rejection, hurt, deprivation and loss and have reacted to the insecurity and pain by becoming aggressive and destructive. The aggressive reaction often starts out as self-defence and the destructiveness arises on the same basis, as a defence against unbearable feelings of insecurity.

Over-harsh reactions and punitiveness drive children to feel that they are totally bad and to internalize intolerant attitudes towards themselves. They may feel so badly about themselves, so ashamed and guilty, that they are unable to take any responsibility for their actions and feelings. Children may bring punishments upon themselves to try to mitigate their sense of guilt or rebel against such severe judgements by acting out in a violent way (Wittenberg *et al.*, 1983).

Destructive impulses may express themselves through envious attacks on others, aggressive behaviour or jealousy. Destructiveness is characterized by spoiling and undermining and is at source an attack on life itself. The destructive attacks may be directed against others or the self, and in certain illnesses a destructive part of the mind attacks its own stable functioning.

It is generally accepted that destructiveness may be stirred up as a reaction to emotional insecurity, deprivation and loss and that reactive forms of destructiveness do occur (Wolff, 1985). Bowlby (1973), for instance, has written widely on separation and loss and describes how the destructiveness seen in disturbed children arises as a direct result of emotionally frustrating and depriving experiences in early life. He describes how children who experience long or repeated separations, and threats of being abandoned or sent away, become very insecure, and develop feelings of hatred, anger and anxiety. The children become anxious about being able to hold in their anger and afraid of further rejection. The resulting tensions make these children prone to irrational, abnormal acts of aggression and anti-social behaviour.

A simple example of insecurity and loss leading to destructiveness comes from therapeutic work with Darren, aged 5 years. He was an emotionally deprived child who for a time was unable to cope with the end of sessions. These stirred up earlier experiences of loss when he had not been helped to manage the frustration. Inevitably, Darren would attack and damage his toys at the end of every session; he had not been exposed to a mother's mental processing of difficult experiences, which would have helped him to tolerate the frustration.

Through long-term therapeutic work Darren was eventually enabled to internalize good mother and father figures who looked after the children, to hold on between sessions and to end with feelings of love and gratitude.

Coping with aggression

There are several broad areas involved in coping with aggression in school. These areas overlap and different combinations of approaches may work for different children and situations. The main areas cover whole-school approaches, a policy for bullying, a policy for persistently troublesome pupils, anger management techniques, working with parents and early intervention.

WHOLE-SCHOOL APPROACHES

The whole-school policy forms the central structure around which individual teachers base their strategies for dealing with individual children. It has been found that such an approach may develop slowly and grow out of existing practice. However, a whole-school policy forms the cornerstone and is essential for developing consistent approaches to undesirable behaviour throughout the school. All children benefit from a consistent approach, as this makes them feel emotionally secure; a clearly defined policy also supports individual teachers.

Generally, rewards are much more effective than punishments, although carefully thought out sanctions are also needed. There are many variations in the use of rewards but one system which has been found to work well when implemented throughout a primary school is described here. A secondary school where both staff and pupils had become trapped in negative attitudes also found that praise, positive attitudes and rewards had an enormous influence for good and in a relatively short period of time turned the whole atmosphere of the school around.

SYSTEMATIC POLICY OF REWARDS

Rewarding children for a wide variety of achievements, academic, social, sporting and artistic among others, does have an effect on school morale. However, it is important to make sure that all the children are able to attain rewards in some area and that the system does not become competitive.

The behaviourist approach used in this general way works by creating a positive atmosphere. There is no evidence to suggest, as is occasionally claimed, that children become overly dependent on what may be thought to be a frivolously over-rewarding approach. At best the children understand that this is a kind of game which adds a light and positive atmosphere to the routine aspects of school life.

All the teachers give out stars for good behaviour and for good work, setting appropriate targets for each child. When the child has gained 10 stars, he or she is given a sticker and 10 stickers lead to a certificate presented by the headteacher. A child can be awarded a sticker for special performance. The final prize for three certificates is a £3 book token. The system carries over from term to term and from year to year.

This approach is combined with an effective strategy within the classroom for stopping minor undesirable behaviour such as shouting out in class. For instance, the teacher writes the offending child's name on the board and every time the child re-offends the teacher puts a tick against the child's name. If the child is given three ticks, he or she has to stay in and write lines at break. If the child is more disruptive, the teacher gives the child a yellow card on which the teacher writes a daily report which has to be signed by the headteacher every day. This means that the child has to wait at the end of school. If there is a more serious offence, the parents are brought in and for the very occasional more disturbed child a report card, written up daily by the teacher and the parent, can be very effective.

Such a systematic approach throughout the school of rewards and sanctions has been found to be effective with 95% of children, and for the remaining 5% it is necessary to intensify the system or, as a last resort, to involve the parents. The aim is to help the children to internalize the capacity to regulate their own behaviour so that the rewards can gradually be withdrawn and become unnecessary.

Children with persistent behavioural problems outside the normal range respond to more immediate rewards. The children are given stars for attaining their own personal target set by the teacher. For instance a child may earn a star for concentrating on a piece of work for 5 minutes. When the child has earned 15 stars he or she is allowed to play for 10 minutes on the Nintendo; an extremely popular reward.

The whole-school policy is clearly written down and, as outlined above, is highly effective. The one problem found so far is that some teachers find it quite difficult in practice as there is a need to be very systematic.

Other strategies which have been found to be useful with children who lose their temper easily or tend to lash out aggressively include a 'comfort' area of large cushions within the classroom and the use of a nominated teacher who deals with that child whenever a crisis arises (Practice to Share 2, 1992).

John, for example, was a large Year 6 child who was liable to violent outbursts of temper. He recognized that he could not control this and could hurt other children. When John started to become aggressive he could be directed towards the cushions and would remain there until he had calmed down and was able to talk about what had made him angry and find a more satisfactory solution.

An infant school whole-school policy included the following strategies:

1. All staff are made aware of those children with considerable needs and any particular difficulty.
2. Whilst recognizing the responsibility of all members of staff, there is a limit to the number of adults in contact with a particular child.
3. One person, usually the class teacher, is nominated to deal with 'crisis' situations wherever they occur.
4. The child is not to be confronted by others who may not have the skills for that child.
5. Crises are slowed down to the point where a rational and sympathetic interaction can take place. This might include 'backing off' from losing situations or removing the child to a comfort area (Practice to Share 2, 1992).

ANGER MANAGEMENT

Strategies for anger management are available and it is useful for teachers to be aware of these. There may be suggestions which teachers would wish to incorporate into their own practice. The underlying aims are to help children admit that they have a problem with anger or aggression, to identify provocative situations and to help them find new ways of coping with these situations.

An anger management programme may consist of individual or group sessions. Each session will focus on a different aspect of the problem until gradually an overall picture is built up, including strategies for dealing with anger. Anger as an emotional response is discussed, both in its constructive aspects and how it can cause problems. The child is encouraged to make a list of things which are likely to cause anger or a loss of temper and if possible to put them in order of severity. The importance of a thinking time is discussed and the child is asked to think of ways to slow down his or her response and thereby avoid a violent outburst. These strategies include relaxation techniques, walking away from the situation, stopping to think, trying to avoid the provocation and the use of the comfort area.

It has been found helpful to ask the child to identify any warning signals such as feeling hot or tapping on the desk. If these can be recognized they can be used to form the first step in the anger management strategy by encouraging the child to associate them with the need for a thinking time.

In general, services such as clinical and educational psychology, child and adolescent psychiatry and some child advisory social work services offer anger management programmes. It is always possible to speak to someone on the phone and find out what is available.

STAFF SUPPORT

An essential part of any policy is to emphasize the need to talk to colleagues about problems with disruptive children. Teachers can feel very isolated alone in the classroom and feel that only they have the problem. A supportive attitude towards each other brings enormous rewards, as once problems are shared the teacher realizes that everyone has their own difficulties. As well as the emotional support, the teacher can be given practical suggestions for dealing with the disruptive child which may, for instance include the child spending time in another teacher's class.

Bullying

As a society we have become more aware of bullying in recent years and the possibility of devastating immediate and long-term effects on children. In the past, teachers and parents may have under-estimated the amount of distress and misery caused. There are some tragic instances where children have killed themselves as a result.

The effects of bullying are not trivial, for either the victim or the bully. Bullying can lead to attempted suicide, suicide, truancy, low self-image, anxiety and depressive illness in the victim. Children's ability to learn and their academic achievements are very likely to be affected. A group of adults recently talked about the lasting effects of being bullied and how it had seriously affected their self-confidence, self-esteem and functioning in adult life. Olweus (1993) found that adults who had suffered from bullying as children were more likely to develop anxiety, depression and low self-esteem. A study of heterosexual men who were having difficulties in forming relationships with women discovered that four out of five of these men had been bullied as children (Gilmartin, 1987).

There are also consequences for the bullies if they are allowed to go unchallenged, as there is then a greater likelihood of the aggressive behaviour continuing into adult life (Robins, 1978). Many violent criminals have begun their life of violence and aggression as school bullies (Elliot, 1993). There is also evidence that boys who bully tend to father children who bully.

DEFINITION OF BULLYING

Bullying can be defined as systematic nastiness involving either verbal abuse, psychological pressure or physical violence towards a child. It includes any systematic unkind comments or actions and comprises a continuum of unpleasantness from name-calling, ostracizing and threatening through to kicking and punching. As secrecy is a central feature, teachers are usually unaware unless the child or parent complains. It needs to be taken seriously. As one child said to me, 'I dread going to school every day knowing I have to face a torrent of abuse.' The situation became so unbearable that he had tried to kill himself.

FREQUENCY OF BULLYING

One study found that approximately 10% of children experience bullying and of these only half those of primary age report it and only 35% of secondary age. Even more worrying is that, having reported the bullying, half those children said that the adults did nothing (Johnstone *et al.*, 1992).

For obvious reasons it is difficult to be sure about the frequency of bullying. Elliot (1993) in a study carried out between 1984 and 1986 found that 68% of children complained of being bullied during this time. Approximately 80% of bullies were boys and 20% girls.

The Sheffield Bullying Project (Sharp and Smith, 1991), which is an extensive research survey based on original work by Olweus in Norway, found that 1 in 10 (10%) of children in primary schools and 1 in 20 (5%) of children in secondary schools were being bullied at least once a week. The results from Sheffield are broadly in line with other research findings. Physical violence was involved in more than 25% of the incidents in secondary schools. In addition, 27% of primary schoolchildren and 10% of secondary schoolchildren said that they had been bullied at some time during that term.

The project found a steady decrease in the numbers of children being bullied as the pupils grew older but the number of children who continued to bully remained the same. This means that bullies tend not to change their behaviour but that the number of victims decreases.

BULLIES

There is no typical stereotype of a bully. Both girls and boys bully although it is more socially acceptable for boys to admit to bullying. There is an idea that bullies tend to be large in size, are rather inadequate and use the bullying to gain respect or power. Sometimes this may be true but it is important to realize that children who bully are not easily recognizable. Bullies may be under- or over-achieving and may be secure or insecure; there is no typical picture.

There is strong evidence that many children bully, and in a survey of over 900 secondary schoolchildren in Scotland, 44% admitted to having bullied at some time in their lives (Mellor, 1991). A similar figure was found for primary schoolchildren in Dublin.

However, it does seem true that there are two main reasons why children bully: first, because they enjoy the feeling of power it provides, and secondly, because it reassures them that they are part of the group and all the bad is located in the scapegoated child outside.

Children who bully as part of a group may well see it as having a bit of fun and not allow themselves to realize that it is actual bullying. Additionally, with group bullying no one feels very much responsibility or guilt, because others are involved.

Some children may become temporary bullies following a traumatic event such as a divorce, a new baby in the family, or the death of someone close, or because of frustration. However, bullies need success. Elliot (1993) gives some additional reasons why children might bully, such as because they:

- like the feeling of power;
- are spoilt;
- feel insecure, inadequate or humiliated;
- have been abused in some way;
- are scapegoated or bullied at home;
- are under great pressure to succeed;
- do not fit in with other children;
- feel no sense of accomplishment or success;
- have suffered from some degree of emotional deprivation.

There is evidence that children who have been exposed to particular attitudes and behaviour at home are much more likely to become bullies. These include lack of warmth, aggressive behaviour accepted as normal and regular physical punishment (Olweus, 1993). On the basis of his research, Olweus describes the factors which seem to predispose to bullying:

- A lack of parental warmth and concern in the early years; this predisposes to later aggression.
- Parents who are permissive or tolerant towards outbursts of aggression; this seems to encourage an escalation of aggressive behaviour which then becomes part of daily life.
- Parents who use physical punishment routinely within the home; their behaviour teaches the children that aggression is an acceptable way of resolving conflicts and difficulties.

Children who bully may start by being reasonably popular but Olweus's research (Olweus, 1993) showed that they become less well-liked as they move up through the school. Such persistent bullies are usually strong, self-assured and with a positive attitude towards violence, making them aggressive towards adults as well as children. These youngsters are very unlikely to be able to empathize with the victim, and other methods of stopping their aggressive behaviour need to be found. In some intractable cases this may be suspension.

Other children who bully may be both anxious and aggressive. Stephenson and Smith (1987) found that one child in five came into that category, with poor concentration, low self-esteem and generally few likeable qualities.

Three general statements can be made about children who persistently bully (Action Against Bullying, 1992): (1) they tend to have aggressive attitudes which they do not try to control; (2) they tend to lack empathy and cannot imagine how the victim feels; and (3) they generally lack feelings of guilt and may twist the evidence to convince themselves that the victim deserves to be bullied.

VICTIMS

It is possible for any child to become a victim just by being in the wrong place at the wrong time. It is common for bullies to try to scapegoat the victim and justify themselves by emphasizing some real or imagined difference. However, any real difference may make a child particularly vulnerable. Differences which can lead to bullying include: (1) a different skin colour; (2) a disability; (3) a different religion; (4) a different accent; and (5) a different background. Bullies tend to pick on children who are vulnerable for some reason but the vulnerability may not be obvious to others.

Racist bullying is common and the Sheffield Bullying Project found that half of all name-calling involved racist names and abuse.

APPROACHES TO BULLYING

It is important for teachers to be aware how difficult it is for children to tell them about being bullied. This may be partly due to threats and fear of reprisal from the bullies as well as to feelings of shame and that it must be somehow their fault. The situation is similar to that in child abuse, where children again find it extremely difficult to tell others about what is happening.

There are several different approaches to bullying, with many overlapping strategies. They have all been successful but only if carried out within the framework of a clear whole school anti-bullying policy. These are:

- no blame approach;
- practical approach;
- buddying;
- conciliation;
- circle time;
- anonymous questionnaires.

No Blame Approach

This was first advocated by Maines and Robinson (1992) from Bristol. It is a thoughtful approach which recognizes that many bullies have problems themselves and uses the group as an instrument of change. There are two main strategies: the bullying children are told how the victim feels and are encouraged to suggest ways of helping, and the teacher meets regularly with members of the bullying group.

The teacher begins by talking to the victim about his or her feelings but does not ask questions about the incidents. The teacher asks who was involved, including any bystanders. The teacher then gathers all the children involved into a group (six to eight children works well). The bullying child or children are not blamed but are told and encouraged to think about how the victim is feeling. Details of the bullying are not discussed.

The teacher tells the group that he or she knows that they can help and encourages each member to think about what he or she can do to make the victim happier. The teacher leaves the responsibility with the group and sets up a meeting with each one individually one week later. After one week the teacher meets with the victim and members of the group separately to find out how things have been going and if necessary continues to monitor the situation until the bullying stops.

The practical approach

It is made clear to the bullying child that bullying is not allowed, that the school takes it very seriously and that the school either imposes sanctions or involves the child's parents, depending on the seriousness of the incident. At the same time, steps are taken to involve the bullying child in some positive activity.

Buddying

Buddying sets out to protect the victim and relies on older children who have been trained to counsel and befriend children who are being bullied or are in need of a friend. Buddying boxes are very useful and enable children to ask for help in confidence. More children come forward if teachers do not have access to these boxes. The victim will feel protected by the presence of the more senior student alongside him or her at break times.

Conciliation

Older children volunteer to act as counsellors and are trained and supervised by teachers with some pastoral experience. These young people are given status within the school, and children who are bullied are encouraged to tell one of the student counsellors. The counsellors, after discussion with the teacher, set out to act as conciliators. They find out how the victim feels and then talk to the bullying child alone. As with the 'no blame' approach they ask the bully to imagine how the victim feels, they explain in fact how the victim is feeling, and also try to understand the child's reasons for bullying. In a proportion of cases the bully is offered time and counselling by the student counsellor, under supervision. The victim and bully are then brought together by the counsellor. The effects of the bullying on the victim are discussed and very often the bully or bullies apologize. If the bullying continues the bully is seen again and more work is done.

Circle time

This is a relatively new idea which has proved very successful, particularly in primary schools. The whole class gathers in a circle once a week and the teacher facilitates open discussion. The children are encouraged to talk about any worries or problems and different subjects are taken as a focus for discussion. It is quite common for children to reveal that they are being bullied during circle time. This can then be dealt with using a combination of the above methods.

Anonymous questionnaires

Several schools have devised their own questionnaires asking about the children's experience of bullying. Schools have found that the students will be honest about the true extent of bullying on such questionnaires and have frequently been shocked by the results. The results can be used to plan strategies to counteract bullying, involving both the pupils and the staff, which can bring out the strengths of the school community (That's Life, 1992).

A combination of these methods should work for most children who bully but, for the rare child who continues despite all interventions, referral to a specialist agency may be indicated. This is particularly true for anxious children who are both bullies and bullied (Pearce, 1991).

OUTCOME FOR VICTIMS

The outcome for victims depends on whether the school can stop the bullying. If the school succeeds, the outcome is usually good, but if it fails to act effectively, the victim is likely to be seriously damaged by the experience. There are lasting effects on confidence and self-esteem. One child said, 'I am just rubbish; they dump on me.' Other effects include missing school and under-achievement as well as depression and sometimes attempts at self-harm. It is easier for children to recover if the bullying is stopped but otherwise the experience may become blocked off and remain as a vulnerable area.

Some significant messages found by Action Against Bullying (1992) are: (1) victims and witnesses need to be encouraged to speak out; (2) the most effective approach is to have an active policy which emphasizes that the school will not tolerate bullying; and (3) leadership from the headteacher is crucial to the success of any initiative.

OUTCOME FOR BULLIES

At least two studies have shown that children who bully are more likely to be involved in criminal activity (Tattum, 1993; Olweus, 1993). Olweus, for instance, discovered that 60% of

12-year-old bullies had a criminal conviction by the age of 24.

A WHOLE-SCHOOL APPROACH

The NPC pack, Coping with Aggression (1992), describes some strategies, including the value of a whole-school approach. There may be a fear that talking about bullying leads to more incidents. In reality this is unfounded, although bullying may be reported more frequently. The schools which emphasized prevention were found to have less bullying as a result. The pack suggests an audit to look at the amount of bullying and where it occurs.

For instance, one teacher asked the children to write down what 'bad' behaviour upset them most in (1) the playground and (2) the class. Although avoiding the word bullying, she found that physical violence of various types was mentioned most frequently in the playground. Others had specifically mentioned bullying and associated behaviour such as name-calling, teasing or being left out of games. Classroom upsets had much more to do with being disturbed while working. Clearly, bullying is more likely to occur in unstructured situations outside the classroom. In order to gain a more precise measure of the scale of the problem, classroom discussions were initiated which defined the characteristics of bullying so that everyone could differentiate more accurately between incidents of verbal or physical aggression and bullying.

In addition, each child was given a simplified map of the school buildings and asked to put a cross were bullying took place, and in this way certain trouble spots were identified. The staff were then able to arrange for increased vigilance in these areas.

Such information can be used to show a need to both staff and governors and also to launch an anti-bullying programme throughout the school. It is useful to involve the children as agents of change. One school, as described in the NPC pack, used the Year 6 class to think of ways to promote the anti-bullying campaign throughout the school. They designed and produced posters and planned an assembly for the whole school in which they acted out examples of bullying and also strategies for minimizing bullying.

Drama is a very powerful medium and can quickly involve children. Language Alive, a Birmingham theatre company for schools, has evolved a powerful play incorporating a girl who is seen to be treated harshly and unfairly at home and who then comes to school and systematically threatens a younger boy, extorting money from him. He in turn finds himself stealing from home in order to produce the money. The children are invited to identify with the different characters and think out variations on the scenes. They are then asked to come and act out a different scenario based on their own suggestions. The children quickly become emotionally involved so that the learning process is much nearer to a real experience and remains with them for a long time.

A suggestion already taken up by many schools for reducing the opportunities for bullying and aggressive behaviour is that of eliminating the afternoon break time. The morning sessions then last until 12.30 and school ends at 3.00.

THE NEEDS OF VICTIMS AND BULLIES

As part of the overall policy it is essential that there is an awareness of the needs of the bullied and the bully and that the necessary provisions to meet these very different needs are clearly set out. Victims may benefit from assertiveness and social skills training. Bullies need to learn to control their aggression as well as being helped to develop their capacity for empathy. It is often possible to use the curriculum to work on bullying through drama, role-play, discussion and games. If the needs of the bully are addressed successfully, then the amount of bullying will naturally decrease. For instance, the bully may crave for attention or power. The teacher may be able to find a constructive role which goes some way to meeting these needs, such as giving the bullying child a protective function with regards to a new child or a special needs child. In practice this worked well in an infant school, where a very aggressive boy was asked to look after and work with a statemented Downs' syndrome child.

IMPORTANCE OF POSITIVE SCHOOL CULTURE

Research shows that schools can be effective and that those with the least bullying have teachers who actively disapprove of and take rapid action against it (Stephenson and Smith, 1987). In the Norwegian and Sheffield studies, differences in the amount of bullying were found between different schools and also between different classes within the same school.

The whole-school approach is crucial in promoting a consistent attitude which disapproves of bullying. This provides the foundation for the different strategies set up to deal with the problem. It is equally important to encourage an atmosphere where telling is seen as positive. Within this framework it is possible to set up standards which oppose aggression even where this runs counter to experience within the home or community.

Such whole-school initiatives can have a very powerful effect. In Norway, for instance, a nationwide campaign reduced bullying by 50% over two years (Olweus, 1993). The children enjoyed school more and there was an associated reduction in other anti-social activities, including stealing and vandalism.

SUMMARY OF IMPORTANT AREAS IN WHOLE-SCHOOL APPROACH

1. Start with a definition of bullying and a policy to deal with it.
2. Emphasize prevention.

3. Relate the policy to social education and the policy on discipline.
4. Act on the policy and support colleagues in taking action.
5. Know the school and the dangerous areas; make spot checks.
6. Support the pupils by making them aware that the school takes bullying very seriously and encourage them to report any incidents.
7. Set up strategies to help both victims and bullies.
8. Use the curriculum and continue to publicize the policy to the pupils, staff, parents and governors.

In conclusion, bullying does matter. Research has found that it is widespread with severe long-term effects on both victim and bully. Schools can have a very powerful effect on reducing bullying through a consistent attitude of disapproval and rapid action. As with other forms of violence against children, doing nothing is likely to reap a bitter harvest in later years (Flood, 1994).

PERSISTENTLY TROUBLESOME CHILDREN

This description refers to children who have an established pattern of disruptive or aggressive behaviour. As mentioned previously, the numbers of these children are increasing, particularly in areas of social deprivation, and although it is important not to produce self-fulfilling terms, it is also important to recognize genuine problems.

It is important to have a clearly defined policy for known 'troublemakers' concerning the consequences if the child transgresses which are agreed with the parent and child. Written contracts can be useful combined with rewards for keeping to the contract.

Some children are unable to manage in an unstructured situation such as a lunchtime play and become aggressive, and yet manage well within the structure of the classroom. These children would be greatly helped if they could be protected from unstructured situations and be given tasks which would remove them from the playground. Possibilities include small indoor clubs, specific helpful activities around the school or being used as an infant 'playleader'.

There are several strategies for a small disruptive group within the class, including separating them out, giving them responsibility, excluding them individually to an adjacent class by arrangement, individual behaviour contracts and a clearly defined policy as to what action to take if a child disrupts, such as immediate removal to the head or deputy.

However, the possibility of keeping disruptive children in at break times has enormous implications for staff. It does need to be recognized that all strategies for dealing with persistently disruptive children put serious additional burdens on the teachers involved as well as having implications for school and LEA budgets. It is very likely that statementing procedures will prove necessary for the majority of these children in order to provide the additional resources required to meet their particular needs.

If none of these strategies works and the child has continuing relationship and behavioural difficulties, it is worth recommending referral to a specialist agency such as a child psychiatry or child guidance team.

WORKING WITH PARENTS

In order to provide a safe holding environment for the child it is essential for the teachers and parents to work together. In some cases, as mentioned above, this may not be possible but a philosophy of partnership where teachers and parents are seen to have different but equally important roles is extremely helpful.

A good example comes from a nursery school but is applicable in all schools (Practice to Share 2, 1992). The school's aim is to develop an integrated educational system that supports and involves parents in the education and care of their children. As part of this they have developed an in-service programme for parents, including help with behavioural problems. Parents are invited to attend regular meetings to learn how to cope with and understand difficult behaviour as well as addressing a wide range of issues of mutual interest.

In this school the children's behaviour was identified as a particular priority because of a variety of behavioural problems. Parents were seeking advice on specific problems, staff felt there was often a mismatch between parental expectations and the 'normal' behaviour of a 3- or 4-year-old and finally there was a recognition of the importance of establishing a consistent approach between school and home.

As a result all teaching and support staff need to clearly define a policy on what is considered acceptable and unacceptable behaviour, share good practice and devise appropriate rewards and sanctions. All new parents have a copy of the behaviour policy and are supported on a daily basis with complementary school and home reward systems.

Although such a parent programme may help to gain the co-operation of some difficult parents, there may well be some who will need very careful handling. These can range from parents with very unconcerned attitudes to those showing active aggression, and their behaviour may have nothing to do with the school directly but result from mental illness or disordered personality functioning. Some parents may connive at or even encourage a child to stay away from school in order to fulfil their own needs. In these cases, it is often helpful to find the most appropriate senior member of staff to deal with that parent and for them to be involved on every occasion.

EARLY IDENTIFICATION

The early identification of children with problems enables treatment strategies to be instituted as soon as possible and gives the child the best hope for a good outcome. Some assessment of the nature and severity of the problem is necessary in order to set up the appropriate treatment. Experienced teachers are very competent in recognizing those children who can be helped within the school, often using a joint approach and working closely with parents and those children who need a more specialist input.

References

Bowlby, J. (1973) *Separation, Anxiety and Anger*. London: Hogarth Press.

Elliot, M. (1993) *Kidscape: Stop Bullying*. London: Kidscape.

Flood, S. (1994) Bullying: cause, effect and prevention. *Young Minds Newsletter*, No. 17.

Gilmartin, B.G. (1987) Peer group antecedents of severe love-shyness in males. *Journal of Personality*, **55**, 467–89.

Hill, J. and Rutter, M. (1994) Personality disorders. In M. Rutter, E. Taylor and L. Hersov (eds) *Child and Adolescent Psychiatry, Modern Approaches*. London: Blackwell Scientific Publications, pp. 668–96.

Johnstone, M., Munn, P. and Edwards, L. (1992) *Action Against Bullying*. Glasgow: SCRE.

Klein, M. (1975) Envy and gratitude. In M. Khan (ed.) *Envy and Gratitude, Collected Works*, Vol. III. London: The Hogarth Press, pp. 176–235.

Maines, B. and Robinson, G. (1992) *The No Blame Approach*. Bristol: Lame Duck Publishing.

McCord, W., McCord, J. and Howard, A. (1961) Familial correlates of aggression in non-delinquent male children. *Journal of Abnormal Social Psychology*, **62**, 79–93.

Mellor, A. (1991) Helping victims. In M. Elliot (ed.) *Bullying: A Practical Guide to Coping in Schools*. London: Longman.

Olweus, D. (1980) Familial and temperamental determinants of aggressive behaviour in adolescent boys: a causal analysis. *Developmental Psychology*, **16**, 644–60.

Olweus, D. (1993) *Bullying at School: What We Know and What We Can Do*. Oxford: Blackwell.

Patterson, G.R. (1982) *Coercive Family Process*. Eugene, Oregon: Castalia Publishing Company.

Pearce, J. (1991) What can be done about the bully? In M. Elliot (ed.) *Bullying: A Practical Guide to Coping Schools*. London: Longman.

Practice to Share 2 (1992) *Coping with Aggression*. Oxford: National Primary Centre.

Richamn, N., Stevenson, J. and Graham, P. (1982) *Preschool to School: a Behavioural Study*. London: Academic Press.

Robins, L. (1978) Sturdy childhood predictors of adult antisocial behaviour: replication from longitudinal studies. *Psychological Medicine*, **8**, 611–22.

Sharp, S. and Smith, P.K. (1991) Bullying in UK schools: the DES Sheffield Bullying Project. *Early Child Development and Care*, **77**, 47–55.

Stephenson, P. and Smith, D. (1987) Anatomy of a playground bully. *Education*, 18 September, 236–7.

Tattum, D. (1993) Child, school and family. In D. Tattum (ed.) *Understanding and Managing Bullying*. Oxford: Heinemann.

That's Life (1992) *Practical Steps to Tackle Bullying*. London: BBC Television.

West, D.J. (1969) *Present Conduct and Future Delinquency*. London: Heinemann.

Wittenberg, I., Henry, G. and Osborne, E. (1983) *The Emotional Experience of Learning and Teaching*. London: Routledge and Kegan Paul.

Wolff, S. (1985) Non-Delinquent disturbances of conduct. In M. Rutter and L. Hersov (eds) *Child and Adolescent Psychiatry: Modern Approaches*. London: Blackwell Scientific Publications, pp. 400–13.

CHAPTER 7
Eating Disorders

Anorexia nervosa

Anorexia nervosa is a mysterious disorder, not yet fully understood, which involves the fear of fatness and an active striving after thinness. It occurs mainly in adolescent girls, who make up 95% of cases, but is also seen occasionally in boys and prepubertal children.

There are striking differences between affluent and poor countries, with the disorder being extremely rare in the less developed parts of the world. For instance, there has been a recent report (Bryant-Waugh and Lask, 1991) describing anorexia for the first time in Asian children, but the eight young Asian girls affected were all living in this country.

Some occupations are associated with an increased risk, especially those where physical appearance is important, such as fashion students and ballet dancers. More cases tend to occur in young women who stay on at school in the 16–18 age group. The prevalence (which is the total number of cases in the general population) is thought to be increasing at present, although in the 1970s it was 1 in every 100,000 people and a rare condition.

The disorder has three main aspects:

- a significant loss of weight due to refusal to eat;
- a distortion of thinking when estimating body size;
- an endocrine disorder, causing the periods to stop in girls and a loss of sexual interest in boys. Starvation is thought to be the major cause (Lawrence, 1984).

Two factors which predict a more favourable outcome are (1) an earlier age at onset, generally between 13 and 17 years, and (2) a relatively recent onset; the shorter the time that the symptoms have been present, the greater the likelihood of successful treatment. Prepubertal children tend to have a poor outcome.

From the available evidence it has become clear that not all anorexics share the same underlying problems. Undoubtedly the condition is related to factors such as sex, age, occupation and the affluence and social attitudes of Western countries, but these in themselves do not explain how the illness comes to take its particular form; an irrational striving after thinness. Two important hypotheses have been proposed, which are not mutually exclusive.

First hypothesis: an underlying personality disorder
Bruch (1974) puts this forward, and in describing the personality disturbance she identifies three main areas of disordered functioning. The first is the disturbed body image, which is usually of delusional proportions; secondly, there is the inability to recognize accurately the bodily sensations of hunger and fullness; and thirdly, there is as she describes it, 'a paralysing sense of ineffectiveness'. Bruch postulates that this then results in a misdirected striving for control; a striving to control food intake, weight and body size.

Bruch believes that these three areas of disordered functioning are a result of faulty personality development from the very earliest stages of life. She suggests that early difficulties in the parent–child relationship prevent the child from developing a secure sense of self and a sense of potency which then inhibits the growth of independence.

This hypothesis has grown out of Bruch's longstanding work with anorexic young women. She found that they were often described as particularly good and compliant as children, but on closer examination it became clear that this was based on the development of a false self. Feelings of insecurity about themselves and their inner worth made them feel they had to please in order to be loved. These young women had not been able to take in a secure sense of being valued for themselves.

The emotional changes and turbulence of adolescence, according to this theory, lead to a paralysing sense of power-lessness and feelings of not being in control. As a result, the drive for a sense of empowerment and control is then turned inwards and is seen as an attempt to maintain a precarious sense of self-esteem. Bruch's theory implies that anorexics with these underlying problems are likely to have been psychologically damaged at an early stage of develop-ment.

According to this theory, the weight loss acts as a smoke-screen for the more hidden problems which centre on how the young person feels about herself. This is supported by Salmons' observation (Salmons, 1986) that, fundamentally, these young people feel badly about themselves and feel bad inside. She believes that this awareness provides the key to understanding the illness.

Unfortunately, once the distorted thinking becomes estab-lished the young person suffers what could be described as a breakdown in normal psychological functioning and very self-destructive ways of thinking and behaving take over. It seems that because of the underlying vulnerability and in-secure personality development the young person is unable to cope with the stress of adolescence and breaks down into the self-destructive illness of anorexia. Part of the reason for the choice of illness could well be to avoid or reverse the physical changes of puberty.

Second hypothesis: anorexia results from a fear of sexuality
This theory, as put forward by Crisp (1980), suggests that the illness fundamentally serves to protect the young person from having to face conflicts about sexuality. Again, the weight loss is seen as a smokescreen for underlying anxieties but it also has a central role in avoiding conflicts about growing up and taking on a mature sexual role. The weight

loss leads to a prepubertal body shape and reverses the hormonal changes of puberty. In this way the feared situation can be avoided. This theory implies a less severe disorder, as although there is a developmental crisis at adolescence, it does not suggest that this occurs on the basis of a longstanding disturbance of personality.

THE INFLUENCE OF CULTURAL ATTITUDES

In Western cultures a slim figure is seen as socially desirable and it seems likely that social pressures largely account for the particular choice of symptoms, focusing as they do on weight and thinness. Bruch's model would offer an explanation in terms of self-esteem, as the young person feels badly about herself and lives in a society which sees fatness as bad and slimness as good. It follows that fatness could easily then be equated with being bad, ugly and unacceptable, and thinness in this context could be equated with being good and acceptable. However, this does not explain the distorted thinking and almost compulsive nature of the illness.

The attitudes to weight and eating found in anorexia have been shown to be present to a much greater degree than the actual illness (Clarke and Palmar, 1983). This finding was confirmed by Hill (1991), who questioned both 9- and 14-year-old girls about their views on weight, physical appearance and ideal shape. The results showed that the two groups were indistinguishable, in that dieting and slimming had become a significant feature of a 9-year-old's world.

Hill was concerned that children seem to be exposed to the same cultural pressures as adults and were not being protected. It seems that these attitudes to body shape have become part of our thinking and are reinforced by the media in the way they portray role models for young people. It is recognized that dieting is a risk factor for anorexia but the outcome for these 9-year-olds is not yet known. However, Hill is clear that it is important for teachers, parents and doctors to be aware of these concerns in young children, particularly as there is evidence that the incidence of all eating disorders is increasing (Rutter, 1991).

It has been suggested by Chernin (1981) that the over-valuation of slimness in Western cultures is also related to the changing role of women and is at source an attack on femininity. The hypothesis is that at an unconscious level men feel threatened by women and boyishness is therefore encouraged.

PSYCHOANALYTIC MODEL

This has similarities with Bruch's hypothesis in that psycho-analytic views place the origin in early mother–child relationships, focusing on experiences of feeding and intim-acy. Davies (1991) describes how the anorexic shows both a fear of an intimate relationship and a desperation for it, which in fantasy may become linked to fears both of poison-ing and of starvation.

Trevarthen (1993) and Stern (1985) describe how a young child has a primary need for emotional contact and sharing. Around the age of 7–15 months the child develops an aware-ness that others have an inner subjective life of their own. This need for intimacy includes taking in a knowledge of the mother's mind. When these basic needs are not met, this may result in a strong sense of greed and a turning away from relationships to a powerful, destructive part of the self. The turning away (as with emotionally deprived children) functions as both a survival mechanism and as a protection from pain. Consequently, the child's sense of self is seriously compromised, often leading to the conformity of a false self during the childhood years.

The conflicts of adolescence may then prove too much for the young person's very fragile self and there may be a breakdown into anorexia. The deep-seated sense of greed stems from early experiences of deprivation and despera-tion, and the refusal to eat represents an attempt to take control of such unacceptable urges.

In more severe cases the destructive self acts as a barrier

around the anorexic adolescent in order to keep out all the painful, unmanageable feelings. It can take over her mind and she may rapidly become trapped inside, too afraid to come out. This powerful, destructive part seeks to undermine all goodness and positive links with other people. It tells lies, for example that starving herself is for her own good. In this situation the healthy part is often very small and the therapist needs to be patient, just being there and reaching out.

Magagna (1993) emphasizes the denial of emotions which she feels occurs in any eating disorder. She describes how young people with anorexia are unable to rely on an inner capacity to tolerate and process emotions. As a result they turn to omnipotent control as their only way of protecting themselves from painful feelings. She shows how this denial of feelings involves cutting off from the more vulnerable parts of the self which in turn delays the development of emotional maturity.

MULTI-DIMENSIONAL MODEL

It makes sense to think of anorexia as the outcome of a range of different circumstances and causes. The symptoms can be seen as the final common pathway for a variety of underlying psychological problems. It is clear that some young women with anorexia are seriously disturbed and have associated personality disorders, whereas others have relatively intact personalities. The disturbed group tend to have more destructive and distorted ways of thinking.

Many of the less ill group seem to precipitate themselves into anorexia in order to avoid the conflicts of adolescence. Interestingly, Lawrence (1984) feels that if they were given more support these young people would manage the stresses without breaking down into illness. Schools could make an important contribution here, provided they were given the resources to set up the necessary counselling and pastoral care.

Depressive symptoms are common once the condition has

become established and a 25% loss of body weight has occurred. It is generally found that the depression is a consequence of and secondary to the eating disorder.

THE ONSET OF THE ILLNESS

Typically, the story is of a young adolescent girl, around the age of 15, who has decided to diet because of concern about being overweight. She may or may not be overweight but continues to diet after a reasonable weight loss has occurred. She avoids all fattening foods, sometimes exercises to extreme and may become preoccupied with food, preparing it for others but not herself. She has become taken over by a striving for thinness which, because of her distorted perception of her body size, never allows her to feel satisfied. She always sees herself as much fatter than she really is, to the extent of putting her life at risk. To achieve her aim she may resort to laxative abuse or self-induced vomiting. If she remains untreated, the physical effects of starvation eventually come to dominate the picture, although this is rare because the majority of sufferers are treated. There is the risk in severe cases that death may occur from electrolyte imbalance and heart failure.

Once serious weight loss has occurred, the refusal to eat becomes very entrenched. In the young person's mind food, which is essential to life, becomes something bad and to be avoided. For these young girls, particularly the group with personality disturbance, it seems that basic trust in a nurturing mother has never been established. These young people have often experienced a disturbed relationship with their mothers, perhaps of an overprotecting or overcontrolling nature, or where the mother's needs have intruded, resulting in a lack of responsiveness to the child's individuality and needs.

> Mandy, aged 15, showed this lack of trust. She suddenly started to diet and rapidly lost more than 2 stones, so that her weight was below 6 stone. She

could not see anything wrong with this and would not believe she was in any danger. There was a small part of her which could see things from an adult and rational point of view, but there was a much stronger part of her which was convinced that food was bad and this part overruled her reason. The confusion stemmed from childhood experiences but at this stage she could not trust either her mother or her therapist.

Another example, taken from the therapy of a 14-year-old boy, shows the usual parental pattern reversed, with a rigid, controlling father and a passive mother (Fortunato and Meltzer, 1977).

Giuseppi was losing weight, refusing food and had all the symptoms of anorexia. It gradually become clear that this boy's refusal to eat stemmed from the fear of his own greedy and destructive impulses, which had resurfaced at adolescence. Neither parent had been able to offer appropriate nurturing and it is known that early failures and deprivation can give rise to deep-seated feelings of greed and destructiveness. It was these he tried to control by not eating. The young man was seeking to control unacceptable impulses within himself. The need to exert control over the inner world or the outer world can be seen as an attempt to modify an inner sense of badness or inadequacy. There is in fact a confusion here between good and bad, for in trying to do what feels right, this young man was actually being very self-destructive. Because of earlier experiences he had not been able to securely internalize a benign, thoughtful parental figure who could help him exercise the necessary control over destructive impulses.

Fortunately, this patient was able to establish a good nurturing relationship with his therapist and quickly put on weight. He continued to work with her, wanting to take as much responsibility as he could for understanding his problems himself. After two years he was able to manage on his own, having internalized a sufficiently caring and thinking parental figure to maintain the good outcome.

TREATMENT

The condition is life-threatening, yet all the anxiety tends to be lodged in other people such as parents, teachers and therapists and is not experienced by the patient. Teachers may be the first to realize that one of their students is losing an abnormally large amount of weight, although anorexics are very skilful at wearing loose-fitting clothes and hiding the weight loss. However, it is vital to take this seriously, as the outlook is generally much better if the condition is treated early. If it seems possible that the student has anorexia and is not being treated, it is advisable to contact the parents and suggest early referral to the family doctor. The patient is likely to deny the problem, but if there is evidence of continuing weight loss it is necessary to stand firm. The family doctor may initially treat the patient and monitor his or her weight, but specialist referral to a child and adolescent psychiatrist is usually indicated.

Effective treatment has to address two areas of concern; first, there is a need for someone to take responsibility for the young person's weight and for keeping him or her alive; and secondly, there is a need for the underlying conflicts to be understood. It is preferable if these roles can be taken on by different people, for example the family doctor or paediatrician to monitor the weight and a psychiatrist or psychotherapist to work on the underlying problems.

The first task is to try to establish a relationship with the young person, who is often hostile, and has been brought along unwillingly. It is important to try to reach beyond the smokescreen of weight loss. Young people respond differently and it is important to be able to offer a variety of treatment approaches. However, it is generally agreed that some form of psychotherapy is essential in the long-term management of these patients, as well as work with the family (Salmons, 1986). Family therapy has been extensively used and has been shown to improve the outcome at one year in younger patients (Russell *et al.*, 1987).

The immediate goals are to keep the young person out of hospital and to begin to establish a trusting relationship. Several writers draw attention to the importance of developing a relationship where the patient can begin to trust and also accept the nurturing from the therapist. There may be a race against time, as once the patient's weight and health deteriorate beyond a certain point, hospital admission becomes essential.

Initially it often seems that anorexic patients are not able to work at a feeling level and it gradually emerges that they do not recognize or trust their own feelings (Salmons, 1986). Once in a therapeutic relationship where trust is developing, the young person is enabled to experience his or her feelings within a safe setting and is sometimes surprised at their strength. The therapist is offering a responsive, thoughtful relationship, comparable to that provided by a mother to her child in order to foster emotional growth.

The abnormally low weight (often a loss of 25% of original body weight) tends to lead to a state of arrested psychological development, and until there is a weight gain it is not possible to make progress in maturational tasks (Salmons, 1986). The illness may also provide a diversion from family problems which may now emerge. Although the condition varies greatly in severity, in many instances, with the support of an understanding therapist, considerable progress may be made in establishing a more secure emotional base and in negotiating appropriate developmental tasks.

OUTCOME

There are different views as to what constitutes recovery; for some workers a sustained weight gain is the main criterion, whereas others apply more rigorous measures. Results are also complicated by the fact that some anorexics are very much easier to treat than others. This needs to be kept in mind when evaluating treatment approaches. For instance, Minuchin (1978) make optimistic claims for family therapy but their patients were all young, living with their families and had only a brief duration of symptoms; a group with a good outlook in any circumstances.

At the other end of the spectrum, 41 more seriously ill patients who all needed hospital admission were followed up after 20 years (Ratnasuriya *et al.*, 1991). A good outcome was found in 30%, an 'intermediate' outcome in 32%, and a poor outcome in 38%. Of these, 15% had died from causes related to anorexia and another 15% had developed bulimia nervosa. In this series the numbers were small and they were not representative of the range of anorexic patients, as a number had already failed to respond to treatment in other hospitals. However, this study highlights the serious nature of anorexia when it takes a chronic course.

As already described, they also found that a poorer outcome was associated with a later age of onset, poor adjustment to circumstances, a history of neurotic and personality disturbances, disturbed relationships within the family and a longer duration of illness.

It was found that patients could recover after 15 years, but the rate of recovery decreased sharply after that, until after 20 years 40% of these more disturbed patients were still seriously incapacitated or had died. The deaths were from electrolyte imbalance or suicide. Of equal significance was the amount of incapacity; one-third were leading socially restricted lives with great dependence on their families. Attitudes to sexuality, marriage and childbearing were still difficult for half the patients. These results are comparable to those of other long-term studies, which have shown that about half of all anorexic patients remain underweight and have continuing social and sexual difficulties.

The outcome is generally related to severity, with young women with serious disorders of their personality at one end of the spectrum and young women with relatively normal personalities at the other. In general, over the whole range of illness 50–60% will make a full recovery.

PREVENTION

Prevention of eating disorders must depend to some extent on changing social attitudes to body shape. Bodily appearance and self-esteem are closely related in all adolescents.

Role of teachers and school

Salmons *et al.*, (1988), on the basis of their study on body-shape dissatisfaction in schoolchildren, suggest that primary prevention should focus on education in positive attitudes to body shape. This means promoting an understanding and acceptance of the individuality of shape as well as thinking about sensible eating choices. In schools they suggest an emphasis on helping children to resist cultural pressures for a very thin shape and to accept the biological range of size and shape. In trying to help young people accept themselves as they are, a positive attitude from teachers can be of great service in making the children feel good about themselves.

These recommendations rely on teachers being able to take on yet another area of concern but hopefully some schools may be able to incorporate work on attitudes to body size and eating into an already existing curriculum area. Positive attitudes towards the children and building up their self-esteem are hopefully already part of the school philosophy.

As already mentioned teachers may be the first to recognize the problem and be involved in encouraging the family to seek help. In an ideal world schools would also provide support and counselling services to help vulnerable young people through the difficulties and emotional turmoil of adolescence.

Bulimia

Bulimia nervosa (usually called bulimia for short) and anorexia nervosa are often seen as separate but closely related disorders. The symptoms and underlying psychological problems overlap and again this disorder is much more common in women. Up to one-third of young women with bulimia have a past history of anorexia nervosa. Studies show that between 1% and 2% of young women in the UK suffer from bulimia (Fairburn and Beglin, 1990).

KEY FEATURES

The three main aspects of bulimia are:

- episodes of overeating;
- compensatory behaviour;
- disturbances of attitude.

Episodes of overeating
The central feature of bulimia is a powerful and irresistible urge to overeat. There is an abnormal preoccupation with food, and periodic binges of overeating occur which are felt to be unpleasant, excessive and beyond voluntary control. The fattening effects of the food are then usually counteracted by self-induced vomiting, purging or episodic starvation. Depression and self-depreciating thoughts almost inevitably follow a binge. Although weight fluctuations occur and bulimics tend to share with anorexics a pathological fear of becoming fat, most patients remain within their normal range for weight.

Some bulimics will eat huge amounts of food over one to two hours. These binges tend to be secret, may be pre-planned and are often followed by depression, guilt or even suicidal behaviour. In a few cases the binges occur several times a day and the greater their frequency, the greater the likelihood of depression.

Compensatory behaviour
Young people with bulimia often try to prevent the weight gain that would normally follow a binge by taking laxatives, vomiting or exercising.

Disturbances of attitude
Although usually of normal body weight, bulimics tend to see themselves as fat and ugly. They believe that by losing weight they will feel better, and often starve themselves between binges. A sense of failure, low self-esteem and lack of control are common.

ONSET AND ADDITIONAL FEATURES

The onset is generally in mid-adolescence to late adolescence or early adulthood and there is a high prevalence of depressive symptoms. It has been found that bulimic women are at risk for suicide attempts and the condition is associated with low self-esteem, self-mutilating behaviour, and alcohol and drug abuse (Freeman and Munro, 1988).

As in anorexia, there is the determination to take control of body weight and a fear of fatness but the patient may not be thin, in women periods often continue, and in general the patient is less ill. To make the diagnosis the condition has to be clearly established over a period of time as bingeing, vomiting and laxative abuse may occur as a passing phase in a young woman of this age.

FAMILY CHARACTERISTICS

In contrast to the overprotecting and overcontrolling parents often found with anorexics, the families of bulimic women are found to be characterized by low cohesiveness between family members and a lack of emphasis on independent or assertive behaviour. There are high levels of conflict within these families, together with a low emphasis on the open expression of feelings (Johnson and Flach, 1985).

UNMET EMOTIONAL NEEDS

In bulimia the patient may feel a compulsion to eat in order to fill an inner sense of emptiness which at source is psychological and not physical. Lovett (1990) describes this in a bulimic young man who was aware that he ate 'in order to feel full'. However, once taken in the food is then experienced as bad because it is fattening and he wants to get rid of it. For the patient the whole cycle is unsatisfying and depressing, as his underlying emotional needs have not been addressed or understood and he feels driven to continue this process.

TREATMENT

Freeman and Munro (1988) report that bulimia is reasonably easy to treat and their own study showed that it is amenable to treatment by once-weekly structured behavioural therapy over a period of four months in either individual or group form. Their impression was that tackling the symptoms of bingeing, self-induced vomiting and laxative abuse directly was the most important therapeutic element, and any subsequent attitudinal change occurred as a consequence of the behavioural change and not the other way around. Overall, 75% of the 92 women patients were symptom-free after 15 weeks.

Treatment with anti-depressant medication has been used but the available evidence suggests that therapeutic approaches, including behavioural, individual or group therapy, produced greater overall change and more stability in maintaining that change. Cognitive therapists have identified some unhelpful beliefs held by bulimic women such as 'being fat is the worst thing of all' or 'I need to take control of everything in my life', and their work sets out to challenge these beliefs.

Claire was treated using individual psychotherapy which concentrated initially on her symptoms but then moved on to thinking about her relationship with her family and her feelings about herself. There was a good outcome after six months of treatment at fortnightly intervals. Claire developed bulimia at the age of 15 and the family relationships illustrate the lack of cohesiveness described. Her parents had separated when she was aged 3 and she had no contact with her father. Claire now lived with her mother and stepfather and unfortunately had a very bad relationship with her stepfather. At the same time her mother seemed to have little awareness of her daughter's needs or feelings, and she tended to treat Claire as a stranger within the house. Virtually all communication had broken down.

Eventually, after three months of treatment, Claire felt able to write a letter to her mother explaining her feelings and her wish for a closer relationship. Her mother responded and from these tentative beginnings a closer relationship developed. As the relationship improved so did Claire's symptoms and her bulimia and self-induced vomiting gradually stopped altogether.

OUTCOME

Predictably, the group of bulimics who have a personality disturbance which is associated with high rates of impulse disorders such as drug or alcohol abuse, self-mutilation, shoplifting or attempted suicide form a difficult group to treat successfully. Again, the group of bulimics without personality disorders are much easier to treat and in fact the study quoted by Freeman and Munro had patients with very low rates of impulse-related behaviours. In their series, 75% of patients achieved a good outcome in terms of control of symptoms and attitudinal change.

Clearly, bulimia presents a serious and prevalent health problem. Untreated, the symptoms are likely to continue for many years, and Garner (1987) not surprisingly found that many bulimics still had symptoms at the end of treatment. For bulimic as well as anorexic young women, issues of control, self-image and independence are usually central and treatment approaches may need to address all these issues in a flexible and appropriate way. Both anorexia and bulimia are based on a lack or incompleteness of healthy feeding and intimate relationships leading to varying degrees of failure to develop sound and healthy identifications.

ROLE OF TEACHERS AND SCHOOL

Teachers and schools have a preventative role to play in discussions about sensible eating habits and fostering positive self-esteem in all children, helping them to accept themselves as they are and building on their strengths. Again, support and counselling for the more vulnerable adolescents can help them to cope with the normal stresses of adolescence and thus lessen the risk of an eating disorder.

Obesity and overeating

This has been defined as a weight 20% above average for age, sex and height. In many cases this is constitutionally determined and there seems to be a fairly constant weight which is naturally maintained. It is well known that people who lose weight through dieting have a strong tendency to regain that weight once they stop. Recent research has shown that it is healthier to remain at a fairly constant weight than go through considerable variations.

However, Bruch (1974) has demonstrated that in some people obesity can be a symptom of psychological disturbance, especially where they use eating to comfort themselves. Various family situations may contribute to overeating in predisposed children. For instance, Andrew was a rather neglected child whose younger brother was preferred and at times of additional stress he turned to food to compensate for the lack of affection.

EMOTIONAL DEPRIVATION

Emotionally deprived and rejected children may turn to food to fill an emptiness within. These children eat voraciously without gaining weight and tend to be small and look uncared for. It is often the school who draws attention to the child's huge appetite; It is as if the child can never eat enough. Of course, food is not what they really need and intensive support from a network of professionals is essential to prevent further emotional damage to the child.

OVERPROTECTIVE PARENTS

Some overprotective parents may overfeed their child without being aware of their underlying wish to keep the child in a close and dependent relationship. This leads to an overweight, emotionally immature child who is vulnerable to bullying.

ROLE OF TEACHERS AND SCHOOL

There are possibilities for the prevention of obesity through interventions in schools, such as health education, as well as identifying children with emotional causes for referral to the family or school doctor. Weight at the age of 11 years has been found to be as good a predictor of obesity at the age of 36 years as is weight at the age of 20 years. This means that children who are overweight at the age of 11 are likely to be overweight at the age of 36.

Eating disorders in young children

Serious eating problems do occasionally occur in young children, usually in the form of a refusal to take in food. Two other rare disorders called rumination and pica also reflect serious conditions.

PICA

Pica is the name given to the eating of substances that are not food, such as paper, cloth, carpet, wood or soil. It is found in children with brain damage or mental handicap but it also occurs very occasionally in children of normal ability. In the latter case it is always a very worrying symptom and tends to indicate severe levels of neglect, emotional deprivation and distress. The pica is usually part of an overall picture of disturbed behaviour and the children come from impoverished and disorganized homes. In all cases, referral to the family doctor is essential and he or she will often refer the child on to the local child psychiatry service for more intensive work with the family. In severe cases admission to hospital may be necessary.

RUMINATION

Rumination occurs in babies between the ages of 3 and 12 months and consists of the continuing regurgitation of food into the mouth without any physical cause. There is an associated failure to gain weight. In the majority of cases this indicates problems in the relationship between mother and child and consequently requires early intervention.

FOOD REFUSAL

Many young children go through short-lived phases of

refusing to eat which resolve spontaneously. However, a much smaller number show a continuing difficulty with accompanying weight loss and failure to thrive.

MOTHER–CHILD RELATIONSHIP PROBLEMS

In small children these longstanding eating problems reflect underlying difficulties in the mother's relationship with the child and are often based on a primary confusion as to whether the food being offered is good or bad. This often comes about when the mother has a severe psychological disturbance which she cannot help communicating to the child. She may be extremely anxious or conveying more disturbing psychotic (disturbed sense of reality) feelings which affect her state of mind and her ability to be responsive to her child.

In these circumstances young children may try to protect themselves by shutting off from everything coming from outside. Very young children cannot separate the body and mind in the way that older children can. This means that the baby may be aware in some way that the disturbing sensations are coming from the mother but due to immaturity has no way of distinguishing taking in milk or food from taking in damaging feelings. The result is that the baby shuts off emotionally as well as refusing to take in food. There is the danger, unless urgent treatment is given, that the child, having cut off from the mother, may turn to an omnipotent or perverse part of himself or herself, leading to a very serious disturbance in personality development.

Bentovim (1970) has also described how distorted parent–child relationships may produce feeding problems which prevent children taking in sufficient food for normal growth. In these cases careful work is needed, often with both mother and child, preferably by a trained child psychotherapist.

> Barry was a 5-year-old referred for severe difficulties with eating. He had vomited as a baby, and this

had led to numerous hospital admissions, although no physical cause was found. Later he refused feeds so that it took hours to feed him. When first seen by a psychiatrist he was an attractive but delicate-looking child, underweight for his height, who chose to draw his family in the first session. All the family members were drawn in a similar way, except for his mother, who was portrayed with large bulging eyes which made her appear terrified but would also frighten a young child. In fact she was an extremely anxious women, not eating vegetables or fruit herself, and was very guarded. Barry's eating improved following work using a psychother-apeutic approach, when both he and his mother felt more understood and there was a safe place where the anxiety and fear could be held in mind and modified.

Failure to thrive

Failure to thrive describes children who show an abnormally slow growth in height and weight. The result is a small, underweight child. In at least two-thirds of cases no physical cause is found. The diagnosis of non-organic failure to thrive clearly indicates that emotional factors are central, usually varying degrees of emotional deprivation. These children often live in areas of high social deprivation where inadequate nutrition is relatively common. Referral to a consultant paediatrician is generally necessary to exclude organic factors and to initiate an appropriate multi-disciplinary treatment plan for the emotionally deprived child.

In practice the diagnosis of non-organic failure to thrive is made on a combination of factors, including the national norms for height and weight and the emotional state of the child. An alert, responsive child who falls just below the 10th centile (which means 90% of children are taller and heavier) is much less likely to be given this diagnosis than an apathetic, withdrawn child who is subject to hostile parenting. The teacher is very well placed to draw these small, unhappy children to the notice of the school doctor.

Deprivation dwarfism

Emotional deprivation early in life may be associated with stunted physical growth and emotional disturbance. The term 'deprivation dwarfism' has been used to describe children whose growth has been affected by emotional factors. Once removed from the depriving environment these children show rapid compensatory growth. However, many emotionally deprived children do not have stunting of growth.

In cases of failure to thrive due to emotional causes a team approach is usually necessary involving the paediatrician, family doctor, social worker and child psychiatrist. The initial approach is to offer intensive support to the family if this seems at all possible and monitor the effects on the child. In very severe cases it may be necessary to remove the child permanently and seek an adoptive home. In less severe cases respite care or weekly boarding at a suitable residential school may offer a viable alternative. Hopefully, with continuing long-term support the child will be enabled to recover from some of the effects of the deprivation and to remain at home.

References and further reading

Bentovim, A. (1970) The clinical approach to feeding disorders of childhood. *Journal of Psychosomatic Research*, **14**, 267–76.

Bruch, H. (1974) *Eating Disorders: Obesity, Anorexia Nervosa and the Person Within*. London: Routledge and Kegan Paul.

Bruch, H. (1978) *The Golden Cage: The Enigma of Anorexia Nervosa*. Cambridge, Mass: Harvard University Press.

Bryant-Waugh, R. and Lask, B. (1991) Anorexia nervosa in a group of Asian children living in Britain. *British Journal of Psychiatry*, **158**, 229–33.

Chernin, K. (1981) *Womansize: The Tyranny of Slenderness*. London: The Woman's Press.

Clarke, M.G. and Palmer, R.L. (1983) Eating attitudes and neurotic symptoms in university students. *British Journal of Psychiatry*, **142**, 299–304.

Crisp, A.H. (1980) *Let Me Be*. London: Academic Press.

Davies, S. (1991) Greed. Tavistock Open Lecture.

Dowdney, L., Skuse, D., Heptinstall, E., Puckering, C. and Zur-Szpiro, S. (1987) Growth retardation and developmental delay amongst inner-city children. *Journal of Child Psychology and Psychiatry*, **28**, 529–41.

Fairburn, C.G. and Beglin, S.J. (1990) Studies of the epidemiology of bulimia nervosa. *American Journal of Psychiatry*, **147**, 401–8.

Fortunato, G. and Meltzer, D. (1977) Psychotherapy of an adolescent case of anorexia nervosa. *Journal of Child Psychotherapy*, **4**, 111–20.

Freeman, C.P. and Munro, J.K. (1988) Drug and group treatments for bulimia nervosa. *Journal of Psychosomatic Research*, **32**, 647–660.

Garfinkel, P.E. and Garner, D.M. (1982) *Anorexia Nervosa: A Multidimensional Perspective*. New York: Brunner-Mazel.

Garner, D.M. (1987) Psychotherapy outcome research with bulimia nervosa. *Psychotherapy and Psychosomatics*, **48**, 129–40.

Hill, A. (1991) Attitudes to dieting in young children. *The Guardian*, 12 April.

Johnson, C. and Flach, A. (1985) Family characteristics of 105 patients with bulimia. *American Journal of Psychiatry*, **142** (11), 1321–4.

Lawrence, M. (1984) Anorexia nervosa: an update. *Newsletter: Association for Child Psychology and Psychiatry*, **6**, 2–10.

Levenknon, S. (1985) Psychotherapy as a compensatory experience with the anorexic patient. *International Journal of Eating Disorders*, **4**, 693–9.

Lovett, J.W.T. (1990) Bulimia nervosa in an adolescent boy boxer. *Journal of Adolescence*, **13**, 79–83.

Magagna, J. (1993) Individual psychodynamic psychotherapy. In

Lask, B. and Bryant-Waugh, R. (eds) *Childhood Onset Anorexia Nervosa and Related Eating Disorders*. Hove: Lawrence Erlbaum Associates, pp. 191–209.

Minuchin, L. (1978) *Psychosomatic Families: Anorexia Nervosa in Context*. Harvard: Harvard University Press.

Ratnasuriya, R.H., Eisler, I., Szmukler, G.I. and Russell, G.F.M. (1991) Anorexia nervosa: outcome and prognostic factors after 20 years. *British Journal of Psychiatry*, **158**, 495–502.

Russell, G.F.M., Szmukler, G.I., Dare, C. and Eisler, I. (1987) An evaluation of family therapy in anorexia nervosa and bulimia nervosa. *Archives of General Psychiatry*, **44**, 1047–56.

Rutter, M. (1991) Services for children with emotional disorders: needs, accomplishments and future developments. *Young Minds Newsletter*, No. 7.

Salmons, P.H. (1986) Outpatient psychotherapy in anorexia nervosa. *Midland Journal of Psychotherapy*, **2**, 68–73.

Salmons, P., Lewis, V., Rogers, P. *et al.* (1988) Body shape dissatisfaction in school children. *British Journal of Psychiatry*, **153** (suppl. 2), 27–31.

Silver, H.K. and Finkelstein, M. (1967) Deprivation dwarfism. *Journal of Child Psychology and Psychiatry*, **27**, 647–56.

Stern, D.N. (1985) *The Interpersonal World of the Infant*. New York: Basic Books.

Theander, S. (1970) Anorexia nervosa: a psychiatric investigation of 94 female cases. *Acta Psychiatrica Scandinavia*, **214** (suppl.), 1–194.

Trevarthen, C. (1993) The self born in intersubjectivity: the psychology of an infant communicating. In U. Nesser (ed.) *Ecological and Interpersonal Knowledge of the Self*. New York: Cambridge University Press.

CHAPTER 8
Emotional Disorders

This is a term which is used to cover psychological reactions to stress which persist and cause continuing distress to the child. In general, disturbances in children can be divided into two broad groups known as emotional and conduct disorders. In the former, the child suffers, whereas in the latter the child's behaviour affects other people and causes disturbance to those around. Although this distinction was first made 30 years ago, more recent work has supported these findings in terms of the two dimensions of behaviour identified (Achenbach and Edelbrock, 1983). First, there is 'internalizing' or 'overcontrolled' behaviour which describes anxious and socially withdrawn children and secondly there is an 'externalizing' or 'undercontrolled' behavioural dimension which refers to inattentive, overactive and aggressive behaviour.

Although the two conditions overlap, with many children showing symptoms of both, children with mixed conduct and emotional disorder tend to be closer in cause and outcome to those with conduct disorder. There are also considerable differences between the two conditions in terms of the clustering of symptoms, response to treatment, family characteristics, association with learning difficulties, long-term outcome and distribution between the sexes, and it is useful to consider them separately.

Emotional disorders occurred in about 2.5% of children in the Isle of Wight study (Rutter *et al.*, 1970) and in 5% in an inner London borough. The prevalence also rises in adolescence, becoming greater among girls.

Emotional disorder in childhood implies a more general disorder with a variety of characteristics such as feelings of inferiority, shyness, self-consciousness, social withdrawal, anxiety, hypersensitivity, crying, chronic sadness and depression. In addition, it includes more specific conditions with symptoms very similar to adult neuroses such as anxiety states, depressive disorders, obsessive-compulsive conditions, phobias, 'conversion' hysteria and hypochondriasis. The main symptoms here are caused by abnormal levels of anxiety which may be expressed directly as an anxiety state or indirectly as fears, phobias or hysterical symptoms.

However, many of these disorders in childhood are of a more general kind and show little continuity with neurotic disorders in adult life. It is therefore preferable to use the term emotional disorder for this group of less well-differentiated conditions which often run a milder course.

The diagnosis is based on the pattern of symptoms which will inevitably involve an emotional disturbance at its centre. There is a persistence of these disturbed emotions outside the range of normal for the child's background and accompanied by impairments in the child's personal or social functioning.

There is a suggestion that most or many instances of phobia or anxiety state arise on the basis of an unconscious conflict. For instance, a 6-year-old boy with school phobia may appear on the surface to fear something to do with the school. However, further investigation may reveal that the child feels very insecure and has not negotiated the emotional stage of being able to separate from his mother and unconsciously feels that his life is at risk if he does separate. All children with this condition are different and each situation needs to be considered in its own right.

It may be more useful to think of there being an underlying key problem rather than an unconscious conflict. This may be to do with unresolved infantile feelings or maladaptive ways of coping which rely on unhelpful underlying fantasies.

> Becky, a 5-year-old girl, was paralysed by anxiety, and because she had been unable to slowly take in a growing sense of inner security, she had turned to unhelpful parts of herself in order to survive. In the normal process of development the mother takes on

a holding function for the baby and holds the baby together through states of unintegration. Babies gradually internalize a mother with this holding function which then enables them to be able to hold and process powerful feelings and states of mind for themselves. There is a slow process of growth through dependence to independence based on a secure internal structure.

Becky had had a difficult birth, spending time in a special care unit, and had not been able to internalize a good and holding maternal presence and structure. As a result she used her talents inappropriately in order to create a false independence and hold herself together as a pseudo-adult. She had turned to an omnipotent part of herself as a substitute for a secure emotional base. She became very grown up and always had to be firmly in control. However, this was to ward off lurking doubts and terrors which were never far away. Becky's emotional pain had not been able to be processed and it was almost impossible for her to be in touch with the small, vulnerable part of herself.

A child with such deep-seated problems needs intensive psychotherapy in order to understand and modify her destructive defences. After two years of therapy Becky was enabled to feel safe enough to allow a space in her mind for thinking, to start to hold on to experiences and not be overwhelmed. She is now doing well, making friends and enjoying school.

This case is a good illustration of how it is always necessary to go beyond the surface level and not only identify symptoms but try to understand their meaning and function in the context of the child's whole life experience. Such an evaluation allows a more accurate appreciation of the depth of the child's difficulties and the nature of the treatment needed. Becky's problem probably started at birth with the lack of a holding experience in the special care baby unit.

Children's fears and anxieties

Many children will develop fears at some stage during their development but these fears are usually transient and manageable. Children's fears tend to change with age. However, a persistent fear can interrupt a child's capacity to adapt easily and successfully to the usual stresses of life. Tiny babies experience anxieties related to their sense of self and security. These may be expressed later as a fear of falling, falling apart and disintegration, or falling forever. These very primitive anxieties remain with us in the depths of our minds and only surface occasionally, such as when we are under stress or have to face a new challenge. Starting something new, such as a new course or school, elicits both hope and feelings of excitement and expectation as well as stirring up very early anxieties.

By 8–9 months babies may become afraid of specific objects and strange situations, and may show a fear of strangers. As toddlers and young children they may develop fears of spiders and other animals or be subject to imaginary fears. These include fears of the dark, ghosts, monsters and other imaginary creatures. A fear of ghosts is found in children in all cultures, and seems to be a universal although primitive phenomenon. There is a general tendency for imaginary fears to decrease with the onset of adolescence and for more realistic fears such as fears of physical illness or danger to increase.

Development of attachment

Bowlby has pointed out that it is not only the presence of certain situations which leads to fear but also the absence of certain conditions, in particular the absence of the mother. Young children need the presence of their mother in order to feel secure and through this to develop a sense of inner security which provides the foundation for further

167

emotional development. On the basis of a secure relationship with the primary care-giver, usually the mother, children develop the capacity to make stable attachments to other people. It has been found that the period from birth to 2 years is crucial in the development of secure attachment and that children are more likely to suffer emotional damage if moved from their attachment figure during that time.

Anxiety

Anxiety is part of everyday life, whether consciously felt or experienced as a state of increased tension. However, excessive states of anxiety, alone or in combination with depression, are present in almost all emotional disorders. A distinction has been made between 'objective' anxiety, which is related to a specific situation, and 'neurotic' anxiety, which is out of proportion to any real danger and is frequently related to unconscious problems and insecurities.

A diagnosis of anxiety state may be made when there is an abnormal degree of free-floating anxiety present which is not attached to a specific situation. Such a state can develop in children who are quite resilient and stable. More frequently, it arises on the basis of a more anxious temperament, as an accentuation of a pre-existing tendency to respond to ordinary stresses with undue anxiety. Lastly, the influence of chronic environmental stress must not be overlooked as a possible cause for the predisposition to anxiety.

Anxiety states may be caused by a frightening event such as a hospital admission or the death of a close relative. Some children grow up in particularly anxious households where parents convey a sense of anxiety to their children. In these cases the anxiety is not held in mind and processed for the child but prolonged and made worse by the parents' own anxieties and indecision.

Symptoms related directly to the anxiety itself include: feelings of alarm, awfulness and fear; and physiological disturbances such as the frequent need to pass urine, dia-rrhoea, nausea and sleep disturbance. Indirect symptoms of anxiety may be shown through clinging behaviour caused by a regression to more babyish behaviour or sometimes may be accompanied by a more angry reaction, leading to attacks on the mother. Young children always tends to blame the mother when things go wrong. In the children's minds she is the one who should be keeping them safe. Abnormal anxiety can lead to poor school attainment and to physical symptoms which may be the cause of frequent absences.

TREATMENT: THE ROLE OF TEACHERS

Treatment approaches need to be based on the assessment of underlying factors. In the majority of cases it is important for teachers to be involved in the treatment plan so that they can support the child in a meaningful way. This is particu-larly relevant for children who become very anxious in new situations and need to be given time to adapt. These chil-dren need to be protected from too many changes and helped to develop more effective coping strategies.

In some cases the children will need individual psychotherapy in order to reach the underlying causes of the anxiety, as with Becky. Other children may benefit from a cognitive approach which helps them to recognize and counter the negative thinking which underlies many of these irrational anxieties. Sometimes, talking to parents about how to relieve the stress on the child may be sufficient in itself.

Phobic states

A phobia is an emotional disorder where there is an intense dread and an irrational fear of specific situations, such as height or open spaces, or of specific objects, like dogs or spiders. Many children pass through a phase between the ages of 3 and 6 years when specific fears are common, especially those related to animals or to being alone in the dark. They usually grow out of these by later childhood. Phobias may be part of a generalized anxiety state or may be discrete fears with no other symptoms of disturbance. School phobia is not necessarily a fear of school and is discussed in more detail later. Agoraphobia (a fear of leaving home) does not occur in children.

Treatment includes allowing the child to talk about the fears, counselling of the family and often a process of desensitization when the child is encouraged to approach the feared situation or object in a graded way within a safe environment. Animal and insect phobias, which usually start before the age of 6 years, respond particularly well to desensitization. In general, children's fears and phobias respond rapidly to sensible handling (except for school phobia) and do not cause much of a problem.

School refusal

School refusal, or school phobia as it is sometimes called, has particular relevance for teachers, as many may be called upon to try to help a child with this condition. It manifests with fear and a great reluctance to go to school. This is because of the amount of anxiety which is generated by the thought of school, although a fear of school itself may not be the major underlying cause. The main fear is often one of leaving home and being separated from the mother. School refusal needs to be distinguished from truancy, which is the deliberate avoidance of school for reasons other than severe anxiety. Apart from truancy, the other main causes of school non-attendance are a physically ill parent or a parent with a psychological need for the child to stay at home.

Although the exact prevalence is unknown, school refusal is relatively common (probably about 5% of all referrals), with more girls being referred than boys in the younger age groups and more boys in early adolescence. There is evidence that increasing teachers' awareness leads to more referrals. In the younger children problems related to separation predominate whereas older children may show evidence of quite serious and more varied disturbance. Young people from families where the mother is very anxious and there is parental discord and inconsistency are particularly likely to manifest additional symptoms of acute anxiety, depression and personality disorder.

Typically it is the quieter and more conscientious children who are affected. There is a tendency for them to be rather passive and dependent with good academic achievements, and to come from families with a high incidence of neurosis. School phobic children may agree to try to attend school but as the time approaches they often become increasingly anxious and panic-stricken, unable to leave home. If they actually manage to reach the school they may feel so terrified that they are unable to go in. Unfortunately, even if they manage to attend for one day, the panic tends to come back the next morning.

In the majority of cases the child is suffering from unresolved problems related to separation from the mother (Gittelman-Klein and Klein, 1980). These issues are stirred up by any new challenge or change, and school refusal typically occurs at times of transition such as starting school or changing to secondary school. The three peak times of onset are 5–7 years (associated with starting school), 11–12 years (transfer to secondary school) and 14 years.

A central problem is that the child has not developed a secure emotional base or sense of identity, usually because of these difficulties in separation. Many of the mothers are not adequately supported and have emotional difficulties themselves. The children tend to be overprotected and over-dependent. As a result, the relationship may develop into a cycle of hostility and dependence. The fathers are either absent or peripheral and in particular are not able to be consistently firm about school attendance and facilitate a secure separation between mother and child.

Sometimes school refusal manifests itself through physical

complaints such as abdominal pain, nausea, headache or limb pains. These symptoms either reflect the physical accompaniments of anxiety such as nausea or diarrhoea or demonstrate a process of somatization (anxiety manifested in bodily terms) as in the case of the limb pains. Because of immaturity and not having been helped to deal with difficult feelings directly, the child may find it easier to experience the anxiety as a physical rather than a mental pain. This is not a conscious decision and both the child and parents may find it difficult to accept that there is nothing physically wrong despite all investigations being normal. The pain is very real.

Associated with these physical symptoms is the salient feature of reluctance to attend school. However, this may not become apparent unless the right questions are asked. In addition, the symptoms tend to vanish once the child returns home and over weekends.

In other cases the diagnosis is not clear because of seemingly valid reasons for not attending such as a difficult teacher or problems with a subject. It is only when these have been dealt with and there is no improvement that the diagnosis becomes more obvious.

Many children with school refusal have difficulty in coping with life at school. They are more vulnerable to stress, have difficulty in making relationships with other children and tend to become anxious away from home. Any additional stress may precipitate a complete breakdown of school attendance and accounts for the peak incidence at the times of change, 5 years and 11 years.

ANGER AND AGGRESSION IN SCHOOL REFUSERS

In many cases these children have not learnt to cope with frustration and may show inappropriate anger and aggression if not given their own way. For instance, they may display outbursts of verbal or physical aggression towards their parents and may refuse to co-operate with professionals who are trying to help.

Paul, for instance, the youngest of three boys, showed a typical picture of school refusal. There was no father and, being the baby of the family, he had been overprotected and indulged. There was a long history of difficulties in separating from the mother and when he was referred at the age of 6 the situation was urgent.

Every morning the mother had to take Paul to the head's office, where Paul started to scream in anger as the mother prepared to leave. He clung to her and had to be physically prised away. However, once in the classroom Paul settled down to work as if nothing had happened. It was always very distressing for the mother and stressful for the teachers involved.

The teacher provided a very helpful report. She perceptively described how Paul had difficulties in managing his feelings of frustration, fear and anger. He was easily upset, emotionally demanding, clinging and angry with his mother at the same time. She felt that Paul had difficulty in forming close relationships with his peer group or other adults and in the playground he wandered aimlessly. Academically he was under-achieving and was difficult to motivate. When Paul was angry with a strong need to see his mother he had been known to run out of school on several occasions.

This is a fairly typical picture of how school refusal can manifest in a young child where separation problems predominate. There will always be individual differences and Paul, for instance, had idealized his absent father. He was emotionally insecure and had not internalized secure parental figures as a base on which to build. These differences will be taken account of in the treatment plan.

Individual work was undertaken with Paul and his mother as well as some family work. The teachers were supported in their approach and a simple behavioural system was set up with rewards for separating from mother. Paul has improved, although some problems still remain. He is now making progress academically and in relating to other children but he is still difficult to handle and can be demanding.

Paul's problems at referral were severe and it is a tribute to the commitment of the teachers concerned that he was able to be maintained within an ordinary school. It is clear how such problems affect all areas of the child's functioning and how crucial it is to arrange early referral and intervention if the child is not to be severely handicapped by emotional problems in adult life.

However, anger as a response occurs more frequently in adolescents, related specifically to their developmental stage and also to their greater awareness and frustration at not being able to function at a level appropriate to their age.

It is because of the longstanding overprotection and overindulgence that these children have not been helped to come to terms with the inevitable frustrations of life and particularly with not being able to have everything their own way. The anger is often precipitated by outside intervention. These may be children who have rarely shown anger in the past and are not used to having their wishes thwarted. However, once symptoms develop and other people become involved who challenge the established pattern, these children are very likely to react with overwhelming anger as well as panic. The anger is usually directed towards the parents, particularly at the mother, who tends to be most closely involved.

DEPRESSION AND SCHOOL REFUSAL

Another complication in making the diagnosis occurs when symptoms of depression are also present. These are more frequent in older children from families with high levels of anxiety, inconsistency and marital disharmony. Ben demonstrates some of the diagnostic difficulties in the older age group.

Ben was a withdrawn 13-year-old when he came to see a child psychiatrist. There was a six-month history of Ben missing half-days, with the explanation that these absences were caused by problems in his relationship with the form tutor. The school had tried hard to help and had changed his form tutor but his attendance had become worse. When the referral was made some eight months later, Ben was refusing to get out of bed, was very low in mood and was losing weight. The teacher had not realized that Ben was beoming more and more depressed.

Ben was the older of two brothers in a family where the father was weak and ineffectual and mother was the more dominant partner who had to take on all the responsibility. The gradual onset and Ben's rationalization of his difficulties, thinking it was the tutor, had led to a delay in making the diagnosis. Depressive symptoms then set in which further complicated the picture. These were related to his difficulties in establishing a secure self-image without an adequate father figure with whom to identify.

Ben was treated with anti-depressants, counselling, family work and a temporary placement in a small teaching unit where he received individual attention. He had become very behind in his school work and this placement gave him a chance to catch up in a setting where he felt safe and could cope. Ben's depression lifted, he was gradually enabled to build up his self-esteem and work continued on trying to help Ben develop a more secure sense of identity.

Ben's problems did not resolve completely following the anti-depressants. Berney *et al.* (1981) in their survey found that school refusal and anxiety often continued after the depression had been treated.

TEACHER'S ROLE

Teachers have a central role in recognizing the symptoms, supporting the child and parents and referring onwards if the problem does not resolve quickly. Their knowledge of the child and family is invaluable as part of the assessment. They can provide essential information as to how the child is functioning and recognize any recent changes in mood or behaviour. Teachers may have to take the lead in initiating a referral as the parents may be unsure of how to obtain help.

In this condition treatment is needed as a matter of urgency. There is always the possibility that mismanagement may lead to a potentially reversible condition deteriorating into a more permanent state of mental disturbance. The first task is to re-establish a pattern of regular school attendance, either at the child's own school or at a smaller teaching unit. Otherwise the child very easily gets behind in work, loses contact with friends and becomes more enmeshed within a neurotic family.

Clearly, the teaching staff are central to the part of the treatment plan involving school attendance and I have found unfailing co-operation and commitment. The child often needs support on first arrival and it can be helpful for the teacher to receive the child at the school gate. In some cases the child with treatment is able to continue at school but sometimes attendance at a smaller teaching unit is necessary before the return to ordinary school. Very occasionally there may be a need for admission to a child psychiatric unit as an inpatient.

Fortunately, the majority of parents are willing to co-operate with the recommended treatment plan, but there may be the occasional one who refuses. In that case very little can be done to help the child, unless the parents can be persuaded to accept help. The only other option is to invoke the Children Act, but there would need to be clear evidence that the child was being seriously emotionally damaged. In practice this is not usually a realistic option as emotional damage is difficult to prove.

OUTCOME

Overall, approximately one-third of children do not return to school. The majority of these will be the older adolescents who are more difficult to treat and who are near to school leaving age. A considerable proportion of these young people continue to have difficulties in making relationships and in holding down a job. In addition, it seems that some are at risk for later psychiatric disorder (Tyrer and Tyrer, 1974).

Hysteria and conversion disorder

As already described, anxiety includes both the feeling of fear and the associated bodily symptoms such as nausea, abdominal pain, frequency of micturition and diarrhoea. However, there is another set of physical symptoms which are caused by anxiety but unrelated to the autonomic response. These include limb pains, abnormalities of gait, psychogenic paralyses, disorders of sensation, blindness, deafness, pain, pseudoseizures and fugue (trance-like) states. The term conversion disorder is used for these on the basis of the hypothesis that emotional conflict has been converted into a physical complaint. Young people may not experience feelings of anxiety but exist in a tranquil state known as 'la belle indifference'. When describing severe incapacitating pain they may smile and often their response is incompatible with the symptoms. However, children and young people are often anxious about their symptoms, unlike adults.

Conversion disorder is quite an uncommon condition and occurs in only 1–2% of referrals to a child psychiatrist (Goodyer, 1981). It is three times as common in adolescents (more girls than boys affected) than in children, where there is an equal incidence.

It is crucial not to miss an organic disorder, and Slater (1965) described how, in about 75% of patients, organic pathology had been misdiagnosed as hysterical conversion disorder in adults attending a neurological clinic. The commonest presentation in those who later developed organic disease was difficulty in seeing. Rivinus *et al.* (1975) found that visual loss, a fall in school performance, disturbances in posture and changeable symptoms were significant indicators in 12 children who were thought to have psychiatric illness but actually had organic disease.

True cases of conversion disorder differed in having a more rapid onset and a more frequent family history of hysterical symptoms. There may be an association between a child's symptoms and a relative's recent illness with the same part of the body being affected. Pseudoseizures have been found to occur quite commonly in young women who have been sexually abused and this diagnosis should always be considered.

> A brief example is provided by an 18-year-old girl from an Asian background who was admitted to hospital with a sudden paralysis of her left arm and leg. On examination the paralysis did not conform to any known neurological lesion and nothing abnormal was found. It was later ascertained that an arranged marriage was being actively pursued by the family. Her symptoms quickly resolved after counselling and it became clear that she had felt very ambivalent about this marriage. In fact she went on to meet the young man and felt much happier about the situation.

In this case the outlook was good. There was an acute and recent onset of symptoms in a girl who had a stable previous personality and a resolvable conflict. All of these factors are important in predicting the process of recovery.

Treatment is best undertaken quickly. A psychotherapeutic approach directed towards understanding the conflict or meaning of the symptoms is generally recommended together with any necessary changes in the family or environment. Physiotherapy may be helpful in facilitating the recovery process.

The outcome is good for children with conversion disorders. They usually recover completely, often within a few days if treated promptly. Otherwise there may be a recovery within 3–9 months or, failing this, a slower process extending over two years.

Epidemic hysteria

This occurs much more frequently in girls and most typically in adolescents within a relatively closed community such as a boarding school. The girls who start the outbreak are usually quite disturbed emotionally, whereas those who are affected later on are usually normal. The social atmosphere of the institution is responsible for the spread of symptoms.

The epidemic tends to take the form of fainting attacks, falling, overbreathing, convulsions or weakness. The first step in containing the spread is to isolate the key figures who started the attack and reassure the others. In order to prevent a recurrence it is necessary to study the tensions and group dynamics within the institution and take account of the personality problems of the one or two key figures.

Obsessional disorders

These are very rare in childhood. Compulsive behaviour which is part of normal development, such as avoiding the lines on the pavement, has to be distinguished from abnormal compulsive behaviour. The incidence of actual disorder is around 0.2–1.2% of children and adolescents seen in a psychiatric clinic (Hollingsworth *et al.*, 1980). People often hide their symptoms and it is thought that up to one-half of adult patients started to have symptoms during adolescence. Obsessional behaviour in adolescents sometimes precedes the onset of schizophrenia, although only about 4% of people with longstanding symptoms go on to develop schizophrenia.

Obsessions can be defined as intrusive thoughts which take over the mind and cannot be reasoned away or dismissed despite the knowledge that they are irrational and unreasonable. Compulsions are the actions arising from these thoughts. Both are usually unwanted and disturbing. It has been suggested that obsessional behaviour is used as a defence against and as a way of controlling severe anxiety. One of the mechanisms involved is the use of magical thinking. Clearly, if the person does not carry out the prescribed act, the sense of anxiety mounts, often to an unbearable extent. There is a feeling that some disaster will occur unless the compulsion is enacted. In adolescents there may be an irrational fear of dirt, with a feeling that it is something terribly dangerous that can harm oneself or others. This may lead to prolonged washing rituals.

> Sarah was an emotionally vulnerable 13-year-old who, with the onset of adolescence and the stress of changing school, suddenly developed severe obsessional thoughts related to fear of dirt and contamination. She started compulsive washing of her hands which would continue for up to 45 minutes, unless she was stopped. Her hands became red and raw. She lived in a world of continual fear of dirt and germs, afraid of them spreading everywhere and causing disaster. Sarah became very upset by her symptoms and her school work was severely affected. She was a vulnerable girl and the stress of events had proved too much for her. Fortunately she was referred early and was treated using the behavioural approach of response prevention combined with increased emotional support from her parents. Once her mother consistently stopped her excess washing and gave her more individual attention, her symptoms cleared up quite rapidly.

It is thought that the outcome is likely to be good in a mild case, but more severely affected patients with longstanding symptoms often need longer-term and even inpatient treatment at times. The most frequently described treatment is response prevention combined with family work. Medication (clomipramine) tends to be particularly helpful in cases where there is clear evidence of anxiety and depression (Marks, 1983). Here the outlook is improved where the obsessional symptoms are secondary to a depressive illness. In general, clomipramine has not been found to be so useful for obsessional-compulsive behaviour *per se* in adolescents, although the results of two recent studies have challenged this by showing that clomipramine was effective even in the absence of coexisting symptoms of depression (Flament *et al.*, 1985; DeVeaugh-Geiss *et al.*, 1992).

The best outcome was found in children with the shortest history before hospital admission. An inpatient sample showed reasonable results with a total relief of symptoms in seven cases and a reduction of symptoms in the remaining six patients (Bolton *et al.*, 1983).

Zeitlin (1987) found a positive association between obsessional disorder in childhood and in later life. In his series 70% of children with symptoms went on to develop obsessional symptoms as adults.

Teachers can help by recommending early referral to a child psychiatrist and encouraging the parents to support a programme of stopping compulsive behaviour and of engaging in family work.

Depression

Although unhappiness and depressed mood are reasonably common, actual depressive disorder is rare in childhood. Sadness of mood occurs with equal frequency in children with conduct disorders and in those with emotional disorders. Feelings of unhappiness and misery are not confined to any one psychiatric grouping. Clearly, psychiatrically disturbed children are often unhappy. This kind of unhappiness is not a clinical depression but needs attention and treatment.

Increasingly, childhood depression is being diagnosed using similar criteria to those used in adult disorder. These are a depressed mood or loss of enjoyment in life plus four out of a possible eight symptoms, all lasting for two weeks or more. The symptoms are: (1) loss of appetite; (2) disturbed sleep; (3) loss of interest; (4) loss of energy; (5) agitation or slowing down; (6) feelings of guilt; (7) difficulties in concentration; and (8) suicidal thoughts. The main feature is therefore a depressed mood which persists despite changes in the outer world. The child may slow down in thinking or in activity, show unnecessary feelings of guilt, feel unable to cope with school, feel that life is not worth living or, even more seriously, develop suicidal thoughts. However, a depressive illness as described here is rare, although being increasingly recognized in recent years (Harrington, 1992).

There is an increase in the prevalence of depression during adolescence which links with findings on suicide, which show a sudden increase at this age. More adolescent girls than boys become depressed in a ratio of 2:1, but more boys actually kill themselves.

ASSOCIATION WITH OTHER DISORDERS

Nearly half of all children with conduct disorder also show some evidence of a depressed mood. However, this change in mood is felt to be secondary and a result of the primary conduct disorder. Schaffer (1974) described how 75% of children who killed themselves had a history of anti-social behaviour.

Many young people with anorexia or bulimia have associated depressive symptoms. Some of these have an actual clinical depression and this is the group where there is often a history of depression in the family. Hysterical conversion symptoms such as psychogenic paralysis may occur together with depressed mood in adolescents, particularly where there has been a bereavement and depression in close relatives. Clinical depression in these groups needs to be treated in the usual way.

CAUSES

Genetic factors are known to play a large part in manic-depressive disorder, where the individual shows major fluctuations in mood. However, whether there is a genetic basis for other depressive disorders is not yet known. Biochemical abnormalities have also been described in depressed adults, such as a relative lack of noradrenaline or serotonin in the brain, and there is evidence supporting both of these hypotheses. It could be that genetic factors give rise to the underlying biochemical changes. However, depression in children may well be very different from that in adults. Certainly, manic-depressive illness is extremely rare in children and adolescents. It is known that some children treated with stimulants react by becoming tearful and that anti-depressants are not very effective in children.

In children depression most frequently occurs as a reaction to very stressful circumstances. It is often found in children from unhappy or disturbed homes as well as in those who are facing emotional deprivation or rejection. Children who become depressed frequently come from families with high rates of psychiatric disorder, have difficulties in social relationships and experience failure in school. In addition, difficulties at school, such as learning difficulties, bullying or relating to other children, as well as experiences of loss, can all give rise to depression.

Bowlby described one of the earliest situations of loss with the sudden onset of what appeared to be depressive symptoms in young children separated from their mothers. After two days the child would become withdrawn and extremely distressed for long periods with inconsolable crying.

Traumatic situations can also cause depression. It is common in post-traumatic stress disorder, which may follow any traumatic event such as a mugging, a violent attack or a car accident. Many children who have suffered from sexual abuse show symptoms of depression, particularly after they have talked about what happened. It is quite common for children to block the abuse out of their minds because the trauma is overwhelming and they are not able to think about it. The unbearable feelings all come flooding back when they tell someone and at that stage they will benefit from and urgently need specialist help.

> Any serious trauma or loss can cause depression. A 10-year-old girl whose parents had divorced became depressed after her house suddenly collapsed due to subsidence. This was totally unexpected and without any preparation she had to move house and school. She was unable to cope with the stress, became depressed and took an overdose. She was a vulnerable child, being sensitized to loss by the divorce of her parents. However, she responded well to counselling sessions with the child psychiatrist where she was supported in gradually being able to come to terms with what had happened.

TREATMENT

Clearly, a full assessment of the child and the child's circumstances needs to be undertaken as a basis for treatment. In the majority of cases psychological treatments such as individual therapy, cognitive therapy and family work are most effective.

Anti-depressant medication is generally not effective in children and is best avoided as a routine treatment. Anti-depressants are more frequently used for adolescents but have been found to be less effective than for adults. Although child psychiatrists tend to use anti-depressants to treat the more severe depressions, the research evidence to support this practice is lacking (Bramble, 1992). If tricyclic anti-depressants are used in children, an ECG should be taken to exclude conduction defects of the heart, as any such defect is a definite contraindication. Increasingly, the newer anti-depressants such as fluoxetine are being used for adolescents.

Any obvious stresses need to be addressed. A psychotherapeutic approach is usually indicated to help the child feel understood and to come to terms with the traumatic or stressful events. More recently, cognitive therapy has been successfully used to counter negative ways of thinking.

In the most severe cases it may be necessary to try to remove the child from very unhappy home circumstances, for instance if the child experiences continuing rejection which cannot be modified. These decisions are extremely difficult but worthwhile for the long-term future of the child.

> Claire was a very unhappy, withdrawn 3-year-old whose parents both had severe personality disorders. They had no concept of a child's emotional needs and treated her as an extension of themselves. Despite intensive counselling and support the parents were unable to change and she was eventually freed for adoption, as her development was being severely impaired. It was very rewarding to see how she blossomed from a silent, unhappy child curled up alone in a corner into a friendly, confident and happy little girl within her new home.

OUTCOME

Where depression is the only diagnosis, the majority of children recover following treatment. Some will recover spontaneously but in other cases the depression may last for long periods if not treated. Children whose depression is a result of stress generally do well, provided the causes of the stress are removed. Where the child has reacted to severe disturbances in the family, the outlook is less good. The worst outlook in terms of personality development is for those children who suffer from chronic depression as a result of rejecting or depriving home circumstances where nothing can be done.

Recent studies have tended to show a poorer outcome; bearing in mind the small numbers of children affected, they found that despite an initial recovery the depression tended to recur and there was a high risk of future psychiatric referral (Harrington, 1992). It could be that these children came from more chronically disturbed families; high rates of alcoholism and anxiety disorder have been found in the families of depressed children. It has also been found that adolescents who suffer from depression are at an increased risk of future depressive or manic-depressive illness. Genetic factors are probably relevant, as there are high rates of depression among first-degree relatives of both child and adolescent patients.

THE TEACHER'S ROLE AND PREVENTATIVE MEASURES

Schools can help through teachers being aware and recognizing children who come outside the range of normal in terms of looking sad and unhappy. If the child's problems are known to be severe or supportive measures within the school do not help, then referral to a child psychiatric clinic is indicated and the teacher can initiate this referral.

Depressed children tend to come from families under stress or where there is psychiatric disorder, so that preventative measures would include all interventions which help to relieve stress and support the parents and children. These include home visiting by health visitors, home–school liaison teachers and Home-Start as well as playgroups and nurseries for the under-fives, and after-school activities and holiday schemes for older children. In more serious cases, respite care provided by social services can offer much-needed support on a regular basis for both parents and child.

Mania

Mania is the opposite of depression and is characterized by a state of excitement, over-talkativeness, euphoria, excessive activity and impaired judgement. It is very rare in childhood and rare in adolescence (Carlson, 1990). There can be a diagnostic problem, as acute manic illness in adolescents is often diagnosed as schizophrenia. This is because it can be difficult to differentiate between them in the early stages and it is important to keep both diagnoses in mind. The condition is so rare that it is only necessary to touch on it briefly.

Drug treatment is always necessary and either phenothiazines or lithium are effective. Lithium takes up to seven days to manifest any anti-manic effect and has serious side-effects, so that blood levels need careful monitoring. Lithium tends to be the treatment of choice (Green, 1991). Carbamazepine can be used instead of lithium in unresponsive patients, as can sodium valproate in the same dosages as are used for epilepsy.

The long-term outlook is guarded for those very few people who have an episode of mania in childhood or adolescence. They are more likely to suffer continuing illness with rapid mood changes between mania and depression, leading to quite severe social impairment. Recent studies have shown that if a patient responds to lithium on the first occasion, the response is less good on the second. It therefore makes sense to keep patients on maintenance lithium for relatively long periods of time. For adolescents this means maintaining the medication at least through any important examinations such as A levels.

There is a mental mechanism called the manic defence which is very different from the illness described above. Children and adolescents may become excited, over-talkative or overactive in order to stave off or avoid something which is upsetting them. If someone is there who can help them settle and quieten down, then the youngster may be able to be more in touch with the underlying stress or upset.

Suicide

Although a few children will make suicide attempts, suicide itself is very rare in children under the age of 12 years;

however, it does occur. Suicide occurs more frequently in adolescents and has now become the major cause of death in that age group. Official figures in 1993 showed an 83% increase in suicides in England and Wales among 15–24-year-old men between 1982 and 1992. The numbers of suicides rose from 262 in 1982 to 412 in 1992.

The Samaritans ascribe this increase to new pressures on young men who are no longer sure how they are supposed to behave or respond within relationships. This insecurity about their role causes an additional pressure which is then added to the inevitable anxieties related to finding a job and starting new relationships. The Samaritans report that men find it more difficult to express their feelings, and particularly feelings of distress or failure. There is a tendency to bottle these up which may prove to be disastrous. In general, women find it easier to talk about how they feel and to see things in perspective.

It has been found that the majority of suicides were planned and the few that were impulsive were associated with alcohol. More boys than girls kill themselves and boys who make suicide attempts have more severe psychiatric disorder than girls who make similar attempts. However, younger children from 5 to 12 years, often from very disturbed homes where they have experienced rejection and/or abuse, do sometimes show suicidal behaviour such as trying to stab or hang themselves. Their behaviour can be seen as a desperate cry for help and needs urgent specialist attention.

Schaffer (1974) studied 30 young people under the age of 15 who had committed suicide. The most frequent precipitant was being disciplined by parents either for delinquency or for truancy. A small number were influenced by reading about a suicide. About half of the group had discussed or threatened suicide within one day of their death. He found that social isolation was a possible factor, either because of depression or because of difficulty in relationships. Over half the boys had missed school on the day before their death, some being long-term school refusers and others being away less than seven days.

Schaffer found that despite small numbers, the children could be placed in one of four categories. These were: (1) children whose behaviour was impulsive or erratic; (2) those who were difficult to reach and uncommunicative; (3) those who were irritable and over-sensitive to criticism; and (4) those who were perfectionist, setting high standards and being self-critical.

Of the 30 young people 22 showed evidence of anti-social behaviour, 21 showed evidence of depression and 17 showed both. One-third were either receiving or on a waiting list for psychiatric treatment. Over half the group had a family member who had been given psychiatric help. These findings suggest that a high proportion of young people who kill themselves are depressed and come from unsettled homes. It seems that these are particularly vulnerable young people, often struggling with feelings of rejection, where being told off and criticized by an angry parent is the final straw in a long series of destructive events.

Orbach (1988) feels that there is a striking similarity between self-destructive behaviour in children and adults. Common patterns of development are described which tend to end in 'the closed world of suicide.' These are as follows:

1. A build-up of pressure on the young person which feels intolerable. The pressure may be caused by rejection, family confusion and loss of appropriate boundaries, unresolvable problems or loss. The pressure may feel intolerable because of adverse early experiences resulting in poor coping skills, rigid and blinkered thinking or distorted concepts of the world.

2. The young person aims to resolve this intolerable pressure, wishing for oblivion, and may initially use alcohol or drugs.

3. This is accompanied by a depressed attitude consisting of despair, hopelessness and alienation.

4. The initial attempts to cope lead to consequences such as isolation, school phobia, aggression, rebellion or delinquency.

5. There is a continued wearing down of emotional strength, leading to the idea of suicide as a way out.
6. The warning signs of self-destructive thinking appear, such as suicide attempts, preoccupation with death or talking about killing oneself. Suicide now seems the only way out of an unbearable situation.
7. Other people's reactions to this self-destructive thinking are important. If this is not taken seriously it may increase the pressure on the young person and confirm his or her often distorted view of life.
8. There may be a continuing build-up of pressure and frustration until the final breakdown, when the young person's mind may go blank but is taken over by the determination to commit suicide.

Suicide attempts

Although suicide in young people is still rare, attempted suicide and suicidal thoughts are more common. This is not a matter for complacency, as at present one in every 100 young women aged between 15 and 19 years makes an attempt at suicide (Lyons, 1993). More girls than boys make suicide attempts and every overdose, however small, needs to be taken seriously. The seriousness of the attempt cannot be judged by the number of tablets.

CAUSES

Many of the young people involved come from broken or disturbed home backgrounds. The attempt is often precipitated by an argument either with a boyfriend, girlfriend or parent, and this seems to be the last straw, often meaning total abandonment, to these young people under stress.

It is not possible to isolate a single cause, except to say in general terms that all psychiatric disorders in young people are becoming more frequent, possibly because of increased levels of stress throughout society. The third edition of *Europe in Figures* (Nicholson-Lord, 1992) shows that the UK has the highest divorce rate and that our working hours are the longest in Europe. He writes that these figures point to a society suffering from more than its fair share of stress.

The results of stress include family break-up, which we know has serious effects on young people. One in five adolescents are now affected by the divorce of their parents. In addition, there has been a steep rise in youth unemployment and homelessness as well as reported increases in sexual and emotional abuse and bullying (Lyons, 1993). These social changes are affecting young people at the same time as they are having to negotiate the developmental tasks of adolescence.

BUILD-UP OF STRESS AND PRESSURE

The culmination comes when internal and external pressures combine to become too much to bear. There is often one incident which acts as the final straw, frequently one which means rejection to the young person, such as a broken relationship or an argument with parents. In these cases, unable to cope with any more stress, the young person's mind suddenly switches into an abnormal state where the wish to die takes over.

For the majority of young people, therefore, the overdose is impulsive and taken on the spur of the moment. There is often a sudden change in mental state when the young person snaps and is momentarily overwhelmed by a flood of feelings, moving into an abnormal frame of mind. In this altered state everything seems negative and there is a very real wish to die. The altered state of mind usually disappears quite rapidly after the overdose and may be inaccessible to memory unless the young person is seen very soon afterwards. This accounts for the fact that many young people regret the overdose almost immediately, once their mental state has returned to normal, and will tell someone what they have done.

As 90% of suicide attempts are by overdosing, the young person will need urgent medical attention. The most appropriate help is at the local hospital, where both medical and psychiatric services are available. It is vitally important that any youngster who takes an overdose, however small, is listened to and taken seriously. Kerfoot (1988), in his long-term follow-up, found that the youngsters least likely to make a further attempt were those whose parents accepted that their child was trying to communicate and made it clear that they wanted to understand what was wrong.

More worrying are those who do not tell anyone and who continue to wish to kill themselves, often taking more tablets at a later stage. Some of this group may be clinically depressed, some may need inpatient treatment in order to keep them safe and certainly no young person should be discharged while continuing to have suicidal thoughts. Those who have attempted suicide are most at risk of trying again within one year.

PRESSURES RELATED TO SCHOOL

It has been found that the number of attempted suicides increases during the school term times and decreases during school holidays (McGibbon *et al.*, 1992). This finding must relate to the additional stress caused by the day-to-day pressures of school. It has also been noticed that the number of attempts increases in May and June, just before the GCSE examinations.

Several well-publicized newspaper reports have shown a link between being bullied and suicide attempts. Name-calling is common in all schools but it is when one child is systematically singled out for verbal or physical abuse that a dangerous situation may arise, particularly if the child is vulnerable for other reasons.

> An 11-year-old boy with specific learning difficulties, having just started at secondary school, was finding writing very difficult. He worked for hours

but was only able to produce a short piece of written work. In addition, he was being systematically bullied by a small group of boys. With great difficulty he wrote about how he was being bullied and how desperate he felt as part of English homework. It was a very moving piece. Somehow his teacher did not pick up his cry for help and the next day he almost killed himself. Fortunately, he hesitated and told his mother before it was too late.

THE SCHOOL'S ROLE

Children who attempt suicide are often vulnerable because of either innate or environmental factors. The more secure the children feel within the school, the less the risk of self-harm in response to arguments or feelings of rejection. For a variety of reasons, schools may go through times of particular stress, which inevitably will affect the children. One example is where a decision to opt out of local authority control split the staff group down the middle. In these circumstances the number of incidents of self-harm suddenly increased, which was, we felt, probably a direct result of the feelings of stress and insecurity within the school.

PREVENTION

Schaffer in the USA tried to set up a preventative programme by looking first at the most important risk factors. He found that for young men these were (1) a previous attempt, (2) mood disorder, i.e. depression, and (3) substance/alcohol abuse. For young women, only one factor seemed important and that was a mood disorder.

Having isolated these factors, Schaffer set up a screening programme in schools and felt he was successful in identifying young people at risk. However, he was unable to proceed with his planned intervention because the parents refused to pay for the preventative treatment. Given the necessary resources, such a programme may be more successful in the UK, where treatment is free.

Hawton (1986) suggests that the most hopeful way forward is to give young people coping skills within school, as he feels that it is very difficult to identify those at risk without complicated questionnaires. This sounds a good idea, as it would benefit all children, but it raises the recurrent question as to who would undertake the work.

A proportion of young people who start to experience suicidal thoughts would contact a counsellor if one were available, particularly if it was someone they knew as a teacher. Youngsters in this group will often contact their psychiatrist or community nurse, if they have one, rather than take an overdose. Overall, however, it is only a small proportion of those at risk who would be able to pause and think and ask for help. It seems that 24-hour telephone line services are of limited usefulness in the adolescent age group.

School counsellors and form and special needs teachers are extremely helpful in supporting young people who have taken overdoses. They are willing to work closely with the child psychiatric team and are often a crucial part of the network set up to try to prevent further episodes of self-harm.

References and further reading

Achenbach, T.M. and Edelbrock, C.S. (1983) *Manual for Child Behaviour Checklist and Revised Child Behaviour Profile*. Burlington: Department of Psychiatry, University of Vermont.

Berney, T., Kolvin, I., Bhate, S. *et al.* (1981) School phobia: a therapeutic trial with clomipramine and short-term outcome. *British Journal of Psychiatry*, **138**, 110–18.

Bolton, D., Collins, S. and Steinberg, D. (1983) The treatment of obsessive-compulsive disorder in adolescence. *British Journal of Psychiatry*, **142**, 456–64.

Bramble, D.J. (1992) The use of antidepressants by British child psychiatrists. *Psychiatric Bulletin*, **16**, 396–8.

Carlson, G.A. (1990) Child and adolescent mania: diagnostic considerations. *Journal of Child Psychology and Psychiatry*, **31**, 331–42.

DeVeaugh-Geiss, J., Moroz, G., Biederman, J. *et al.* (1992) Clomipramine hydrochloride in childhood and adolescent obsessional compulsive disorder; a multicentre trial. *Journal of the American Academy of Child and Adolescent Psychiatry*, **31**, 45–9.

Flament, M.F., Rapoport, J.L., Berg, C.L. *et al.* (1985) Clomipramine treatment of childhood obsessional compulsive disorder. *Archives of General Psychiatry*, **42**, 977–83.

Gittelman-Klein, R. and Klein, D.F. (1980) Separation anxiety in school refusal and its treatment with drugs. In L. Hersov and I. Berg (eds) *Out of School—Modern Perspectives in School Refusal and Truancy*. Chichester: Wiley, pp. 321–41.

Goodyer, I. (1981) Hysterical conversion reactions in childhood. *Journal of Child Psychology and Psychiatry*, **22**, 179–88.

Green, W.H. (1991) *Child and Adolescent Clinical Psychopharmacology*. Baltimore: Williams and Wilkins.

Harrington, R.C. (1992) The natural history and treatment of child and adolescent affective disorders. *Journal of Child Psychology and Psychiatry*, **33**, 1287–302.

Hawton, K. (1986) *Suicide and Attempted Suicide in Children and Adolescents*. London: Sage Publications.

Hollingsworth, C.E., Tanguay, P.E., Grossman, L. and Pabst, P. (1980) Long-term outcome of obsessive-compulsive disorders in childhood. *Journal of the American Academy of Child Psychiatry*, **19**, 134–44.

Kerfoot, M. (1988) Deliberate self poisoning in childhood and early adolescence. *Journal of Child Psychology and Psychiatry*, **29**, 335–44.

Lyons, J. (1993) Adolescent suicide and self-harm: new approaches. *Young Minds Newsletter*, No. 14, 14–15.

Marks, I.M. (1983) Are there anticompulsive or antiphobic drugs? Review of the evidence. *British Journal of Psychiatry*, **143**, 338–47.

McGibbon, L., Ballard, C.G., Handy, S. and Silveira, W.R. (1992) School attendance as a factor in deliberate self poisoning by 12–15 year old adolescents. *British Medical Journal*, **304**, 28.

Nicholson-Lord, D. (1992) Britons show stress of longest European Community working hours. *The Independent*, 23 September.

Orbach, I. (1988) *Children Who Don't Want To Live*. London: Jossey-Bass.

Rivinus, T.M., Jamison, D.L. and Graham, P.J. (1975) Childhood organic neurological disorders presenting as psychiatric disorder. *Archives of Disease in Childhood*, **50**, 115–19.

Rutter, M., Tizard, J. and Whitmore, K. (eds) (1970) *Education, Health and Behaviour*. London: Longman.

Schaffer, D. (1974) Suicide in childhood and early adolescence. *Journal of Child Psychology and Psychiatry*, **15**, 275–92.

Slater, E. (1965) The diagnosis of hysteria. *British Medical Journal*, **1**, 1395–406.

Tyrer, P. and Tyrer, S. (1974) School refusal, truancy and neurotic illness. *Psychological Medicine*, **4**, 416–21.

Zeitlin, H. (1987) *The Natural History of Psychiatric Disorder in Childhood*. Institute of Psychiatry Monograph No. 29. Oxford: Oxford University Press.

CHAPTER 9

Children Who Are Abused: Physical, Sexual and Emotional Abuse, Neglect

The definition of child abuse as the avoidable impairment of any aspect of growth and development or of physical and mental well-being is now widely accepted. Thus it includes physical, sexual and emotional abuse as well as neglect, failure to thrive and impaired development. Although there is often considerable overlap between the different forms of abuse, the specific issues raised make it important to consider each separately. However, it needs to be acknowledged that the predictable consequence of any form of child abuse is lasting emotional damage.

Surprisingly, child abuse was not recognized until the early 1970s, when it was known as 'the battered child syndrome'. Each year, several thousand children are abused in one or more of the above ways. Teachers in inner city areas are particularly likely to be called upon to become involved with abused children and such situations are very emotionally demanding. However, it is important to know what to look for and how to take appropriate action.

Violence and children

It is now becoming increasingly recognized that normal people under the widespread influences of socio-economic disadvantage, the cultural sanctioning of violence and the break-up of the family can be at high risk for child abuse and neglect (Wolfe, 1991). The relationship between early childhood events and outcome in adult life is receiving increasing attention in child abuse research (Cicchetti, 1989). Researchers are aware that abuse can be defined not only in terms of physical acts to the child but also in terms of the psychological impact on the child (Wolfe, 1987; Zuravin, 1991).

Zulueta (1993) offers a comprehensive review of the issues related to violence within relationships. She looks at theoretical models such as patterns of attachment in human beings and situations where attachment goes wrong.

Some of the other relevant research findings are as follows:

- Students aged 18–23 years who were physically abused in childhood used threatening and violent behaviour towards their partners more often than those who had not been abused (Browne, 1993). There was a strong correlation between students who had been abused as children and those who had behaved violently towards parents or siblings during the previous year (Browne, 1993).
- Gayford (1975) found that 80% of battered women in shelters had witnessed their mothers being assaulted by their fathers during childhood.
- Researchers agree that the effects on children of witnessing violence within the family are usually serious and result in the children learning and internalizing aggressive styles of response and becoming abnormally aroused by aggressive situations (Flood, 1993).
- Patterns of violence are commonly passed from one generation to the next (Flood, 1993).

THE PATH FROM VICTIM TO OFFENDER

Some of the research findings which relate having been abused to becoming an offender can be summarized:

- Only one in every 14 children abused will go on to become an adult abuser (Flood, 1993).
- Two out of three offenders in secure accommodation in the USA have been abused (Browne, 1993).

- American research has identified six factors which can be used to predict the most likely characteristics of an assailant in New York. These are, in order: (1) male, (2) black (which reflects socio-economic factors and not any intrinsic ethnic factor), (3) young, (4) has a history of physical abuse as a child, (5) neglected as a child, and (6) sexually abused (Browne, 1993).

POSSIBILITIES FOR TREATMENT

During the assessment period which follows proven abuse it is important to identify parental expectations so that a treatment package can be planned which is relevant to and meets the needs of the family. Wolfe (1991) describes interventions which promote parental sensitivity and responsiveness to the child's behaviour as well as improving the parents' discipline and anger management skills. Interventions need to address the needs of the parents and the child. The following guidelines apply to abused children:

- There is no one model for the treatment of abused children but all treatment needs to address the problems of low self-esteem, poor social relationships and poor understanding of others. If available, treatment by a child psychotherapist offers the best hope of working through the past traumatic experiences and improving future relationships.
- All children should receive counselling after having been abused. At present, only 10% of those being taken into care receive it (Browne, 1993) and many others who continue to live at home are not offered any help at all.
- Child victims should not be involved in criminal proceedings; it can be harmful to them and is unnecessary (Browne, 1993). My experience fully supports Browne's contention, as these court appearances are adversarial and often very traumatic.

POSSIBILITIES FOR PREVENTION

As the factors within society which facilitate abuse are unlikely to change, Wolfe (1991) suggests that mental health professionals play a larger role in helping parents and children establish healthier relationships which are free from violence. He believes that the prevention of child abuse is best achieved by strengthening the child's developmental abilities at the same time as working on a more positive parent–child relationship.

Research has shown that the cycle of abuse can be broken. Egeland *et al.* (1987) found that those abused mothers who managed to break the cycle showed the following factors:

1. They experienced a significant relationship with someone in childhood.
2. They had a clear memory of the abuse.
3. They had received some form of counselling or psychotherapy.

This research underlines the importance and protective effect of a good relationship with at least one significant person as well as the need for the child to be offered specialist treatment.

Physical abuse

NON-ACCIDENTAL INJURY

A wide variety of injuries can be caused by physical child abuse. In babies and young children this is commonly known as non-accidental injury and often takes the form of fractures of the ribs or the bones of the arms or legs. However, more severe injuries may be found involving brain damage. Every year young children are severely handicapped or even die as a result of child abuse. Nursery teachers may be involved in recognizing and reporting abuse in children under 5 years.

Child abuse can occur at any age and teachers generally are in one of the best positions to recognize the signs. They may find unusual bruising or marks on a child, particularly when the child changes for swimming or PE. Many cases of non-accidental injury in older children are picked up by teachers. The injuries in older children tend to be bruises in unusual places, strap marks or bizarre injuries such as cigarette burns or bites. In children known to be at risk it is extremely helpful if teachers keep a written record detailing the size and location of the bruising or other injuries as well as notifying social services as a matter of urgency.

Clearly, teachers will need to go through their own internal procedures which should involve consultation with the headteacher but they are also required to notify social services about any unexplained injury or bruising to a child. It is vital they do so in order to protect the child. In many instances the child will not tell the truth about how the injury was caused, often out of fear of further abuse or punishment. Social services, in conjunction with doctors who specialize in child abuse, will then become involved and decide whether child abuse has occurred and what further action needs to be taken.

Domestic violence is known to be linked with the abuse and neglect of children and this has been used to detect children at particular risk before abuse has occurred (Browne and Saqui, 1988).

DIAGNOSTIC CRITERIA

The main diagnostic criteria for non-accidental injury are as follows:
1. Delay in seeking medical advice.
2. The account of the accident is vague and inconsistent.
3. A discrepancy between the account and the degree of injury.
4. Abnormal parental behaviour with a lack of concern for the child.

5. The interaction between the child and parents is abnormal.
6. Finger tip bruising, especially over upper arms, body, sides of face, ears or neck.
7. Bizarre injuries, e.g. bites, cigarette burns or rope marks.
8. Sharply demarcated burns or bruises in unusual areas.
9. Injuries around the mouth, e.g. torn frenulum of inside lip.
10. Retinal haemorrhage.
11. Multiple subdural haemorrhages.
12. Peri-anal or genital injury.
13. Long bone fractures in children less than 3 years.
14. Previous injuries, e.g. old scars or healing fractures.
15. The child's expression which is deadpan and watchful; 'frozen awareness'.

EFFECTS OF PHYSICAL ABUSE

Physical and mental pain in the form of violence, threats of abandonment, humiliation and evoking feelings of guilt are all ways of abusing a child. The violence may be directed towards the child's body but unfortunately the experience often causes lasting emotional damage, becoming implanted in the child's mind, sometimes for a lifetime. It is important to remember that violence and trauma are likely to have permanent effects.

TREATMENT

This is where the child psychiatry team has a role to play in helping the child to work through the experience of physical and emotional abuse. Children who have been subjected to severe or recurrent violence and abuse will need specialist psychotherapeutic treatment. Children who have experienced lesser degrees of neglect may be able to respond to more favourable experiences without the need for treatment, but each child's responsiveness and emotional development will need careful monitoring.

THE CHILD PSYCHIATRIST'S ROLE

Child psychiatrists can also help in these cases by giving an expert view on: (1) whether the behaviour of the adults in injuring the child can broadly be regarded as being caused by stress factors acting upon a normal personality or whether there is abnormality and pathology within the personality of one or both parents; (2) whether the psychological state and mental health of the child comes within the normal range or whether there is evidence of disturbed functioning; and (3) the parenting capacities of the abusing parents.

THE TEACHER'S ROLE

Co-operative work between professionals in many disciplines is essential for successful child abuse work and this includes teachers. Teachers have a responsibility to notify social services of any suspicious or unexplained bruises or other injuries on the children. In addition, teachers are able to provide information about the child's level of maturity, ability to relate to others, emotional state and behaviour, whether the child appears well cared for, and intellectual level and ability to learn. The teacher often has first-hand knowledge of the family.

Teachers are usually invited to case conferences where crucial decisions as to the child's future may be taken. They have an invaluable role in providing information as to how the child is progressing in school. However, the actual responsibility for planning and intervention lies with social services and the courts.

Neglect, failure to thrive and impaired development

NEGLECT AND IMPAIRED DEVELOPMENT

Neglect is a chronic condition which often shows itself most obviously in the young child's failure to gain weight, but there are also deeper, more lasting effects on the child's emotional and personality development. More profound neglect will also affect the child's growth in height.

Failure to thrive is often thought to be only a failure to gain weight but it also implies a failure to flourish emotionally. Thus a baby may gain weight from a bottle propped on a pillow but the neglect becomes obvious from other signs such as the lack of normal emotional responsiveness and delayed development related to the lack of stimulation.

Need for attention and stimulation

A baby's healthy development depends on the parents' responsiveness as described in Chapter 3. Sensory deprivation can drive adults out of their minds; not surprisingly, it can prevent babies from ever getting into theirs.

Without stimulation the child's mind does not come to life or develop a sense of exploration, curiosity and play. Similarly, for pre-school children language development is of fundamental importance and is directly related to how much adults talk to, listen to and respond appropriately to the child by following through the child's cues.

It is the lack of human contact, attention and responsiveness that is intellectually stunting, and a proportion of children in schools for children with moderate learning difficulties will have ended there through emotional deprivation alone. An apparent link between stunting of height caused by deprivation and poor intellectual attainment has been demonstrated (Dowdney and Skuse, 1987). The opposite of love for these children is not hate but indifference. The lack of the necessary emotional care results in attention-seeking behaviour, which more accurately should be renamed 'attention needing'. This is in contrast to the deadpan face and withdrawn behaviour of a physically abused child.

Treatment

Effective treatment depends on early detection. Health visitors have a vital role to play in making the diagnosis through the surveillance of young children and the follow-up of those who do not attend their clinic appointments. However, they need training and supportive medical colleagues. In some areas of high social deprivation there are such large numbers of children suffering from relative deprivation that the health visitors accept poor child-rearing practices as the norm.

Unfortunately, there are insufficient resources to meet the needs of these deprived communites, caught in the cycle of deprivation. No one agency can tackle such a problem on its own. A combined approach bringing in social services, housing, welfare benefits, nursery education, teachers, paediatricians, child psychiatry services and the voluntary agencies, e.g. Home-Start, Newpin, and the NSPCC, may be able to help, but even more effective would be a specifically designed project with funding, involving all these agencies. At least then some planned intervention could be offered to these deprived families and their children.

FAILURE TO THRIVE

A hospital or community paediatrician is most likely to make the diagnosis of failure to thrive once possible organic causes have been excluded. If, despite community support, the child fails to thrive within the home, hospital admission may clarify the diagnosis. Children suffering from undernutrition gain weight rapidly, more than 50 g per day on a normal hospital diet. Older children often will not thrive until they are in a place where they feel safe, such as a foster home.

Family centres are extremely useful as they support both the mother and child and focus on helping mothers to give attention to respond to and play with their children. Selwyn (1993) looks at the psychodynamic aspects, including unmet needs in the parents.

Sadly, if the child's needs cannot be met within the home, long-term foster care may be the best alternative, depending on the age of the child and the possibilities for adoption. King and Taitz (1985) showed that catch-up growth for both height and weight was much more likely to occur in long-term rather than short-term foster care. Children are more likely to feel secure in a long-term placement.

Emotional deprivation and abuse

EMOTIONAL DEPRIVATION

Emotional deprivation is said to occur when a child's emotional needs are not met over a period of time, resulting in fundamental disturbances in personality development. The child is likely to have serious long-term difficulties in making close, intimate relationships, experiencing insecurity and unhappiness as well as showing learning and behavioural problems.

The disturbance is manifested in adult life as a personality disorder with continuing difficulties in making relationships and much suffering. The term 'cycle of deprivation' comes from the awareness that these parents are trying to do the best for their children but have not had their own emotional needs met and therefore cannot fully meet their child's needs.

Emotionally deprived children are likely to show a range of behavioural problems from attention-seeking behaviour, bedwetting, over-friendliness to strangers, lack of normal bonding, an inability to establish close relationships and show affection, to more aggressive and destructive behaviours, including lying, stealing and bullying. The behavioural and relationship problems, if mild, may slowly resolve but some children will need long-term help from the child psychiatry team. The most disturbed children will benefit from work with a child psychotherapist.

If a diagnosis of serious neglect is made, social services will need to be involved. Emotional deprivation will inevitably be part of the picture and the child psychiatrist can usefully be asked to make an assessment of both the child and parents as well as giving an opinion on their capacity to parent. As with physical abuse a case conference will be held involving other agencies but social services carry the final responsibility for ensuring the welfare of the child.

Unfortunately, at present the options for older children are often quite limited. Foster placements for older children are often impossible to find so that the conference is left with a choice between returning the child to an unsatisfactory home or placing the child in a children's home where he may be subject to more violence and abuse from older, more disturbed children who increasingly fill these homes. These are not easy decisions.

Outcome

The outlook for these older children is not good. Women who have experienced neglect as children tend to end up with violent partners and men who have been physically abused as children tend to become abusive fathers. This links with recent and growing evidence that boys (and increasingly girls) who are abused are at risk of dealing with the trauma by identifying with the aggressor and abusing other children in their turn.

However, these outcomes are not inevitable, and appropriate treatment can go a long way to modify the effects of violence and neglect. The most successful treatment involves long and painful work with a professional trained in child psychotherapy skills who can help the child work through at least some of the traumatic and depriving experiences (Boston and Szur, 1983). The child's developing personality is likely to have been damaged to a greater or lesser extent and these children need help in establishing trust and a basis of security within themselves as well as being given the opportunity to internalize more caring and thoughtful parental figures.

Children with more serious emotional damage who cannot manage to live successfully within a family are often described as 'unintegrated'. These children will need the specialist help of a therapeutic community school if there is to be any hope of healing the trauma and promoting more normal personality development.

EMOTIONAL ABUSE

Emotional abuse is difficult to prove but is often found in conjunction with physical and sexual abuse. In essence it consists of emotional cruelty. The adults involved may or may not be aware of what they are doing. It occurs when the child is made to feel unwanted and bad. The emotionally abused child may be threatened and living in fear or insecure, afraid of abandonment, or feeling rejected and unwanted. The child's self-esteem may be systematically undermined by cruel comments, making the child feel badly inside.

> Jimmy aged 6 years, was very upset by his parents' separation and started to soil. His mother had limited emotional resources and punished him. Jimmy became more insecure, anxious and angry, with the result that the soiling became worse and he began to have temper outbursts. The situation deteriorated as Jimmy's mother turned more and more against him, seeing him as bad and rejecting him. Jimmy became withdrawn and miserable, unable to learn. Despite intensive support to the family and trying to help mother see that Jimmy was not being naughty, her harsh, punitive and rejecting attitude continued. In these circumstances we felt that Jimmy was suffering from emotional

abuse which was seriously affecting his emotional development and his mental well-being.

After a court case the judge ruled that Jimmy should live with his father, although continuing with weekly access visits to his mother and sister. Fortunately, Jimmy had not been irrevocably damaged and he responded well to his new home. The soiling stopped quite rapidly and he gradually became a much happier child, no longer withdrawn but able to make friends and also to learn.

Treatment

In all cases of suspected emotional abuse an assessment is essential. Social services will have to be involved and may already know the family. If at all possible, interventions need to be set up in order to try to improve the situation for the child within the family. Only if this fails does one then consider whether other options would improve the child's life and lead to a better outcome. The Children Act (1989) is clear that any legal intervention must ensure that the proposed action will in fact improve the situation for the child.

Sexual abuse

It is difficult to face the facts and cope with the emotional impact of any form of child abuse, but sexual abuse is particularly difficult to face. This is seen in the enormous amount of denial which occurs both in professionals and in families; a denial that sexual abuse could possibly have occurred.

A working definition of child sexual abuse (CSA) is the exploitation of a child for sexual gratification. This includes any sexual contact from inappropriate fondling to full intercourse and also includes abuse perpetrated by older children or siblings.

The number of cases reported each year is steadily rising.

There is no doubt about the serious consequences of CSA. Mullen (1990), for example, has shown how sexually abused children have a 2 to 12 times increased risk of developing adult mental illness. In general terms, CSA is more likely to harm a child's normal development than any other form of abuse. It is therefore essential that all children who say they are being abused should be taken very seriously and social services notified. Children rarely lie in these circumstances.

In the majority of cases the abuser is male but increasingly boys from the age of 6 to 7 upwards are being found guilty of sexually abusing another child, as are an increasing number of girls who have been abused themselves. In a significant minority of cases the abuser is female and often the mother.

LONG-TERM OUTLOOK

The long-term outlook varies with the nature and duration of the sexual abuse but all children will benefit from some therapeutic input following disclosure of the abuse. With the more serious forms there will be lasting damage unless treatment is provided. In addition to the sexual abuse there may be evidence of neglect and emotional and physical abuse to be considered. CSA is sometimes part of a much wider range of emotional abuse and problems within a family. Not surprisingly, it has been found that prolonged sexual abuse within the family, accompanied by violence and involvement in child pornography carries the worst outlook.

TYPE OF ABUSE AND TARGETING OF CHILDREN

As the number of cases continues to increase, there are increasing numbers of young children and boys being affected. The type of sexual abuse depends to some extent on the age of the victim. In younger girls and boys of all ages, anal abuse is particularly common. The perpetrator is usually someone known to the child who will have targeted and groomed this child for abuse. The sexual abuse usually starts with inappropriate fondling and touching, gradually moving towards intercourse over time. The child is likely to have been threatened and made to feel guilty and responsible, which makes it more difficult to tell. In girls from the age of 6 to 10 years, vaginal abuse occurs with increasing frequency. However, more than half of all sexually abused children will have no physical signs on examination, having been subjected to masturbation, oral sex, fondling or pornography.

NUMBERS OF CHILDREN SUFFERING FROM SEXUAL ABUSE

It is difficult to find accurate information about how often abuse occurs but certainly there is much sexual abuse that is not reported. However, figures quoted from Barbor and Piller (1987) provided by the NSPCC show that estimated numbers of children aged 0–14 who had been physically abused in England and Wales increased from 9114 in 1985 to 9590 in 1986. Similarly, for sexually abused children aged 0–16 the increase was from 2932 in 1985 to 6330 in 1986.

The great increase in numbers of children suffering from reported sexual abuse which started in 1986 is continuing, with more cases being reported every year. In March 1991 the NSPCC reported that cases of suspected CSA had risen by 20% (Brindle, 1991). It comes as a shock to find that one-third of all sexually abused children are under 5 years of age.

HOW CHILDREN LET OTHERS KNOW

Sometimes children do tell other people what is happening in a direct and straightforward way. This is relatively rare, as they have usually been threatened or given presents to keep them quiet. These inducements force the child into a nightmare world of secrecy, shame and guilt. In fact all the main studies emphasize that delay in telling is a major feature of

CSA (Jones and McQuiston, 1989). This is mainly due to the shame and guilt involved. It has become clear that being sexually abused in itself provokes great guilt in the children, as if it was somehow their fault, which it very definitely is not. After a time some children will confide in a friend, who may then turn to the teacher for help. As in all cases, the teacher needs to let social services know. Teresa's story is fairly typical.

> Teresa, aged 13, was admitted to hospital following an overdose but then became extremely reluctant to return home. She was also describing frightening nightmares where she was chased by a man. We strongly suspected sexual abuse but Teresa always denied this. However, 18 months later she confided in a friend at school that she had been abused by her mother's partner. The friend alerted the teacher and social services were then involved by the school.

ALERTING SIGNS

It is still unfortunately quite common for children to try to alert people to their plight and for those people to turn away and not allow themselves to see what the children are showing. Some of these alerting signs are as follows:

1. Younger children may become precociously sexually aware, trying to touch adults' breasts or genitalia in a quite inappropriate way.
2. Younger children may try to imitate sexual acts such as fellatio, cunnilingus or sexual intercourse while playing with other children.
3. Younger children may show the sudden onset of inappropriate sexual behaviour such as compulsive masturbation or poking objects into the vagina.
4. More verbal children may drop hints about the abuse or talk about it happening to other children; they may write a story about it for their teacher.

5. Adolescents may run away or take an overdose for no apparent reason.

THE TEACHER'S ROLE

It is important to make careful notes of any warning signs, noting the date and exactly what the child said or did. Teachers are often in the position of observing the abnormal behaviour or receiving confidences. If the child does confide about abuse it is important to ask any necessary questions in order to clarify exactly what the child is saying but without putting words in the child's mouth. For example, a child may say 'daddy hurt my bum'. This statement is open to different interpretations and it is important to ask the child to tell you exactly what daddy did, if he or she can, or to draw what happened. It is also important to find out whereabouts the hurt is. One boy told his teacher that daddy hurt him inside his bottom. This, taken with other physical evidence, seemed to indicate with a fair degree of certainty that sexual abuse was taking place. The teacher's evidence is crucial, as by the time an investigatory interview took place this boy had probably been threatened and he subsequently said nothing.

Guidance as to how agencies should work together has been issued by the government (Department of Health, 1991). If the teacher has any suspicion or concern it is best to discuss this with social services. Again, teachers need to go through their own internal procedures, including discussion with the headteacher, before notifying social services.

PRESENTING SYMPTOMS SHOWN BY SEXUALLY ABUSED CHILDREN

Many of these have been described under alerting signs but in general there are three types of presentation:

1. Symptoms caused by localized injury or infection as a result of the abuse such as soreness round the vagina,

vaginal infection, unexplained urinary tract infection, anal pain and bleeding.

2. Symptoms resulting from the emotional effects, e.g. emotional regression, loss of concentration, wetting, soiling, anorexia, depression, behavioural problems, attempts at self-harm or running away. A change in behaviour is an important indication that something is wrong.

3. Sexualized behaviour or inappropriate sexual knowledge in young children. (It is necessary to bear in mind that this may have been gained from inappropriate exposure to the parent's sexuality or from watching pornographic videos.) However, this is still of great concern, as the child's sexuality has been inappropriately stirred up.

PSYCHOLOGICAL EFFECTS WHILE ABUSE IS OCCURRING

These tend to manifest as unexplained emotional disorders or deterioration in the child's behaviour. Children may become anxious and fearful or develop eating or sleeping problems. Other children may become more withdrawn and depressed or alternatively become aggressive and start to lie and steal. A fall-off in school work is common, although occasionally a student may work even harder as a way of dealing with the repeated trauma. Children under 5 may develop temper tantrums, whereas adolescents may make suicide attempts, run away, take drugs or become beyond parental control. There is a recognized association between sexual abuse as a child and outcomes such as pregnancy in adolescence, prostitution and anorexia.

EMOTIONAL EFFECTS AFTER DISCLOSURE OF ABUSE

Studies show that about two-thirds of abused children will show the kind of emotional or behavioural changes described above.

Another considerable proportion will also develop post-traumatic stress disorder. There are three aspects to this: (1) flashbacks when the events of the abuse suddenly fill their minds, (2) states of increased arousal such as nightmares, anxiety and panic, and (3) an avoidance of any reminders and emotional numbing. A proportion of children will retract their statements, sometimes due to pressure from the family. It is now recognized that some families influence the child to 'accommodate' to the abuse through their emphasis on secrecy and hiding the truth. Some parents do not support their abused child and may accuse the child of lying, especially in cases where the family is likely to be broken up and the partner may have to face prison.

OUTWARD EFFECTS OF CSA ON CHILDREN AND YOUNG PEOPLE

These can be summarized as:

1. Behavioural disturbances – aggressive and/or destructive behaviours, substance abuse, running away, self-destructive and suicidal behaviours.
2. Emotional disturbances – depression, anxiety, guilt, shame, feelings of isolation, phobias.
3. Bodily disturbances – difficulty sleeping, nightmares, aches and pains, appetite disturbances, anorexia, psychosomatic problems, daytime wetting and bedwetting, soiling.
4. Low self-esteem.
5. Age-inappropriate sexual behaviour – a preoccupation with sexual matters, excessive masturbation, over-sexualized behaviour, fear of sexuality (Tufts New England Medical Center, Division of Child Psychiatry, 1984).

PSYCHOLOGICAL EFFECTS OF SEXUAL ABUSE ON THE
VICTIM

There is always a gradual process of adaptation for all family members when abuse takes place within the family. The situation which makes abuse possible starts long before the actual abuse occurs. There are various factors which have been found to be present in abusing families.

On occasions the abuser is emotionally close to the victim and uses this position to gradually sexualize the relationship (this is known as grooming). In other instances the abuser may be unpleasant and rejecting towards the child well before the abuse starts and in these cases there is a feeling of sexual aggression towards the child.

The abuser creates situations where the targeted child is alone with him or her and gradually escalates the sexual behaviour from excessive touching to fondling to oral sex or penetrative intercourse at a later stage. Younger children may not be aware of the abuse at first and become very confused by the mixture of affection and abuse. Other children value the attention and are torn by their wish for warmth and affection, although realizing somewhere within them that what is happening is wrong.

Children are often coerced into acquiescing by being told frightening stories about what will happen if they tell anyone, e.g. 'if you tell you will be taken away from home', or by more open threats (Lister, 1982). At the same time, the child's sexual feelings may well have been stirred up and taken advantage of by the abuser. The result is that the child now feels guilty, which makes it even more difficult to tell.

Making children into victims
Children who suffer abuse over a period of time find ways of adapting but at a great cost to themselves. Their adaptation often involves taking on a victim psychology. These children describe how they feel different, bad and dirty but continue to blame themselves. This leads to a very poor self-image and very distressing feelings of isolation and of having been

psychologically damaged. These children live in a state of high stress, facing a situation from which there seems to be no escape. This has been called 'learned helplessness' (Peterson and Seligman, 1983). This process tends to occur in all situations where people are living in a state of ongoing stress and fear and is also seen in wives who are repeatedly abused by their husbands.

Long-term effects

The long-term effects are well documented and include mental illness, anxiety and depression, sexual problems, including inhibition and failure, extremely low self-esteem, marital problems and difficulties with parenting. Unless appropriate treatment is provided, many sexually abused young people are permanently damaged by the experience, with continuing unresolved problems throughout their adult life (Mullen, 1990; Sheldon, 1988).

In those cases where CSA is symptomatic and part of a much wider range of emotional abuse within a family, the outlook is particularly poor. An additional factor is that many of the victims have grown up in families where normal social roles are very distorted, leaving them confused about their own role and seeing others as confused about theirs.

How psychological effects are mediated

CSA is an impingement on the child, both physically and mentally. The child's mind is raped and this is not dependent on what happens physically. CSA is particularly damaging to children and the effects are mediated through the destructive effects on the child's internal world (Trowell, 1990). The child is not ready for a sexual relationship and any form of sexual abuse represents a violent intrusion into the child's normal unfolding pattern of development.

This intrusion is likely to cause a split in the child's mind. The abuser forces in an experience which does not make sense and which replicates the nightmare world of madness. A terrible secrecy and fear have entered the child's life.

Many abused children try to deal with this by splitting off the unthinkable 'mad' experience and trying to carry on a normal life with the rest of their mind (Trowell, 1990).

The outcome for these children depends on whether they are able to tell someone and whether the family believes them, as well as on their developmental level. If the experience remains secret and not able to be told, it is likely to be split off and encapsulated within the young person's mind.

If the abuse continues, some children find another way of coping by believing that what is happening is normal. This response unfortunately interferes with their thinking and can lead to a loss of contact with reality in part of their minds.

However, if the abuse only occurs on one occasion and children come from a stable home, they are usually able to recover without permanent damage. Similarly, brief abuse by a stepfather, relative or family friend may be able to be survived without such mentally destructive effects. Although psychosexual development may be distorted, it is not shattered, and with treatment these young people may be able to work through the feelings and eventually allow the experience to fade in their minds. However, even then there may be some residual effects on psychosexual development and on the capacity to make intimate relationships. Survival implies that the children may come through scarred but not devastated.

In many cases the abuse continues over a significant period of time and the child feels unable to tell, with the result that the experience does become split off from other more normal experiences, blocked off and encapsulated. This can be compared to a walled-off bubble in the mind which at times is in danger of bursting and releasing overwhelming and devastating feelings.

Some unforeseen episode in life such as starting a sexual relationship at adolescence or getting married may cause the feelings to burst out, or more unusual situations such as one's own child reaching the age at which the abuse occurred.

A young woman who had dealt with the abuse by cutting off her feelings and encapsulating the experience suddenly started to feel she was going mad and turning against her boyfriend. He was pressing her to start a sexual relationship and they had just become engaged.

As these unconscious links became more conscious, the walled-off feelings came nearer to the surface and eventually burst out in an unmanageable way. The memories flooded back and she became distraught. There was no way she could integrate such traumatic and disturbing experiences, which had overturned all her expectations of a father, with the other normal experiences of her life. Fortunately she was able to benefit from psychotherapeutic help.

If the child's parenting and care are good enough, the encapsulated part may not be obvious and it may remain as an untouched and walled-off area within the mind. This may be the best solution for those many abused people who have found a mode of surviving and where to open the subject up would prove to be too damaging.

If therapy is being considered it is important to try to judge whether the person is strong enough to manage the overwhelming feelings without breaking down. It may be possible to touch on some of the issues and some of the pain without breaching the walled-off area, leaving the individual free to return for more help later on if necessary.

AGE AT WHICH ABUSE OCCURRED

The age at which the abuse occurs has an effect on the outcome.

Pre-school children
Boys and girls from 0 to 5 years are undertaking major

developmental tasks, including working through the normal fantasies related to their understanding of sexual relationship. Sexual abuse at this young age can be catastrophic and seriously interfere with further development. Pre-school children who are abused before they have a consistent sense of themselves as separate people and before they have the vocabulary to describe what has happened are particularly at risk (MacCarthy, 1988).

These children are very vulnerable to being overcome by disturbing emotions and physical sensations but with the added difficulty of not being able to express their problems in words. They are likely to have experienced feelings of profound powerlessness while being abused, which it is important not to replicate. The victims may communicate great distress but be unable to describe their symptoms clearly because they did not have access to words at the time of the abuse (Campling, 1992).

Junior schoolchildren

During these years children show rapidly developing skills. However, sexual abuse at this time may push the child towards either a sadistic or masochistic pattern of behaviour. Some children react by taking on a masochistic victim role but an increasing number of both boys and girls are taking on an aggressive sadistic position. They identify with the aggressor displaying violence towards others but also show a sexual delight in their violence. This can be seen in children as young as 7–8 years.

In addition, the emotional side of sexual development may well be seriously affected by the abuse. Abuse violates normal physical and psychological development. Sometimes a boy may be precipitated into homosexuality or into very violent sadistic sexual behaviour.

Some children are left desperately searching for love as adults and find themselves once again in an abusive relationship. These vulnerable people tend to relate to the world and their problems either in a masochistic way or with despairing acceptance.

Behavioural research confirms the serious consequences of CSA in children. Tufts' New England Medical Center, Division of Child Psychiatry (1984) found that 40% of a sample of 58 abused children aged between 7 and 13 years scored in the seriously disturbed range, as did 47% of the sample of Tong *et al.* (1987) of the same age range.

Secondary schoolchildren

Abuse at this age particularly affects the young person's future expectations and evolving sexuality. Sex becomes associated with violence, fear and guilt. Young people frequently feel tremendous shame if they were sexually excited by the abuse, especially if the abuser took advantage of this (Cahill *et al.*, 1991).

Many abused people cope by denying or avoiding their sexual feelings (John, 1980). Others feel confused and unsafe and use their sexuality in chaotic, inappropriate and self-defeating ways.

MAKING THE DIAGNOSIS

This is made on the basis of the alerting symptoms and signs, the interview with the child carried out by someone with expertise in the field and an assessment of the family. A physical examination of the child is also undertaken by a skilled professional, either a paediatrician or a police surgeon, but it is known that this will be negative in 50% of cases even though abuse has occurred (Jones and McQuiston, 1989).

Reliable diagnosis requires an experienced professional team approach. However, even if there is physical evidence the diagnosis needs to be approached with caution and humility and needs confirmation from the multi-disciplinary investigation. The most important single feature, if available, is the statement by the child (Robinson, 1991).

In Barbara's case both the police and the psychiatric services were convinced that sexual abuse had taken place but the Crown Prosecution Service felt that there was insufficient evidence to proceed with a prosecution of the man involved.

> Barbara, an 8-year-old, was sexually abused for nine months before she finally told her mother. She had been told not to tell and did not want to upset her mother. Mother's new partner set out systematically to groom her by involving Barbara in games which focused on picking her up in sexually inappropriate ways when her mother was absent. The sexual behaviour gradually built up over time, edging nearer to full intercourse. For instance, he would make sure that Barbara's mother was cooking and would then take Barbara into the bedroom and abuse her.
>
> Barbara changed, becoming unhappy and moody, not wanting to be left with mother's partner and flaring up easily, until eventually she snapped. She broke down in tears and mother persuaded Barbara to tell her what was the matter. Mother instantly believed her, as it made sense of all Barbara's behaviour. The partner left, although he denied the allegations and social services and the police conducted an investigation. They were convinced by Barbara's testimony which was also videotaped, but the case did not go to court and the man is free.

TRUE OR FALSE ALLEGATIONS OF ABUSE

A child's spontaneous statement about sexual abuse is likely to be true. Children very rarely lie in this situation. It has been found that about 98% of children's allegations are true (Jones and McQuiston, 1989). However, one has to be aware in custody and access disputes that there is a higher incidence of false allegations in these circumstances.

THE ABUSER

In the majority of cases the abuser is someone very well known to the child, such as the father, grandfather, step-father, uncle or mother's partner. It is really quite rare for a child to be abused by a stranger.

FEATURES OF FAMILIES WHO SEXUALLY ABUSE

Once the interview and examination of the child have been completed, the professionals need to have made a decision as to the probability of sexual abuse having occurred. It is necessary to bear this in mind when assessing the family, as without this initial assessment of risk a very secretive family, by their silence, could leave the child even more exposed. Finkelhor (1984) describes four pre-conditions in the family for sexual abuse to occur:

1. Are there factors which may motivate the individual towards sexual abuse? For example, (a) is there a confusion of roles within the family, (b) is there sexual arousal towards children on the basis of one or other parent having experienced traumatic events in childhood such as sexual abuse, or (c) is there a problem with normal sexual outlets because of excessive anxiety, sexual inhibition or failure?
2. Are there factors present which would predispose to internal prohibitions being overcome, e.g. alcohol or drug abuse, limited intellectual ability or a family with very poor boundaries?
3. Are there factors present which would predispose to external prohibitions being overcome? For instance, is there illness or absence of a protective parent? Is there a distant or rejecting relationship between the abuser and the child, such as a step-parent or boyfriend?
4. Are there factors present which may make the child more vulnerable? It has been shown that children with physical or intellectual disabilities are particularly vulnerable to abuse.

To summarize, it seems that the abuse may well start within families where abusers have problems themselves, and are unable to form normal, satisfying relationships. Against this background there is additionally a loosening of the usual prohibitions against sexual contact between an adult and a child.

There are two kinds of family which seem to predispose to abuse. First, there is the family with high levels of secrecy and an almost complete absence of conflict. This is linked to a great fear of separateness and anxiety about the break-up of the family. Here the child is needed to hold the family together at the expense of the child's own needs.

Secondly, there is almost the opposite; the family with high levels of violence, conflict and neglect where boundaries between family members are almost non-existent. This is the atmosphere where both physical and sexual abuse can occur and may involve more than one family member. It is based on a cycle of deprivation, with the parents coming from similar chaotic and deprived childhood backgrounds.

TREATMENT

Both individual and group therapy have been found to be helpful. All children who have been sexually abused should be offered therapeutic sessions as soon as possible. If group therapy is an option, a short period of individual therapy may be necessary first to deal with some of the issues and prepare the youngster. Walford (1989) found that this took between two and six months. Group therapy is complementary to individual therapy and can help with feelings of isolation and feeling different which are commonly experienced (Walford, 1989).

Individual therapy alone or followed by group therapy is the treatment of choice. Some larger academic centres both here and in the USA have set up treatment programmes for children and parents using group work (Bentovim et al., 1988; Furniss et al., 1988; Giarretto, 1981; Sgroi and Dana, 1982).

It is important for those treating these young people to be extremely sensitive in their work, much of which has the underlying aim of facilitating a change in feeling and attitude from victim to survivor (Davenport and Sheldon, 1987). One of the problems is finding ways of managing the rage and hatred stirred up by the abuse.

Survivors may direct these feelings towards the abuser alone or towards the parent or society which failed to protect them. The hatred may be displaced, often on to those close to them or on to the professionals trying to help. It is important for those working with these young people to recognize and hold the anger in mind when it is directed at them without retaliating (Winnicott, 1949). Sometimes this hatred becomes projected in an all-embracing way so that the young person feels hated by everyone and comes to lead a very restricted life (MacCarthy, 1988).

EFFECTS OF INTERVENTION

It is important to ensure that the interventions are less harmful than the abuse itself. The system is now much better so that children no longer have to suffer multiple interviews, although in some cases more than one is still necessary. Other harmful effects relate to the break-up of the family, with the abused child being taken into care.

THE NEEDS OF THE CHILD VERSUS THE NEEDS OF THE LEGAL SYSTEM

Finally, there is the legal system, which if misinterpreted can result in the child's mother being given counselling and support while the child is left without any help or treatment. The Crown Prosecution Service (CPS) is still saying that from the time the child talks about the abuse until the case comes to court, the child should not receive any therapy or counselling because that will contaminate the evidence (Howarth, 1991). This seems to be because the CPS is afraid that the therapist will coach the child. In fact, child psychiatrists and psychologists are trained to listen to the child and if professionally competent there is no way they would seek to coach the child in any way.

In addition the legal system continues to cause undue stress on children through delays, postponements and the length of time they have to wait before the case comes to court. Until the court case is over, children cannot start to put the abuse behind them, work on their feelings and gradually allow the experience to fade in their minds. I find this a particular problem in that the present system is adding to the child's suffering and artificially prolonging severe distress.

Whether the present court system is the best way of dealing with sexual abuse is very much open to question. However, overall, very few cases are ever brought to court (Howarth, 1991). As a consequence many children are left feeling that the abuser has got away with the abuse and is free to continue to abuse other children. Clearly, this is a very difficult area and it is essential to ensure that people are not convicted of crimes they did not commit, but many child psychiatrists feel that the scales are too heavily weighted against the child. In many instances there seems to be a good case based on the child's evidence and symptoms and yet there is no prosecution.

TREATMENT OF CHILD SEXUAL ABUSERS

Before any realistic treatment can be undertaken, child sexual abusers need to acknowledge that their behaviour is wrong and extremely damaging to the child involved. That is the first essential step in any treatment programme. Many abusers have manipulated the truth in order to justify their behaviour, and tell themselves that what they are doing is not particularly harmful to the child.

The probation service offers treatment groups for sexual abusers and many groups do excellent work, although the long-term outcome for offenders is not yet known and not all abusers are able to respond to this approach.

References and further reading

Barbor and Piller (eds) (1987) *Report on The Medical Aspects of Child Abuse*. Liverpool: The Children's Research Fund.

Bentovim, A., Elton, A., Hildebrand, J. *et al.*, (1988) *Child Sexual Abuse Within the Family*. London: Wright.

Boston, M. and Szur, R. (1983) *Psychotherapy with Severely Deprived Children*. London: Routledge and Kegan Paul.

Brindle, D. (1991) Child sexual abuse cases rise. *The Guardian*, 19 March.

Browne, K. (1993) Victim to offender: breaking the cycle. *Young Minds Newsletter*, No. 16, 14.

Browne, K. and Saqui, F. (1988) Approaches to screening for child abuse and neglect. In K. Browne, C. Davies, and S. Stratton (eds) *Early Prediction and Prevention of Child Abuse*. Chichester: Wiley.

Cahill, C., Llewelyn, S.P. and Pearson, C. (1991) Treatment of sexual abuse which occurs in childhood: a review. *British Journal of Clinical Psychology*, **30**, 1–12.

Campling, P. (1992) Working with adult survivors of child sexual abuse. *British Medical Journal*, **305**, 1375–6.

Cicchetti, D. (1989) How research on child maltreatment has informed the study of child development. In D. Cicchetti and V. Carlson (eds) *Child Maltreatment: Theory and Research on the Causes and Consequences of Child Abuse and Neglect*. New York: Cambridge University Press.

Davenport, S. and Sheldon, H. (1987) From victim to survivor. *Changes*, **5**, 379–82.

Department of Health (1991) *Working together: a guide to arrangements for interagency cooperation for the protection of children from abuse*. London: HMSO.

Dowdney, L. and Skuse, D. (1987) Growth retardation and developmental delay amongst inner-city children. *Journal of Child Psychology and Psychiatry*, **28**, 529–41.

Egeland, B., Jacobvitz, D. and Papatola, K. (1987) Inter-generational continuity of abuse. In R. Gelles and J. Lancaster (eds) *Child Abuse and Neglect: Biosocial Dimensions*. New York: Aldine de Gruyer.

Finkelhor, D. (1984) Four preconditions of sexual abuse: a model. In D. Finkelhor (ed.) *Child Sexual Abuse: New Theory and Research*. New York: Free Press.

Flood, S. (1993) Violence and young minds: an introduction to some of the key issues. *Young Minds Newsletter*, No. 16, 10–16.

Fountain, D.M. and Moore, B. (1989) Therapy for adult victims of childhood sexual abuse in a district setting. *Psychiatric Bulletin*, **13**, 437–9.

Furniss, T., Bingley-Miller, L. and van Elberg, A. (1988) Goal-orientated group treatment for sexually abused girls. *British Journal of Psychiatry*, **152**, 97–106.

Gayford, J. (1975) Wife battering: a preliminary study of 100 cases. *British Medical Journal*, **25** (1), 94–7.

Giarretto, H. (1981) A comprehensive child sexual abuse treatment programme. In P.B. Mrazek and C.H. Kempe (eds) *Sexually Abused Children and their Families*. Oxford: Pergamon.

Howarth, V. (1991) Our treatment of children. *Young Minds Newsletter*, No. 8, 1–5.

John, D. (1980) *Beyond Sexual Abuse: Therapy with Women who were Victims in Childhood*. Chichester: Wiley.

Jones, D. and McQuiston, M. (1989) *Interviewing the Sexually Abused Child*. London: Gaskell.

King, J.M. and Taitz, L.S. (1985) Catch up growth following abuse. *Archives of Disease in Childhood*, **60**, 1152–4.

Lister, E.D. (1982) Forced silence: a neglected dimension of trauma. *American Journal of Psychiatry*, **139**, 867–72.

MacCarthy, B. (1988) Are incest victims hated? *Psychoanalytic Psychotherapy*, **3**, 113–20.

Mullen, P.E. (1990) The long-term effects of child sexual assault on the mental health of victims. *Journal of Forensic Psychiatry*, **1**, 13–34.

Peterson, C. and Seligman, M. (1983) Learned helplessness and victimisation. *Journal of Social Issues*, **39**, 103–16.

Robinson, R. (1991) Physical signs of sexual abuse in children. *British Medical Journal*, **302**, 863–4.

Selwyn, R. (1993) Psychodynamic aspects of failure to thrive: a case study. *Journal of Child Psychotherapy*, **19** (2), 85–100.

Sgroi, S.M. and Dana, N.T. (1982) Individual and group treatment of mothers of incest victims. In: S.M. Sgroi (ed) *Handbook of*

Clinical Intervention in Child Sexual Abuse. Massachusetts: Lexington.

Sheldon, H. (1988) Child sexual abuse in adult female psychotherapy referrals: incidence and implications for treatment. *British Journal of Psychiatry*, **152**, 107–11.

Tong, L., Oates, K. and McDowell, M. (1987) Personality development following sexual abuse. *Child Abuse and Neglect*, **11**, 371–83.

Trowell, J. (1990) The Ramifications of Child Sexual Abuse. BTPP Lecture, Dudley Road Hospital, July.

Tufts' New England Medical Center, Division of Child Psychiatry (1984) *Sexually Exploited Children: Service and Research Project*. Final Report for the Office of Juvenile Justice and Delinquency Prevention. Washington, DC: US Department of Justice.

Walford, G. (1989) Group therapy for sexually abused children. *Newsletter, Association for Child Psychology and Psychiatry*, **11**(6), 7–13.

Winnicott, D. (1949) Hate in the countertransference. *International Journal of Psychoanalysis*, **30**, 60–75.

Wolfe, D. (1987) *Child Abuse: Implications for Child Development and Psychopathology*. Newbury Park, CA: Sage.

Wolfe, D. (1991) *Preventing Physical and Emotional Abuse of Children*. New York: The Guilford Press.

Zulueta, F. (1993) *From Pain to Violence: The Traumatic Roots of Destructiveness*. London: Whurr.

Zuravin, S. (1991) Suggestions for defining child physical abuse and neglect. In R. Starr and D. Wolfe (eds) *The Effects of Child Abuse and Neglect: Issues and Research*. New York: Guilford Press.

CHAPTER 10

Hyperactivity, 'Dyslexia', Drug and Solvent Misuse, Bereavement

Hyperactivity

The term 'hyperactivity' has been used in different ways and has generated considerable confusion over the years. It seems most useful to use the word 'overactive' to describe a child who moves about a great deal but where the activity is not part of a defined disorder.

Hyperactivity is best reserved for a specific disorder which involves much more than very active behaviour (Taylor *et al.*, 1991). Hyperactive children show a pattern of continuous chaotic movement combined with impulsive behaviour, a lack of self-control and an inability to settle or concentrate. These children tend to flit from one activity to another in a motiveless way and this, together with their impulsive behaviour, frequently causes trouble within a school setting. In addition, severely hyperactive children have problems with relationships and making friends as they are unaware of other people's feelings.

There is a clear distinction between a normal active child, full of energy and life who can concentrate when necessary, and a hyperactive child, whose activity is disorganized and who is unable to settle down and concentrate for more than a minute or two. Children with a conduct disorder may also show overactivity and have difficulty in concentrating.

CRITERIA USED IN THE USA

The criteria used for diagnosing hyperactivity in the USA are very different from those in the UK, with children who we would consider were showing a conduct disorder being given a diagnosis of hyperactivity or attention deficit hyper-activity disorder (ADHD). The diagnosis of ADHD is made on the basis of the presence of overactivity and lack of atten-tion only. These children are commonly prescribed stimulant medication in the USA, with the possibility of side-effects such as difficulty in sleeping, tearfulness, lack of appetite and diminished growth rate. Fortunately, these side-effects are not common. In the UK, hyperactivity, because of its very specific definition, is a rare condition with a prevalence at any one point in time of about 1.7% (Taylor et al., 1991).

OVERACTIVE BEHAVIOUR

The causes generally fall into four main categories: (1) temperamental variation; (2) reaction to stress; (3) associ-ated with conduct disorder; and (4) hyperactivity as a disorder in its own right.

Temperamental and genetic factors
As part of their temperament, children tend to have a consistent way of doing things which involves their activity level, ability to adapt to change, attention span, persistence and mood. Temperamental factors can be the cause of serious problems in the relationship between mother and baby. A smiling, responsive baby is much easier to live with than a miserable crying one, and a grouping of negative characteristics such as lack of adaptability, misery and poor attention span give rise to a typical picture of the difficult child. Some parents find a very active child particularly stressful, whereas others might see the child in a more pos-itive way as energetic and lively.

Genetic factors may be involved in hyperactivity. Boys are affected four times more than girls and this seems related to the fact that young female brains are more stable and are less likely to be affected by any form of developmental delay.

Reaction to stress
Children may respond to worrying situations and stress by becoming very active. Constant activity is one way of keeping unbearable anxiety at bay and may only occur in particularly stressful situations. If this seems possible it is important for parents and teachers to explore and remove any sources of stress.

> Rachel was a little girl who had some learning diffi-culties and also great difficulty relating to other people. She was taken to a small nursery group at the age of 3 and spent the whole time racing round the room, which was totally unlike her. It quickly became clear that Rachel was unable to cope and her mother recognized this and withdrew her for a time.

Overactivity associated with conduct disorder
Children with conduct disorders are quite frequently over-active in certain situations and have difficulty in concentrating but they lack the continuing restless, chaotic quality which is found in true hyperactivity. In the UK, chil-dren with a conduct disorder who are also very active would probably be treated with a behavioural approach in the first instance, involving firm discipline together with a system of rewards.

The overactivity which is seen in some children with a conduct disorder is often a result of some degree of emotional deprivation. The origins of this behaviour can be seen in very young children. Observations of young babies have shown that they may use muscular activity to hold themselves together when their mother is not emotionally available to them.

> One baby of 4 months was observed to have devel-oped a pattern of moving his arms and legs almost continually. His young mother was preoccupied with her own life and needs and was not able to empathize with her baby's need for attention. It was

felt that he had turned to constant activity and movement in order to hold himself together. As this little boy became older and able to walk, the continual movement of his limbs developed into a pattern of very active behaviour; he was always on the go and never seemed to become tired.

The continual activity also served to protect him from having to face the bad feelings inside himself. He had not been enabled to internalize a good, loving mother and had not had the experience of being loved for himself. This is an example of how a pattern of overactivity may build up on the basis of emotional deprivation. In these circumstances the child may well go on to develop a conduct disorder with defiant, aggressive behaviour both at school and at home.

Hyperactivity as a disorder in its own right

True hyperactivity is a continuing pattern of behaviour made up of disorganized activity, inability to concentrate and impulsive actions lacking in self-control. In this case referral to the family doctor or child psychiatric service is indicated for further assessment.

HYPERACTIVITY AS A DISABILITY

In the UK about one child in 2000 is diagnosed as hyperactive and may be treated with stimulant medication. In general, hyperactivity is seen as a disability with the potential to adversely affect normal psychological development. Hyperactivity has a great impact on learning, severely affects the child's ability to relate to others and affects how people see the child; these children are often unpopular and regarded as a nuisance. However, despite these risk factors the majority of hyperactive children mature and grow up into normal adults.

Parents are usually first to recognize that there is a problem but the diagnosis tends to be made after the child starts school. Because young children's activity levels cover a very wide range, it is generally only possible to diagnose severe hyperactivity before the age of 3 or 4 years. The general level of activity makes up one aspect of a child's temperament and varies considerably between the ages of 2 and 4 years. Some children are particularly active and a child with a high activity level will run about most of the time. However, by the age of 4 years the majority of children have settled down.

FACTORS ASSOCIATED WITH HYPERACTIVITY

There are four main factors, which are (1) the extreme end of normal temperament, (2) slower than usual development and maturation, (3) severe brain damage, occurring either at birth or later, and (4) a physical disorder such as deafness or loss of vision. It is unlikely that any one factor is totally responsible; physical and psychological factors tend to interact.

It is probable that the majority of hyperactive children, especially those with the milder form, are either at the far end of the normal range or are slow developers. In any event, children with hyperactivity quite frequently show other areas of slower development, such as being late in talking and understanding speech as well as having possible learning difficulties. In fact, they may show the triad of language delay, clumsiness and a slightly lower than average intelligence. The slower maturation means that hyperactive children tend to improve with time and the level of activity falls as they grow older.

FAMILY FACTORS

As with all conditions, the family can be an influence for good or ill upon the hyperactive child. Family relationships in themselves cannot cause hyperactivity but can make the child's behaviour very much better or very much worse. It has been found that parents who manage their child's behaviour well tend to have the children who develop well and that criticism has an adverse effect on outcome (Weiss and Hechtman, 1986).

It is not always possible to deal calmly and firmly with a hyperactive child. Occasionally, parents and child can find themselves in a destructive relationship based on continuing conflict. A negative cycle can start when a parent responds to the overactivity with anger and punishment. The child is then likely to become angry and confrontational. This can continue into a pattern of punishment and resentment so that all warm, loving feelings are lost. The child is left feeling unwanted and bad and may start to show aggressive and anti-social behaviour.

When parents themselves are vulnerable or under stress it is easy to see how such negative cycles develop. The whole pattern needs to be turned around so that good behaviour is encouraged and reinforced. A system of identifying good points, rewarding small steps towards desired behaviour and allowing time for the hyperactive child to let off steam has been found to be effective. Successful parents have managed to find ways of encouraging their child's self-control; they stay calm, set clear, simple rules and are prepared to change them if necessary and engage in many shared activities with their child.

PROBLEM AREAS WITHIN SCHOOL

Some hyperactive children blossom on starting school but others find it particularly stressful and may respond by becoming more disorganized and rushing about even more. These children will probably not look distressed and are more likely to appear cheerful and excited. In addition to causing constant disruption to the class, hyperactive children often have some degree of learning difficulties because of their short attention span and poor self-control. Any child with a clear learning difficulty needs a professional assessment by the educational psychologist.

> Carl had a diagnosis of hyperactivity made while an inpatient at a child psychiatric unit at the age of 6 years. He showed the typical symptoms of overactive behaviour, flitting impulsively from one thing to another with often thoughtlessly aggressive behaviour towards other children. Carl's major problems manifested in school and he had already been excluded from two schools.
>
> Carl was the older of two children and his parents managed reasonably by being very strict and structured. Carl was eventually placed at a school for children with emotional and behavioural problems but they found his demanding, impulsive behaviour very disruptive and difficult to manage. A behavioural approach combined with the use of methyl phenidate (a stimulant) proved to be the most effective treatment and enabled him to continue at the school.

HOW TEACHERS CAN HELP

1. Ensure that the very active child is properly assessed and, where appropriate, a diagnosis of hyperactivity is made. The child will probably need to see an educational psychologist as well as a child psychiatrist.
2. In consultation with these other professionals, decide on the most appropriate educational provision for the hyperactive child. It may be within an ordinary school with additional support and resources where necessary or within a special school. The decision is usually based on the provision that is available locally. Some schools may be willing to accommodate to the individual child's needs within a mainstream school. The school's attitude is very important, particularly in recognizing that the hyperactive child does have a disability and needs special help.

Fortunately, severe hyperactivity is rare as there are no special schools for hyperactive children. For some children with difficulty in concentrating as the main problem, a school for slow learners may be most appropriate. For others where disruptive behaviour is the major problem, a school for children with emotional and behavioural problems may be the best option.

HOW TO HELP THE HYPERACTIVE CHILD

1. Avoid constant telling off. Hyperactive children cannot control their behaviour; they cannot help how they are.
2. Identify the different problem areas and set up strategies to deal with each one individually. Particular problem areas may be (a) learning, (b) attention span, (c) impulse control, (d) aggression, and (e) social relationships.

Learning
In order to learn something new it is helpful to break the task up into very small steps, each of which can be learnt very quickly within a few seconds. The child is then asked to master each step separately.

Also, as these children cannot order their work for themselves it is important to present subjects in a structured way, with the most important points brought to attention and emphasized.

Attention span
The lack of attention and concentration is a real, although not always recognized, disability and is an active block to progress in learning. It is a particular handicap when children are asked to work on their own. Learning involves exploration and curiosity. Hyperactive children cannot explore the world in the way normal children do through

using their curiosity and taking in what they find out. They lack normal curiosity and are unable to sustain interest, which means that they can only explore in a brief, repetitive and fragmented way.

Teachers can help in encouraging the child to take a structured approach towards an increased concentration span. One possible approach is to ask the child to persist at a task for a certain period of time and then to gradually increase the time periods. Each task completed successfully is rewarded and the child is moved on to a task which requires slightly more persistence.

Another skill which teachers can encourage is reflection. Hyperactive children tend to jump to conclusions without thinking. The teacher can ask children to say to themselves, 'stop and think' whenever they are asked questions or given problems. Encouraging children to talk to themselves and develop an inner language is also useful in learning to control aggression and also in learning how to notice several things at once and selecting out the most important. Children are asked to talk to themselves about the problem.

Impulse control

Encouraging children to talk to themselves is helpful in providing some control over the impulsive behaviour. Again, children need to be helped to say to themselves, 'stop and think' before rushing into action. Specific targets can be set, such as not running off at the end of school. The target behaviours can be monitored and achievements rewarded.

Aggression

Children who are not coping and are falling behind very often start to misbehave. It has been found that 50% of children who are severely behind in their reading also show anti-social behaviour involving truancy, aggression and stealing (Taylor, 1985). These children can very easily feel like failures and begin to despair of themselves. As part of this process they may become more likely to lash out and attack other children.

Hyperactive children who are also aggressive need to be helped to recognize that there is a problem. It can be helpful to encourage children to identify situations where they may become aggressive and then encourage them to avoid those situations if at all possible. The next step is to help them develop an inner language through repetition, saying to themselves, 'stop and think: walk away'.

Hyperactive children need adults to help them with self-control. For instance, some children can learn how to take turns if helped by an adult.

Social relationships

Another important area of disability is that hyperactive children often have great difficulty in picking up social cues and are also unable to empathize with other children. Thus gentle and friendly advice from a sympathetic adult as well as explanations of how other children are feeling can be of great benefit and can help with the child's social development.

OTHER TREATMENTS

Medication

As behaviour therapy techniques become more widely used, the need for medication is becoming less, but it is still very helpful in selected cases. Stimulants are the most commonly used drugs for severe hyperactivity. They work by reducing the overactivity and thereby helping the children to be calmer and concentrate better. The child's improved behaviour has important effects on family functioning. The whole family can move into a positive cycle where the child can be praised and valued rather than continuing the negative cycle of difficult behaviour and angry frustrated parents.

Stimulants can also help with the other associated problems such as defiant, aggressive behaviour (Taylor *et al.*,

1987; Barkley *et al.*, 1989) and the quality of relationships with other children (Whalen *et al.*, 1989). It is likely that these positive changes are a direct result of the reduction in hyperactivity (Taylor, 1994).

After diagnosis, teacher and parent baseline behavioural scales can be quickly completed so that the effect of the medication can be monitored. Methyl phenidate is often the treatment of choice. It has a short life and is therefore best given twice a day, in the morning and at midday, in the dose range of 0.3–1.5 mg per kg per day (Prendergast, 1993). Height, weight, pulse and blood pressure need measuring on a regular basis.

Diet

As a general rule, diets which eliminate certain foods are not helpful, except in the very rare case where the child is known to be definitely allergic to a certain food as shown by the development of a rash or a headache. However it has been found that parents who notice a definite change in their child's behaviour in response to a certain food are often right (Taylor, 1994). Dietary treatment is still at an experimental stage, although diets seem of little value for the vast majority of hyperactive children (Taylor, 1985). Some children may show a short-lived improvement but this is often a non-specific response to the extra attention, and the improvement soon falls away.

OUTCOME

The majority of hyperactive children do show improvement over time, with the level of activity reducing as they mature. By adolescence most of the children have slowed down, although there are a few who remain very active. There is also a small group who are at risk of delinquency or developing a personality disorder in adult life. The disorder is more likely to persist where the parents have difficulty in coping and are consistently critical of the child.

Many of the current treatments are designed to reduce the added complications of the disorder such as failure at school, low self-esteem and punitive relationships with close relatives. However, even without these treatments it can be said with confidence that the majority of hyperactive children will improve and many will eventually mature into normal adults.

Dyslexia (or specific reading retardation)

Reading and writing are complex skills. The majority of children are able to read single words by the age of 6 years, and by 10–12 years will have developed sufficient reading skills to cope with ordinary life.

Some children are slow learners, which is often part of a generalized delay in learning due to a mild degree of learning disability. These children show poorer ability in all areas compared to the average for other children of the same age.

Dyslexia or specific reading retardation (SRR) are synonymous and are used to describe a marked discrepancy in actual as compared to expected reading ability based on IQ. This means that the child has specific difficulties in reading but not in other non-verbal areas.

There is evidence, however, that nearly 4% of 9- and 10-year-olds (Rutter et al., 1970) and up to 10% of the same-aged children in an inner city area (Berger et al., 1975) may be affected by this specific form of disability. These rates may seem rather high but similar rates have been found in many different countries (Stevenson et al., 1982). These children typically write letters backwards and have great difficulty in spelling, showing reading skills which are far behind their actual intelligence. There is evidence that dyslexia runs in families, and results of twin family studies have shown a substantial genetic component to the disorder (Highfield, 1994).

Severe reading difficulties cause disability in their own right and the frustration involved often gives rise to associated behavioural problems. The rate of SRR is higher in boys (3:1), whereas general reading backwardness (GRB) occurs with equal frequency in boys and girls. In addition, neurological disorders and developmental difficulties are found much more frequently in the GRB group as compared to children with SRR, whose disability is strongly linked to speech and language difficulties. The two groups also differ in that more GRB children tend to come from socially disadvantaged homes (Rutter and Yule, 1975; Silva *et al.*, 1985). SRR is associated with:

1. delay in acquiring speech;
2. a family history of reading difficulties;
3. conduct disorder;
4. brain injury;
5. a confusion between left and right and poor visuo-spatial ability;
6. episodic hearing impairment (due to recurrent ear infections) and unrecognized visual defects (Hackett, 1993).

PRESENTATION

The majority of children are picked up in school because of the difficulty in learning to read and may be referred in some cases to educational psychologists for advice. Other children with SRR are referred to child psychiatrists with behavioural problems or following attempts at self-harm such as overdoses, because their reading problems have not been properly addressed. The children become either increasingly frustrated or increasingly distressed.

THE TEACHER'S ROLE

Teachers need to be aware of this condition and take it seriously. If a child is showing specific difficulties with reading and writing despite normal intelligence, the special needs procedures need to be instituted as early as possible. If the

SRR seems relatively severe, the educational psychologist also needs to be involved.

Treatment involves appropriate remedial teaching together with explanation and support for the parents. All children with reading difficulties need an intensive daily supportive programme involving at least 30 minutes of individual tuition every day. Without such intensive intervention the children are likely to remain stuck and not show any progress.

Clearly, reading and writing are necessary for taking part in most school subjects and the child with specific reading difficulties is often severely handicapped. It is important to be aware of other areas of vulnerability, such as the effect on the child's self-esteem. Alternative sources of self-esteem need to be encouraged by finding other activities where the child can feel valued and successful. In addition, technical aids, for instance the use of word processors with spell-check, are extremely useful, particularly for examinations.

OUTCOME

Children over the age of 10 years make very slow progress in reading despite adequate remedial help and most will continue to have reading and spelling difficulties. Children with a higher intelligence level and from higher socio-economic backgrounds tend to have a better outcome. Adolescents are at risk of developing behavioural problems which may adversely affect the outcome.

Drug and solvent misuse

Drug and solvent abuse is a continuing and increasing problem as the numbers of young people affected and the number of deaths continue to rise. Between 1989 and 1993, for example, there were more than 400 deaths as a result of solvent sniffing; at least 100 deaths every year (Department of Health, 1994). In 1992 glue or solvent abuse killed 122 children, and of these one-third were sniffing for the first time. Heroin and cocaine misuse is responsible for anything between 400 and 500 deaths each year (Department of Health, 1993).

In the years 1969–1994 young people's exposure to illicit drugs increased dramatically, but, despite more education, young people's knowledge remains limited (Wright and Pearl, 1995). In their survey of 14- and 15-year-olds they found that television continued to be the main source of information.

Peer pressure is a major factor. Young people are encouraged by friends to try out various substances with little realization of the dangers involved (Wright and Pearl, 1995). Research in the USA shows that there is a close correlation between the probability of a young person smoking marijuana and use by a best friend. The most commonly used drugs by adolescents in the UK are tobacco, alcohol and cannabis (Scarth, 1993).

Overall, alcohol is the second most frequently misused drug within this country and acts as a depressant of brain function. Adolescents are most likely to experience problems from acute intoxication but not from dependence, which comes later. There is no direct relationship between adolescent drinking behaviour and a later pattern of adult drinking (Fillimore and Midanik, 1984).

Drug-taking occurs quite extensively, although it is difficult to obtain exact figures. Certainly, drugs such as cannabis, amphetamines, ecstacy and LSD are now widely available to young people and some secondary schools are known to have been infiltrated by an established drug culture where the pupils are even more at risk (Swadi, 1988; Health Education Authority, 1992). The habit typically starts at adolescence, beginning with alcohol, moving on to cannabis and eventually, in some cases, to heroin. Young people tend to use a variety of drugs rather than one only, such as cannabis and LSD; heroin is usually the end of the line and only taken after experimentation with other drugs.

CAUSES OF DRUG-TAKING

Drug-taking may start out of curiosity, but peer pressure and identification with a drug-taking subculture may lead to a regular pattern of drug misuse, although with little dependence. However, those who are unemployed, emotionally troubled or despairing are at greater risk. They may take drugs to lift themselves out of a state of depression or boredom, or a deadening routine. The hoped-for effect is to blank out the suffering and to create a sense of excitement and well-being. Young people may become addicted to drugs in order to block out past deprivations and a bleak present reality.

REASONS GIVEN FOR DRUG AND SOLVENT MISUSE

If the reasons behind the behaviour are understood, it is easier to help. Young people gave the following reasons for using drugs:

- to rebel or shock people;
- to feel part of a group of friends;
- to take risks;
- to have fun;
- to do the 'in thing';
- as part of a night out, e.g. a rave;
- to look and feel grown up;
- to escape from the pressures of life;
- to escape from boredom;
- because drugs are easy to get (Department of Health, 1993).

Fortunately, for the majority of youngsters drug-taking is a passing phase which does not end in dependence or any serious difficulty. However, even if it is only a passing phase the risks of drug-taking are considerable and always present. Excessive use can result in overdosage and the possibility of death. Drug-taking can cause other insidious but serious problems, such as a withdrawal from or deterioration in friendships, a falling off in school or work perform-ance, a lack of interest and enjoyment in life, poor physical health and an increased risk of criminal behaviour.

During adolescence drugs are used equally by girls and boys, but adult men addicted to heroin outnumber women by four to one. As expected, the prevalence of drug-taking is higher in urban areas.

DRUG-TAKING AND DELINQUENCY

There is a complex relationship between drug-taking and delinquency, with a strong association between substance misuse and conduct disorder or delinquency (Johnson *et al.*, 1991). In general, non-addictive use does not lead to criminality. However, the level of delinquency tends to be directly related to the seriousness of the drug abuse; the more delinquent the youngster, the more serious the drug abuse. This relationship is grounded in the nature of the youngster's problems and the neighbourhoods in which they live.

PERSONALITY AND FAMILY FACTORS

Other factors in drug abuse are related to personality and family situation. For instance, youngsters who do not conform easily to generally accepted rules are more at risk for experimentation with drugs. These youngsters often come from broken homes, have poor relationships with their parents and have parents who frequently use drugs.

OUTCOME

The outcome is not necessarily poor; only a very small number of young people eventually become addicted. Of those who become addicted to heroin, 2–3% will die each year. After 10 years it was found that 38% of a group of addicts had given up drugs and the majority of those on maintenance treatment managed to remain reasonably well and did not deteriorate. There is always hope and even the most addictive drug can be given up at any stage.

COMMONLY USED SUBSTANCES

Cannabis (dope, grass, blow, hash, draw, wacky backy)
The cannabis plant contains tetrahydrocannabinol (THC) as the active agent. Marijuana is made of the dried flowers and contains between 1% and 10% THC, whereas cannabis resin, known as hashish, contains 8–15%. The drug is widely used by teenagers and young adults and is usually smoked but can be eaten.

The immediate effects depend to some extent on the individual's mood and expectations but euphoria, increased sensory awareness and a sense of relaxation are common, although feelings of anxiety and hunger may follow. Short-term memory loss, nausea and a vague paranoia are frequently reported. It is important to avoid activities which require concentration, such as driving, while taking cannabis.

In higher doses perceptual distortions, confusion and paranoid ideas may occur. It is known that cannabis can cause an acute toxic psychosis with delusions and hallucinations and that the symptoms of schizophrenia can be made worse by chronic use. Clinical experience indicates that it can be a factor in the onset, the worsening or the prolongation of psychotic episodes.

LSD (lysergic acid diethylamide or acid)
This is said to be the most unpredictable of drugs, as the state of mind and setting play a very important role in the outcome. LSD is a very powerful drug and very small amounts have a marked hallucinogenic effect. It is usually sold as tablets. The main effects are to heighten perceptions, but delusions and visual hallucinations may occur as well as rapid changes in mood. The experience may feel positive

and good but it can also be terrifying. The chances of a 'bad trip' increase with the amount of anxiety beforehand. Heavy use may result in an acute psychotic illness resembling schizophrenia which may continue and become chronic.

Magic mushrooms
These mushrooms, when eaten, give rise to hallucinations and there are about twelve species of fungi with this effect. Other effects include distorted perceptions, euphoria and infectious laughter which last for a period of between four and nine hours. Very rarely, feelings of fear and anxiety may lead to a psychotic episode. It is similar to a mild LSD experience and so 'bad trips' can occur. The greatest danger is of eating a poisonous species by mistake. Some of these can be fatal even in small amounts.

Amphetamines (speed, uppers, sulphate, sulph, whizz)
Amphetamines are stimulants and have the effect of producing feelings of well-being and increased energy, often followed by depression and lethargy. Amphetamines are often mixed with a number of other substances. Apart from the dangers associated with this, amphetamines suppress the need for food and sleep, and their continuing use can lead to damaging physical and psychological effects. Long-term use may lead to a psychosis.

Ecstacy (3, 4-methylenedioxymethamphetamine, E or MDMA)
This comes in tablet form and has effects similar to those of both amphetamine and LSD. It enhances the emotions and is used by young people at raves to increase energy and produce feelings of exhilaration but it can also lead to confusion and disorientation. Sudden death has been known to occur, particularly in those who have become dehydrated and overheated through too vigorous dancing. It is strongly recommended that those using ecstacy drink a pint of water

every hour. The effects of taking a tablet start after 20 minutes and can last for several hours.

Increasingly, a mixture of drugs rather than ecstacy alone is being sold at nightclubs. This is very much more dangerous, as the constituents are unknown.

Cocaine (coke, snow)

Cocaine usually comes as a white powder which is snorted, but it can be injected. One of the major dangers of injecting is that of sharing needles, which is associated with a serious risk of contracting HIV or AIDS. The effects include a sense of euphoria and increased energy which last for about 20–30 minutes and may be followed by tiredness and depression. Because the effects of cocaine tend to wear off quickly, there is a temptation to try to hold on to the feelings of confidence and energy by taking more. Prolonged use can lead to weight loss, paranoia, nasal damage and heart trouble. Large doses are dangerous and can cause a toxic psychosis or even death from heart or respiratory failure.

Crack

Crack is cocaine converted into a form in which it can be smoked. Its name refers to the sound that the crystals make as they burn and give off fumes, turning it into one of the most addictive drugs yet known. The impact of the cocaine in this form is much greater, as it is absorbed throughout the whole surface of the lungs. As a result, here is a sudden explosion of cocaine into the bloodstream. The drug is carried forward to reach the heart and brain with a sudden force which accounts for the instant and overwhelming sense of euphoria which lasts for only a matter of 40 to 50 seconds at the most. The intensity of this euphoria is thought to be responsible for the powerful addictive quality of crack. Side-effects include insomnia, chronic paranoia and severe lung damage.

It takes five months of regular use for heroin abusers to become addicted and 18 months for those abusing cocaine. In contrast, crack users can become addicted after one puff and 75% are known to be addicted after smoking crack three times, usually over a period of two weeks.

In 1985 crack suddenly appeared on the US scene, together with an upsurge in shootings, crime and violence. Crack users often develop paranoid or violent mental states. The dealers have particularly targeted poor black inner city communities, and in this country the effects of crack are being seen in the increased violence and use of guns in London, Manchester and Birmingham.

The treatment of crack addiction is especially difficult. Dr G. Nahas believes that this is because crack stamps the brain with an ineradicable biochemical memory. As yet nothing can remove that memory, leaving the sufferer in a state of longing for another 'high'. The only sure way to cure an addiction to crack is to make certain that it is totally unavailable.

The outlook is poor unless the temptation, in the form of crack, can be removed. However, treatments offering intense support are worth trying. A combined approach with counselling and group therapy, using groups like Cocaine Anonymous in order to talk the sufferers through their problems, is generally recommended.

Heroin (smack, gear or scag)

The numbers of registered addicts increased steadily from 2657 in 1970 to 28,000 in 1993 (Wright and Pearl, 1995). The majority (90%) are addicted to heroin. At a conservative estimate this puts the total number of heroin users at about 70,000. Heroin is usually smoked or injected and costs from £60 to £80 per gram. An average daily amount is 0.25–0.75 g.

Surveys show that the use of heroin and cocaine in school-aged youngsters is low, probably less than 1% (Wright and Pearl, 1995). It is generally the older adolescents who are affected, with a recent increase in those aged 16–20 years; the majority of users are in the 20–30 age group. The death rate is raised where there is intravenous use to 28 times the normal rate. While many users manage to inject themselves without incurring life-threatening damage, the risks of overdosing and, if needles are shared, of HIV and AIDS are very real.

The immediate effect is one of euphoria but this is followed by withdrawal symptoms after anything from 4 to 12 hours. These include dilated pupils, aching limbs, goose-fleshing of the skin, shivering, yawning and tiredness. Heroin (like all drugs) should be avoided during pregnancy because of the harmful effects on the baby.

Many heroin misusers also have a psychiatric disorder such as depression, personality disorder or alcoholism. They tend to be isolated from family and friends, and unemployed, and often have a criminal record.

Treatment is usually offered through specialist clinics or services which focus on drug abuse. Social and psychological support is necessary to help the young person to stay off drugs. Some young people who have become dependent may need a gradual withdrawal programme using methadone as a substitute for heroin.

ROLE OF TEACHERS

It is important for teachers to keep in mind the possibility of drug or solvent abuse when thinking about a young person in trouble or difficulty. If teachers become aware that there may be a problem with drugs it is important to go through the usual school procedures as well as letting the parents know. Teachers need to be aware that the effects of drug misuse are very similar to the normal processes of adolescence. The teacher may notice sudden changes in mood from alert and cheerful to sullen and moody, unusual episodes of drowsiness, loss of interest in school work or in friends and irritability or aggression. If the young person is taking drugs he or she may be able to stop once the underlying causes have been addressed, but for more entrenched problems support from a specialist centre may well be needed.

In some areas headteachers are asking for drug education to tell children from the age of 5 years about the dangers of drugs. They are concerned that some young children have brothers, sisters or parents involved with drugs. There is also evidence that young children in some areas such as South Yorkshire are being introduced to solvent abuse at the age of 4–5 years (Brown and Abrams, 1994).

PREVENTION

Until recently the main approach has been through relatively straightforward educational programmes (Schinke *et al.*, 1991). However, as the use of drugs is still increasing among young people, the need for effective and pragmatic preventative strategies is becoming more urgent. In Lothian, as part of a new preventative initiative, younger children are receiving education in life skills and healthy choices while the older children are offered drug education by their peers and information on how to reduce the harmful effects (Tissier, 1994).

In Westminster the Drug Education Forum, responding to the numbers of 16–18-year-olds taking large amounts of designer drugs and crack, has decided that the emphasis needs to be on the minimization of harm, controlled drug use and integration back into society rather than on abstinence. Workshops have been held for parents, teachers and secondary age children to look at the problems associated with drugs. Recent research in Lothian shows that young people do not want horror stories but factual, unbiased information, preferably from people of their own age group (Tissier, 1994).

SOLVENT ABUSE

This term includes glue-sniffing and refers to the inhalation of fumes from any one of the 30 common household substances which can be abused in this way. Figures released in 1993 show that three young solvent abusers die each week and of these, as already emphasized, one in three is sniffing for the first time. It is a tragic waste of life and young people are not sufficiently aware of the dangers involved. As one bereaved mother said, 'The youngsters need to learn how to resist pressure from their peers. They must learn that they are not cowards if they say "no" and walk away.'

The West Midlands has one of the largest solvent abuse problems in the country. Children as young as 9 have been found sniffing gas, and solvent abuse killed 149 people in 1990 (Department of Health, 1994).

The concept of glue-sniffing is out of date, as butane gas is now causing more deaths than any other substance. It is inhaled directly into the mouth from refill canisters, causing death from an acute heart attack. If this one practice could be stopped, there would be far fewer deaths. Of the other 30 sniffable substances, aerosols and solvent-based glues are also popular. A further danger is of freezing the air passages by squirting the aerosol directly into the mouth, and a number of people have died in this way during their first attempt (Department of Health, 1994).

There are no accurate figures as to prevalence. An estimate is that between 7% and 10% of secondary schoolchildren are thought to have tried solvents, and 2% sniff for a matter of weeks or months and then stop, leaving a minority of 1% who will continue and become long-term users (Department of Health, 1994). The peak age seems to be between 13 to 14 years and it usually starts as a group activity. Children from any social background may be involved, although more children in inner city areas try solvents.

Solvents kill by causing a non-rhythmic beating of the heart. Large amounts of solvent (particularly aerosol gases and cleaning fluids) leave the child's heart sensitized to adrenaline, and if something then happens to release adrenaline, such as a fright or exertion, the child's heart suddenly stops. Instances such as being shouted at, chased or surprised in some way all cause the release of adrenaline ready for the flight or fight response.

The effects of sniffing are similar to being drunk but come on more quickly and disappear equally rapidly. The fumes from glue are mostly formed from toluene, which produces a state of rapid euphoria, of disinhibition and dizziness. This may be followed by hallucinations, fits, coma or unsteadiness. Children often steal to find the money to buy the solvent once they have become chronic users.

Long-term effects
There is no withdrawal syndrome but long-term abusers find it very difficult to stop and can experience tiredness, pallor, forgetfulness and lack of concentration. There may also be weight loss, depression and trembling but these disappear when the sniffing stops. It is possible that heavy solvent abuse over several years may cause moderate, lasting damage to the brain.

Causes
There are many reasons why young people misuse glue and solvents. Some of these are:

- as an alternative to alcohol;
- for the excitement and danger;
- to shock adults;
- as a source of pleasure or a new sensation;
- the substances are not expensive and easily available;
- for the hallucinations;
- to blank out problems, especially for those who carry on and become chronic solvent misusers (Department of Health, 1994).

Treatment
The source of supply needs to be cut off at the same time as the child is given intensive psychological support from professional workers and the family. The underlying reasons for the abuse need to be investigated, understood and remedied as far as possible. Alternative activities may be helpful. It is particularly important to listen to the child.

It can be very difficult to treat solvent abusers who have disturbed early backgrounds, serious behavioural problems and no wish to change. However, many of these sniff as part of a group subculture and can stop if they wish, as they are not dependent on solvents. Psychological dependence can occur, usually when there are family or personality problems, and these youngsters are in danger of becoming solitary sniffers. Tom's story shows how things can go badly wrong once psychological dependence occurs (Hobbs, 1993).

> Tom tried glue-sniffing at the age of 11 after watching a television programme on this subject in 1979. All the children were talking about it and he started sniffing as part of a group. However, Tom was the one who continued, becoming involved in petty crime such as robbing the gas meter.
>
> Two years later Tom had become a lonely, dependent sniffer, often being found intoxicated on wasteland. He had been taken over by the addiction, and as his life deteriorated he found himself spending more and more time in solitary glue-sniffing. He said that he now needed glue in order to feel normal.
>
> After going through two children's homes and an assessment centre Tom found life harder than ever to bear and described how he used more and more glue to blank everything and everybody out. Although he tried to stop several times, Tom was unsuccessful and eventually killed himself at the age of 23 years. The family reported that they found it extremely difficult to obtain specialist help from someone trained in working with solvent abusers.

Role of teachers
It is important for teachers to be alert to the signs of solvent abuse. There are no clear-cut signs but teachers or parents may notice:

- a sudden change in behaviour or a change in friends;
- a chemical smell on clothes or breath;

- sudden changes in mood or behavioural swings;
- redness or spots around the nose and mouth;
- persistent headaches, sore throat or runny nose;
- empty solvent cans;
- secretive behaviour (Department of Health, 1994).

If solvent abuse is occurring, the teacher will need to go through the standard school procedures as well as notifying and counselling the parents as to how to find help. If the child cannot stop easily, referral to a specialist agency or to the local child psychiatrist may be necessary.

Helping children cope with loss, death and bereavement

It is important to recognize that children, like adults, respond to loss and bereavement in their own individual way and that there are no right or wrong responses. Much depends on the age and understanding of the children as to when and how they face the loss. Children as young as 3 years in certain circumstances, such as losing a parent, do have some concept of death. This awareness continues to develop with increasing age (Lansdown and Benjamin, 1985).

On average, about 50 children each day in the UK will lose a parent through bereavement and even more will lose other relatives and pets. As the rates of separation and divorce increase, as many as one in five children may have to cope with feelings of loss very similar to those of a bereavement reaction.

The majority of these children will not receive any outside help, and teachers may find themselves alone and without guidance in trying to support the child.

Different stages following bereavement in adults have been described (Kubler-Ross, 1970; Bowlby, 1980). However, it is unusual for children, as well as adults, to go through these in as clearly defined a manner as described here. Parents and teachers might find it helpful to keep the stages in mind but do not need to worry if the child does not seem to follow them. Children need support in order to allow them to experience whatever their feelings are, which may initially be a mixture of confusion, grief, anger and depression.

FOUR MAIN STAGES OF BEREAVEMENT

1. Shock. There is often an initial stage of shock when it is impossible to fully take in the impact of the death. The bereaved person may carry on with normal tasks but in a rather trance-like state which may last for several hours or even days. It continues until the person is more ready to face the loss.
2. Feelings of anger and unfairness. The bereaved person commonly feels angry with the one who has died; there is anger at being left and at the unfairness of the situation. There may be a wish to blame someone. In school the bereaved child may initially start to have temper outbursts or be unusually irritable. The child may have difficulty in concentrating and sleeping.

    In the early days adults often describe feelings that the lost person is still with them and may have a sense of their presence.

    The opposite of the wish to blame are feelings of guilt. Bereaved people may go over and over the events leading up to the death and recurrent doubts and questions may arise as to whether they could have done something more or even saved their loved ones.
3. Feelings of terrible sadness, sorrow and longing. This is the most painful and long-lasting stage and forms the centre of the grieving process. There is frequently a recurrent need to go through the events leading up to the death in order to digest and slowly come to terms with the loss. The person may wish to be alone to cry, to look at photographs, to go over letters and to remember. This is a very important and often private part of

grieving. Some grief can be shared and some is inevitably private.
4. Rebuilding. This will never be complete as the loss will always be there. However, hopefully the feelings of loss and grief can be worked through and the lost person can be gradually internalized to form a helpful and loved internal presence.

Anniversaries, times of stress and any future losses are very likely to stir up again the strong feelings associated with the original bereavement.

The loss of a mother during childhood may have long-term consequences and has been associated with depressive disorders in adult life (Brown *et al.*, 1986).

THE ROLE OF THE TEACHER

It is important for the teacher to follow the child by acknowledging the loss briefly with a few sympathetic words and then waiting for the child's reactions over the following days and weeks and responding to these. The teacher needs to be realistic about how to help and to recognize that seemingly small things can be very helpful, such as thinking about the child and tolerating the feelings of helplessness without rushing into action. It helps to realize that these feelings are normal and tend to be experienced by everyone.

In addition it is important for the teacher to be aware that the pain and distress are part of the normal process of grieving and that the child needs to be supported to experience these. This means that if the child starts to cry or become upset it is important for the teacher not to say, 'don't cry' or 'cheer up' but to find somewhere where the child can cry. The teacher may well wish to take away the pain and make the situation better, but the key role for anyone at this time is to help the bereaved child to work through the grief and try to bear it rather than attempting to remove or avoid the pain.

If the child comes to talk later on the most important response is to be there and to listen to what the child is saying. It is best not to be worrying about what to say in response, as then the teacher's attention will not be fully on the child. A few supportive words are enough to let the child know that the teacher has taken in what the child has said: something like, 'Yes it is difficult' or, 'I'm glad you came to talk to me'. In short, the teacher's role is to try to be there for the child as a support, a listener and a source of caring, strength and stability.

THE ROLE OF THE SCHOOL

The need for stability leads us on to understanding the importance of the school in the bereaved child's life. At this time when the child may feel that his or her whole world has fallen apart, the security and regularity of the school can be extremely supportive. The predictable routine of school and the familiar, friendly faces help to provide a stable, holding environment as well as engendering a sense of life continuing.

The same factors are important in the child suffering from the separation of the parents. School can be a source of comfort and constancy in contrast to the frequently experienced upset and turbulence at home.

It is helpful if the teacher can talk to a parent or close relative about the effects of the bereavement on the child so that there is a feeling of the school and home working together in understanding what is happening and the plans for the future. The head teacher and class teacher need to work closely together in their efforts to support the child. Dyregrov (1991) has written an excellent book on how to help bereaved children.

PREPARING AND SUPPORTING THE CLASS

It is helpful if the teacher takes the opportunity while the bereaved child is away from school to talk to the class about what has happened and how they can help. This may stir up feelings associated with bereavement and loss in other children and the teacher needs to be sensitive to this.

One simple yet important way of involving everyone and keeping the bereaved child in mind is to send a class card which all the children have signed (Knapman, 1993).

The teacher can take a lead in other ways by explaining the bereaved child's need for normality and suggesting that the children offer only a few words of sympathy. It is important for the children to say that they are very sorry about what has happened but then to allow the bereaved child to get on with the normal routines of school. It is worth letting the class know that some children want to talk about their experiences related to the bereavement and others do not, and both responses need to be respected.

The bereaved child needs to be included and to feel part of the class again as soon as possible. It may be necessary to mention how hurtful it is to be avoided because people don't know what to say.

Lastly, the teacher needs to watch out for the very occasional child who may take the opportunity to make unkind and hurtful comments.

HOW TO TALK TO THE BEREAVED CHILD

There are a few common pitfalls. As already mentioned, it is unhelpful to say, 'Don't cry' or to discourage grieving in any way. Also, it can upset children if adults say, 'You'll soon get over it,' or, 'I know how you feel'. Both children and adults can feel upset and offended by the idea that they will ever get over the bereavement, as in one sense they never will entirely. Remarks like this can put up a barrier and make the bereaved person feel more isolated and not understood. In the same way, the person doesn't really believe that you do know how he or she feels and your words serve to show a lack of understanding (Knapman, 1993). It may be that it is so painful to be in touch with the child's or the adult's pain that we unconsciously try to deny it.

EXPRESSING FEELINGS

After a major bereavement children and adults often experience a confusing range of feelings, including numbness, disorientation, sadness, depression, anger and guilt. Very young children may need a parent or close relative to give a simple explanation of what has happened and to help by trying to put the children's feelings into words. Enabling children to name and identify feelings can help them to feel more in control.

Many children find it easier to express their feelings through play and drawing. Stories can help children to come to terms with painful events and suggest new ways of coping (Gardner, 1993). Other children may express feelings through dreams or through changes in their behaviour. Young children who lose a mother frequently regress, feeling very insecure, and as a result become clinging and may start to wet or soil again. Children of all ages may become very demanding, become easily upset and develop temper outbursts because of the insecurity and loss.

ATTITUDES TOWARDS DEATH AND LOSS

Teachers may be able to help the children develop a more open and healthy attitude towards death (Gisborne, 1995). This can be initiated by any intervention which gives a message that, however difficult, death can be thought about and talked about.

The subject may come up in the normal course of events when a child's pet dies. It is helpful to show that it is acceptable to care for and touch the dead animal. In the same way, children are helped by families who arrange a simple burial for their pet and who are able to express feelings of loss together and help and support each other (Knapman, 1993).

Billings (1992) describes how there is a tendency to overprotect children when a relative is seriously ill and to offer reassurance at times when it would be more helpful to prepare the child for the possibility of death. It is important to provide explanations at the child's level of understanding, but children are less frightened by the truth than by being left alone with an awareness of something happening and not knowing what.

Similarly, it is helpful for the child to attend the funeral, to share in the ceremony and celebration of that person's life as well as the grief. Children generally wish to be included but need to be prepared for what will happen and for the sadness. The presence of children can also be very helpful to others, as it emphasizes the continuity of life (Billings, 1992).

Within the school, opportunities may arise for teachers to talk about death as being part of life and as a normal, natural event. If children can be given the message that death can be discussed and the sadness shared, it may help them to develop a more open attitude and may enable them to cope better when they have to face a death at a later stage.

CHILDREN BEREAVED IN A TRAUMATIC OR VIOLENT MANNER

Children bereaved by the violent death of one or both parents are always traumatized by the event. These children will need expert counselling from the child psychiatric team. A team in London has developed special expertise in this area (Black and Kaplan, 1988). The children need urgent referral for debriefing if this is at all possible, and to be effective it needs to take place within the first few days.

References

Barkley, R.A., McMurray, M.B., Edelbrook, C.S. and Robbins, K. (1989). The response of aggressive and non-aggressive ADHD children to two doses of methylphenidate. *Journal of the American*

Academy of Child and Adolescent Psychiatry, **28**, 873–81.

Berger, M., Yule, W. and Rutter, M. (1975) Attainment and adjustment in two geographical areas II: the prevalence of specific reading retardation. *British Journal of Psychiatry*, **126**, 510–19.

Billings, A. (1992) Helping children to confront death. *British Medical Journal*, **304**, 261.

Black, D. and Kaplan, T. (1988) Father kills mother. *British Journal of Psychiatry*, **153**, 624–30.

Bowlby, J. (1980) *Attainment and Loss: Loss, Sadness and Depression*, Vol. 3. New York: Basic Books.

Brown, C. and Abrams, F. (1994) Anti-drugs drive to aim at children. *The Independent*, 1 June.

Brown, G.W., Harris, T.O. and Bifulco, A. (1986) Long term effects of early loss of a parent. In M. Rutter, C.E. Izard and P.B. Read (eds) *Depression in Young People: Developmental and Clinical Perspectives*. New York: Guilford Press, pp. 251–96.

Department of Health (1993) *Drug and Solvent Misuse: A Basic Briefing*. London: HMSO.

Department of Health (1994) *Solvents: A Parent's Guide*. London: HMSO.

Dyregrov, A. (1991) *Grief in Children: A Handbook for Adults*. London: J. Kingsley.

Fillimore, K. and Midanik, L. (1984) Chronicity of drinking problems among men: a longitudinal study. *Journal of Studies on Alcohol*, **45**, 228–36.

Gardner, R. (1993) *Story-Telling in Psychotherapy with Children*. Northvale, NJ: Aronson.

Gisborne, T. (1995) Death and bereavement in school: Are you prepared? *Education 3–13*, **23** (2), 39–44.

Hackett, L. (1993) Normal development and developmental delays. In D. Black and D. Cottrell (eds) *Child and Adolescent Psychiatry*. London: Gaskell, pp. 6–27.

Health Education Authority (1992) *Tomorrow's Young Adults. 9–15 Year Olds Look at Alcohol, Drugs, Exercise and Smoking*. London: Health Education Authority.

Highfield, R. (1994) Genes traced as a cause of dyslexia. *The Daily Telegraph*, 14 October.

Hobbs, A. (1993) Lingering death of glue sniffer. *The Observer*, 7 February.

Johnson, B.D., Wish, E.D., Schmeidler, J. and Huizinger, D. (1991) The concentration of delinquent offending: serious drug involvement and high delinquency rates. *Journal of Drug Issues*, **21**, 205–29.

Knapman, D. (1993) Supporting the bereaved child in school: feeling at a loss? In P. Alsop and T. McCaffrey (eds) *How To Cope With Childhood Stress: A Practical Guide For Teachers*. London: Longman, pp. 84–92.

Kubler-Ross, E. (1970) *On Death and Dying*. New York: Macmillan.

Lansdown, R. and Benjamin, G. (1985). The development of the concept of death in children aged 5–9. *Child Care Health Development*, **11**, 13–20.

Prendergast, M. (1993) Drug treatment. In M.E. Garralda (ed.) *Managing Children with Psychiatric Problems*. London: BMJ Publishing Group, pp. 85–101.

Rutter, M. and Yule, W. (1975) The concept of specific reading retardation. *Journal of Child Psychology and Psychiatry*, **125**, 181–97.

Rutter, M., Tizard, J. and Whitmore, K. (1970) *Education, Health and Behaviour*. London: Longman.

Scarth, L. (1993) Clinical syndromes in adolescence. In D. Black and D. Cottrell (eds) *Child and Adolescent Psychiatry*. London: Gaskell, pp. 154–82.

Schinke, S.P., Botvin, G.J. and Orlandi, M.A. (1991) *Substance Abuse in Children and Adolescents. Evaluation and Intervention*. Developmental Clinical Psychology: 22. Beverly Hills, CA: Sage.

Silva, P.A., McGee, R. and Williams, S. (1985) Some characteristics of 9-year-old boys with general reading backwardness or specific reading retardation. *Journal of Child Psychology and Psychiatry*, **26**, 407–21.

Stevenson, H.W., Stigler, J.W., Lucker, G.W. *et al.* (1982) Reading disabilities: the case of Chinese, Japanese and English. *Child Development*, **33**, 1164–81.

Swadi, H. (1988) Drug and substance use among 3333 London adolescents. *British Journal of Addiction*, **83**, 935–42.

Taylor, E. (1985) *The Hyperactive Child*. London: Dunitz.

Taylor, E. (1994) Syndromes of attention deficit and overactivity. In M. Rutter, E. Taylor and L. Hersov (eds) *Child and Adolescent Psychiatry: Modern Approaches*. Oxford: Blackwell Scientific Publications, pp. 285–307.

Taylor, E., Schachar, R., Thorley, G. *et al.* (1987) Which boys respond to stimulant medication? A controlled trial of methylphenidate in boys with disruptive behaviour. *Psychological Medicine*, **17**, 121–43.

Taylor, E., Sandberg, S., Thorley, G. *et al.* (1991) *The Epidemiology of Childhood Hyperactivity*. Maudsley Monograph No. 33. Oxford: Oxford University Press.

Tissier, G. (1994) Practice focus: drug services. *Community Care*, 3–9 November, 10–11.

Weiss, G. and Hechtman, L.T. (1986) *Hyperactive Children Grown Up*. New York: Guilford Press.

Whalen, C.K., Henker, B., Buhmester, D. *et al.* (1989) Does stimulant medication improve the peer status of hyperactive children? *Journal of Consulting and Clinical Psychology*, **57**, 545–9.

Wright, J.D. and Pearl, L. (1995) Knowledge and experience of young people regarding drug misuse, 1969–1994. *British Medical Journal*, **309**, 20–4.

Useful addresses

Cruse
Cruse House
126, Sheen Road
Richmond, Surrey
TW9 1UR
Tel: 0181 940 4818

Cruse-Bereavement Care provides counselling, advice and opportunities for social contact for all those who are bereaved. There are many local branches: phone main number for information.

Hyperactive Children's Support Group
71, Whyke Lane
Chichester
Sussex
PO19 2LD

Drug Alert – How To Get Help
PO Box 7
London W3 6XJ

The Institute for the Study of Drug Dependence
1 Hatton Place
London EC1N 8ND
Tel: 0171 430 1991
(A library and information service, producing a list of publications
   and prices.)

The Standing Conference on Drug Abuse
1–4 Hatton Place
London EC1N 8ND
Tel: 0171 430 2341
(The national reference point for services for people with drug
   problems: it produces a booklet, 'Drug Problems: Where to Get
   Help'. There is also a Freefone line; dial 100 for the operator
   and ask for Freefone Drug Problems. This is a recorded message
   with telephone contact numbers throughout England.)

For Scotland phone 0141 221 1175 (Scottish Drugs Forum, 5,
   Oswald Street, Glasgow, G1 5QR.) For Wales phone 0220
   825111 (Welsh Office Drugs Unit, Welsh Office, Cathays Park,
   Cardiff, CF1 3NQ). For Northern Ireland phone 0232 321224
   (Northern Ireland Council for Voluntary Action, 127, Ormeau
   Road, Belfast, BT7 1SH).

Re-Solv (The Society for the Prevention of Solvent and Volatile
   Substance Abuse)
30A, High Street
Stone
Staffs. ST15 8AW
Tel: 01785 817885

CHAPTER 11
Wetting and Soiling

Enuresis or wetting

Nocturnal enuresis or bedwetting occurs in normal children without any psychiatric disorder as well as being associated with emotional deprivation and insecurity or with regressive behaviour at times of particular stress. Daytime wetting is much less common and therefore more worrying in terms of indicating some underlying problem. Rutter *et al.* (1973) demonstrated an association between bedwetting and psychiatric disorder but this does not mean that nocturnal enuresis in itself is indicative of any disorder. Most children are dry by day and night by 4 years of age. Approximate figures are that 10% of 5-year-olds and 5% of 10-year-olds are still wetting the bed.

Children who have never developed bladder control are described as having primary enuresis, whereas those who have and then lose it are described as showing secondary enuresis. Secondary enuresis most commonly starts between the ages of 5 and 7 years, becoming rare after the age of 11. Children who develop secondary enuresis tend to have more pre-existing psychiatric symptoms than children who have never become wet (McGee *et al.*, 1984).

CAUSES

The main causes can be summarized under the headings of physical, genetic and psychological.

Physical
Urinary tract infections are quite commonly found in girls with day and night wetting. Abnormalities of the renal tract or epileptic fits occurring during the night are much rarer causes.

One cause of daytime wetting which always has to be considered is sexual abuse, particularly in girls. This also needs to be kept in mind if a child suddenly starts to wet at night. It is likely that there will be other symptoms or indications if sexual abuse is taking place. The wetting may occur on the basis of anxiety due to the trauma and stress or may be due to a urinary tract infection caused by the abuse.

Several studies have commented on a relationship between enuresis and a delay in speech, motor and social development (Essen and Peckham, 1976; Fergusson *et al.*, 1986). In these cases the enuresis is likely to be part of a general developmental delay and this has also been associated with an increase in psychiatric symptoms (Schaffer *et al.*, 1984).

Genetic
Approximately 70% of enuretic children have a first-degree relative with the condition. It clearly does run in families and delayed neurological maturation is the most likely cause.

Psychological
Many enuretic children come from impoverished, disadvantaged and unhappy homes. The causes here relate to social and emotional deprivation.

> Gary, a 6-year-old, lived with his emotionally immature mother and, because of mother's own childhood experiences, she was unable to provide the emotional care that he needed. As a result a negative cycle built up where Gary showed his insecurity through bedwetting and difficult behaviour,

often when he could not have his own way; he had never been helped to deal with frustration. Gary's behaviour had gradually deteriorated until his mother could no longer cope with the violent tempers.

At mother's request he was moved in to live with an experienced foster mother who had no difficulty in providing genuine emotional care and attention combined with consistent control. Gary soon felt more secure and both his bedwetting and his uncontrolled behaviour gradually improved as he came to feel safe within an emotionally settled home. Very sadly, because of her earlier experiences, Gary's mother was not able to mobilize the inner resources necessary to meet his emotional needs.

A more minor stress may be experienced as temporarily overwhelming in anxious children. However, major causes of stress in children often involve loss or separation from their parents. In these circumstances the children may also regress to more babyish behaviour, such as using baby talk, clinging and needing a lot of holding and cuddling. This behaviour needs to be understood and tolerated, as does the bedwetting.

In the Robertson's film 'A Two Year Old Goes to Hospital' (1952) the little girl is seen trying to hold herself together during her mother's long absences. She becomes sad and withdrawn and, to add to her distress, she starts to wet the bed. The emotional stress of being without her mother has become too much for her.

The experience of wetting is usually distressing for children and for some it may be a cause of great unhappiness. In order to cope with the upset and lack of control, some children turn to denial as a protection for themselves and behave as if they don't care. The family's attitude is crucial and understanding parents help the child to cope. Blame or punishment increases the suffering and makes denial more likely as well as decreasing the chances of successful treatment. The denial is easily misinterpreted as the child being naughty or defiant.

TREATMENT

Treatment is based on the underlying cause. In the majority of cases, examination of a mid-stream urine sample, a good history and physical examination will be sufficient to make a diagnosis.

Once physical causes have been ruled out and a baseline established, the first approach is to use a star chart with praise or a small reward for dry nights. The aim is to obtain some improvement and build on that. Some parents have found that lifting the child before they go to bed also helps towards increasing the number of dry nights, particularly with younger children.

If these approaches are not successful, the next stage is the use of an enuresis alarm. It is usually effective in children over the age of 7 from stable families (Dische *et al.*, 1983). In general, night alarms are the most effective treatment available, and the mini body alarm with a small sensor which attaches to the child's pyjama pants represents an important improvement (Schmitt, 1986). Interestingly, children with primary and secondary enuresis do equally well. Those who do less well are children with family stress, psychiatric disorders, associated daytime wetting and a marked lack of concern about the symptom.

Finally, medication such as tricyclic anti-depressants or desmopressin can be tried but their effectiveness often ceases when the medication is stopped. As there have been occasional reports of sudden death in children on tricyclics, it is essential to take an ECG, asking for a check on whether there is any evidence of a conduction defect, before starting these drugs. Desmopressin is commonly prescribed as a nasal spray at night (and more recently as tablets) and in 80% of cases there was a satisfactory response while the child was on the medication (Aladjem *et al.*, 1982).

Therapeutic optimism is essential in working with children who bedwet. It is important to try each approach for a time and then have a break before trying again. Eventually, the vast majority of these children will become dry at night. Moffat *et al.* (1987) report that successful treatment resulted in the children becoming more assertive, independent, self-confident and happier in themselves. Although successful treatment brings important social and emotional benefits, it generally has no effect on any associated behavioural problems (Schaffer *et al.*, 1984).

Soiling

Faecal soiling is not a frequent symptom but when it occurs it is a sign that something is wrong. It is also a symptom which cannot be ignored. The majority of children are toilet trained and clean by the age of 3 years. Soiling is sometimes also referred to as encopresis and means the passing of faeces into the underwear or an inappropriate place in the absence of any physical disease. It is a particularly distressing symptom for the child, the parents and teachers and can lead to the child being excluded from school. Fortunately the majority of schools are very understanding and make contingency arrangements with the parents in order to keep the child in school and avoid teasing.

Many parents feel angry that their child appears totally unconcerned about the soiling, but in fact the denial of concern develops as a protective shield. These children are extremely distressed by the symptom but as they have no control they often try to cope using the defence mechanism of denial. Children who soil are not able to process these feelings on their own and are therefore unable to be in touch and admit to their distress.

Soiling occurs three times more frequently in boys than in girls. Davie *et al.* (1972) found daytime soiling in slightly over 1% of children over the age of 5 years, and figures of about 1% for boys and 0.3% for girls are generally agreed. By the age of

16 years the majority of young people have overcome the problem and the condition does not persist into adult life. However, this does not mean that the underlying relationship problems have been resolved, and these children may well have continuing personality problems in adult life.

CONTINUOUS SOILING

Soiling is described as continuous if the child has never been properly toilet trained and clean. This is rarely the case, and the majority of children with soiling come into one of the discontinuous categories.

Children with continuous soiling tend to come from families who live in a socially deprived area with inadequate finances and continuing unemployment. The families often show numerous signs of difficulty in coping and the children are often dirty, smell of urine, look uncared for and under-achieve at school. These children have never been adequately toilet trained and the soiling is just one facet of the pervading lack of care and organization in a socially disadvantaged family.

DISCONTINUOUS SOILING

Within the discontinuous group, where normal bowel control has been achieved and then lost, there are two broad categories: those associated with chronic constipation and those without constipation. In general terms, children with constipation tend to come from depriving chaotic homes with inadequate parenting or from overcontrolling homes.

Retentive soiling with constipation
The soiling in this condition occurs on the basis of the retention of large amounts of faeces in the colon and rectum. These children may then become severely constipated, with the result that there is an eventual leakage of liquid faeces

around the hard faecal mass. It is this which produces the soiling and the situation is clearly out of the child's control. Retentive soiling may be due to physical or emotional causes.

Physical causes include conditions which give rise to severe pain on defaecation, such as a tear in the skin of the anus (known as an anal fissure). There is also a rare congenital condition, Hirschsprung's disease, in which the nerve ganglia are absent from a segment of the colon. As a result, this part does not contract properly and the faeces become delayed. The history is of constipation from birth, failure to thrive and the rare passage of large stools.

Emotional causes used to be divided into two main groups depending on the relationship between the parents and child. More recently, a third category, child sexual abuse, has had to be added.

1. Chronic deprivation. The first group comprises children from chaotic, emotionally depriving homes. The soiling is often combined with bedwetting and seems to occur as a result of the deprivation. Levine (1975) describes a significant association between wetting and soiling.

> Gary came from a depriving chaotic home and as a result he was immature, aggressive and soiled. The soiling was secondary to chronic constipation and was successfully treated with laxatives and a carefully monitored behavioural programme set up in two stages. The first stage consisted of rewards for sitting on the toilet. When this routine had been successfuly established it was followed by the next stage of rewards for actually using the toilet.

2. Overcontrolling attitudes. The second group show a large amount of unexpressed anger, built up as a reaction to inappropriate parental control. This has been described as occurring in young children with rather

obsessional parents who use coercive methods of toilet training. However, attitudes have changed, making this situation rare.

Overcontrolling attitudes are associated with soiling in older children who are often rather quiet and inhibited. It seems that the active retention of faeces, leading to chronic constipation, is one way of expressing repressed anger and aggression towards the controlling parent. In these cases individual therapy often has an important part to play in the treatment.

3. Child sexual abuse. Sexual abuse can give rise to soiling, on the basis of either anxiety or chronic constipation in both girls and boys, and needs to be kept in mind (Boon, 1991). It is a reasonably frequent symptom in younger sexually abused children and can be very intractable even when the sexual abuse has been recognized and dealt with.

Stress soiling without chronic constipation (anxiety)
Children without constipation tend to soil because of continuing levels of anxiety. This is a particular reaction to anxiety which is similar to the frequent passage of stools experienced by some people just before examinations and interviews.

This type of stress soiling, where normal bowel control breaks down, occurs in anxious children at times of psychological stress such as hospital admission, additional family tension or examinations at school. In my experience traumatic events such as parental separation or death of one of the parents can lead to the onset of soiling in some children. Causes of anxiety involve rejection, loss and other instances of stress, including the trauma of sexual abuse (Boon, 1991).

Bowel control is usually regained once the stress is relieved, provided the situation has been carefully handled and there is a stable home.

School can be a cause and one unusual example

involved Brian, an emotionally vulnerable boy who had specific learning problems which had not been recognized. Unfortunately, the teacher thought he was lazy and not trying hard enough, as he was a bright child. The pressure from school led to the onset of stress soiling. Once Brian's learning problem was recognized and treated, the soiling stopped.

It occasionally happens that children whose parents separate start soiling. Two examples are Michael, aged 4, and Tony, aged 6, who both started to soil after their parents separated, which was clearly due to the anxiety aroused. Michael experienced hostility and rejection from the remaining parent and was trapped in a state of continuing anxiety and insecurity. Consequently, his stress-related soiling continued until he was eventually removed from the situation and reunited with his other parent.

After his parents' separation Tony very soon developed severe constipation. He had a very controlling mother and it seems that following his initial episodes of soiling due to anxiety, his mother became very hostile and punitive. She was under a lot of pressure herself and could not empathize with her son. Tony, who was a fairly inhibited child, reacted by holding on to his faeces and becoming constipated as a way of expressing his unconscious aggression.

In individual therapy sessions he showed a great deal of anger, blowing up and exploding people and buildings in his play. At the same time he was given laxatives combined with a behavioural programme and work was undertaken with his mother to try to modify her controlling and punitive attitude. This combined approach was successful. Tony demonstrates how two quite different emotional factors can interact and result in continuing aggressive soiling.

FEAR OF THE TOILET

A small number of children develop a fear of sitting on the toilet or even being near it (Ashkenazi, 1975; Doleys and Arnold, 1975). In some cases the children are frightened of monsters attacking them from below and in other cases the children have been sexually abused.

TREATMENT

Treatment is directed towards the underlying cause and involves a combination of approaches, including support and work with the family, laxatives, a behavioural programme and individual psychotherapy. Most children will eventually respond to this combined approach but for very difficult and resistant problems the resources of a day hospital or inpatient unit may be needed.

If the child's soiling occurs in school, teachers will need to be fully involved and in agreement with the treatment plan. Children from more chaotic homes would benefit from additional educational and emotional support within the school, if this is at all possible.

THE TEACHER'S ROLE

Soiling is a particularly embarrassing problem for both parents and children and as such needs sympathetic handling. In mild cases the school may be able to manage while children receive treatment. The best arangement, if possible is for an agreement with children and parents that children will clean themselves and have spare clothes in school.

Some teachers have an arrangement that the parent will come in and change the child when necessary, but this has proved quite disruptive and demoralizing for the parent involved. In severe cases it may not be possible for children to attend their usual school and special educational provi-

276

sion may be needed. Bullying in the form of verbal or physical abuse may become an additional problem.

OUTCOME

Many children respond quite rapidly to appropriate treatment but the risk of relapse remains high and regular follow-up is needed, often for at least two years (Levine, 1983). Children who soil may sometimes need years of treatment.

Older children are more difficult to treat. Bemporad (1978) describes an entrenched problem in 10–14-year-olds who show severe personal pathology in the form of a personality disorder together with disturbed family relationships.

Other children who do badly show symptoms such as soiling accidents during the night, hyperactivity and lack of concentration together with a feeling that they are in the hands of fate, rather than being able to influence the soiling themselves (Landman *et al.*, 1983).

References and further reading

Aladjem, M., Wohl, R., Boichis, H. *et al.* (1982) Desmopressin in nocturnal enuresis. *Archives of Disease in Childhood*, **57**, 137–40.

Ashkenazi, Z. (1975) The treatment of enuresis using a discriminatory stimulus and positive reinforcement. *Journal of Behaviour Therapy and Experimental Psychiatry*, 6, 155–7.

Bemporad, J.R. (1978) Encopresis. In B. Wolman, J. Egon and A. Ross (eds) *Handbook of Treatment of Mental Disorders in Childhood and Adolescence*. New Jersey: Prentice Hall.

Boon, F. (1991) Encopresis and sexual assault. *Journal of the American Academy of Child and Adolescent Psychiatry*, **30**, 479–82.

Davie, R., Butler, N. and Goldstein, H. (1972) *From Birth to Seven*. London: Longman.

Dische, S., Yule, W., Corbett, J. *et al.* (1983) Childhood nocturnal enuresis: factors associated with outcome of treatment with an enuresis alarm. *Developmental Medicine and Child Neurology*, **25**, 67–80.

Doleys, D.M. and Arnold, S. (1975) Treatment of childhood encopresis: full cleanliness training. *Mental Retardation*, **13**, 14–16.

Essen, J. and Peckham, C. (1976) Nocturnal enuresis in childhood. *Developmental Medicine and Child Neurology*, **18**, 577–89.

Fergusson, D.M., Horwood, L.J. and Shannon, F.T. (1986) Factors relating to the age of attainment of nocturnal bladder control: an 8-year longitudinal study. *Paediatrics*, **78**, 884–90.

Landman, G.B., Levine, M.D. and Rappoport, L. (1983) A study of treatment resistance among children referred for encopresis. *Clinical Paediatrics*, **23**, 499–505.

Levine, M.D. (1975) Children with encopresis: a descriptive analysis. *Paediatrics*, **56**, 412–16.

Levine, M.D. (1983) Encopresis. In M.D. Levine, W.B. Carey, A.C. Crocker and R.T. Gross (eds) *Developmental Behavioural Paediatrics*. Philadelphia: W.B. Saunders, pp. 586–95.

McGee, R., Makinson, T., Williams, S. *et al.* (1984) A longitudinal study of enuresis from five to nine years. *Australian Paediatric Journal*, **20**, 39–42.

Moffat, M.E., Kato, C. and Pless, R.B. (1987) Improvements in self-concept after treatment of nocturnal enuresis: a randomised control trial. *Journal of Paediatrics*, **110**, 647–52.

Robertson, J. (1952) *A Two Year Old Goes to Hospital* (film). Ipswich: Concord Films Council.

Rutter, M., Yule, W. and Graham, P. (1973). Enuresis and behavioural deviance: some epidemiological considerations. In Kolvin, I., McKeith, R. and Meadow, S.R. (eds) *Bladder Control and Enuresis*. Clinics in Developmental Medicine, nos. 48–9. London: Heinemann/Spastics International Medical Publications.

Schaffer, D., Gardner, A. and Hedge, B. (1984) Behaviour and bladder disturbance in enuresis: the rational classification of a common disorder. *Developmental Medicine and Child Neurology*, **26**, 781–92.

Schmitt, B.D. (1986) New enuresis alarms: safe, successful and child operable. *Contemporary Paediatrics*, **3**, 1–6.

CHAPTER 12

Autism, Elective Mutism and Schizophrenia

Autism

Autism was thought to be a rare condition, with about 2–4 children in every 10,000 being affected. However, there has been a recent increase and more children are being diagnosed as being on the autistic continuum, with figures of between 10 to 20 children per 10,000 showing some autistic traits (Bryson *et al.*, 1988).

Frith (1991) describes autism as a disorder of communication, socialization and imagination. A fundamental problem is that autistic individuals find it almost impossible to establish emotional contact with others. As a result they are cut off from the normal processes of growth and development through relationships and are also cut off from the outer world to varying degrees. Partly because of difficulties in understanding other people, these children tend to withdraw for protection into their own worlds, which are often mindless and empty. Boys outnumber girls by three to one.

The three main features of autism are: (1) the inability to make normal social relationships, (2) abnormal language development, and (3) repetitive interests and behaviour, including an inability to play imaginatively. Autistic disorders lie on a continuum from very severely affected children to those with milder problems who are often described as having autistic traits. For a diagnosis of autism the symptoms need to have been present before the age of 3 years.

ABNORMAL RELATIONSHIPS

One of the most obvious problems is the abnormality in relating to others. This may be present from birth but some children seem to show a period of normal development up to about 18 months, then language drops away, and the child turns away from relationships and withdraws into a seemingly empty world (Kurita, 1985).

Kanner (1943) originally described 11 children with 'autistic disturbances of affective contact'. He was particularly struck by their lack of emotional contact and commented how one little girl moved among other children like a strange being, as one moves among the pieces of furniture in a room (Hobson, 1991).

Early signs of the disorder are the lack of eye contact, the lack of pointing to show or to mean 'I want' and the lack of reciprocity in relationships (Rogers and Pennington, 1991). Projects are currently being undertaken to help health visitors recognize the very early signs, as the earlier the diagnosis is made, the better the outlook in terms of the response to treatment.

ABNORMAL LANGUAGE DEVELOPMENT

Autistic children are often late in starting to speak and when they do the pattern of language is often abnormal. The child typically does not use the words 'I' and 'you' or may confuse them and tends to copy words and phrases in a meaningless way (this is known as echoing or echolalia). The normal social responsiveness and capacity to imitate which precedes speech does not develop. There is no conversational synchrony as described by Trevarthen and Marwick (1986) and the facial expressions, nodding and gestures which usually accompany the relationship with the mother are typically absent (Le Couteur *et al.*, 1989).

About half of all autistic children do not learn to speak, particularly those who are also mentally handicapped (Rutter, 1978). The more intelligent autistic children may develop normal language but the tone of voice may be rather monotonous and lack the usual emotional inflexions. Many autistic children lie somewhere on the continuum between these two, with some language but often with limited ability to express themselves as well as having difficulty in understanding spoken language.

REPETITIVE INTERESTS, ROUTINES AND RITUALS

Stereotyped patterns of behaviour become more obvious in older nursery age children. There is typically an inability to develop imaginative or fantasy play. Toys may be spun or twirled obsessively or lined up in a meaningless and repetitive way. Some children collect stones or other hard objects and may become extremely attached to them. However, there is little capacity to develop a sequence of play, although older, more able children may develop a pattern of routines with objects or dolls (Le Couteur et al., 1989).

Many autistic children have a strong need for sameness and develop rituals in order to help them cope with the stresses of life. The rituals may take the form of rigid routines of behaviour which help them to master anxiety and feel safer. Stereotyped, repetitive movements are common such as flicking or twisting the fingers.

OTHER BEHAVIOUR ASSOCIATED WITH AUTISM

In addition to the disorder of communication, autistic children may have a whole range of other behavioural problems. These include eating difficulties, overactivity, extreme fears, poor concentration, tantrums and aggression.

AN AUTISTIC CHILD'S WORLD

It is important to recognize that autistic children in a sense, do not live in our world. They quickly withdraw into their own worlds of visual, aural or tactile sensations. These are mindless and without meaning, but are often soothing, satisfying and safe. The pull of these sensations can become quite addictive, making it even more difficult to draw the child into our world of meaning and feelings.

Autistic children have no social skills and no way of learning what is expected of them. They cannot understand other people's emotional expressions, have no concept of empathy and tend to experience other people as things. Very importantly, they need to be allowed personal space, and if this is invaded they are likely to become upset and may attack themselves or start hand-flapping.

Typically, autistic children have no sense of pain and no sense of danger, as these are cut off from awareness. They have no understanding of cause and effect and will not relate a rule learned by rote to themselves. Similarly, more able autistic children may be quite capable at the mechanics of reading but be unable to understand what they have read.

Autistic children are very vulnerable to being overwhelmed by stimuli and any input needs to be carefully modulated. It is as if autistic children have no protective skin to shield them from the impact of people, colours, light and sound.

Because of all these difficulties, autistic children often find the world a dangerous and frightening place. They use their fascinations and obsessions to control anxiety. One autistic boy had a fascination with crystals and could describe everything about them, which had the function of helping him to feel more secure and in control. Routines and rituals also serve to create a safer and known world.

The autistic child's world can be a very limited one, particularly when the child is very dependent on routines in order to feel safe. Autistic children generally need constant supervision and as a result the child's world frequently becomes the parent's world also.

EMOTIONAL CONTACT

Autistic children may show some improvement with increasing age but the fundamental difficulties remain, particularly in the area of relating to others. One young woman described how she was more interested in the sensual qualities of things than in establishing emotional contact. She gave an example of how a glinting speck of dust was more interesting to her than her companion (Williams, 1990).

Sometimes it is possible to make emotional contact but this is often very frightening for the autistic child and it takes very patient reaching out and making sense of things to start to build up an emotional base for further development. A group of child psychotherapists at the Tavistock Clinic are undertaking innovative work in this field and finding that it is possible to move many autistic children forward; in some cases there are very significant improvements (Alvarez, 1992; Reid, 1995).

PSYCHODYNAMIC THEORIES

Tustin (1981, 1986, 1990) has made an important contribution to the psychoanalytic understanding of autism while accepting that both organic and psychological factors play a part in causation. She was a pioneer in this field, but tended to work with a particular group of autistic children. She describes how these children tend to shut out all 'not me' experiences and immerse themselves in a sensation-dominated world. She sees autism as a response to a very early trauma in which children are made aware of bodily separateness before they have the psychological equipment to cope.

Meltzer (1975) describes the dismantling of the autistic child's mind, leading to states of mindlessness. Reid (1990) writes movingly of her work with an extremely withdrawn child and his gradual coming to life. Alvarez (1992) integrates modern psychoanalytic theory with new findings in infant research and brings fresh insights to the understanding of autistic children. All these workers ascribe to a multiple causation theory for autism.

BASIS OF AUTISM

In most cases both organic and psychological factors are involved. Early research on the organic side found that part of the underlying problem seemed to be a difficulty in processing information (Hermelin and O'Connor, 1970). Rutter (1983) concludes that autistic children have a cognitive deficit which results in a difficulty in processing emotional and social cues, although there is no evidence of a deficit in any one sensory system.

There is evidence which supports the view that in some cases organic factors play an important role. This includes the genetic findings, neurological signs in some cases and the frequent onset of epilepsy in later childhood (Deykin and MacMahon, 1979). However, no organic cause has been identified which would explain the complexity of the psychological findings.

Baron-Cohen (1988) has concentrated his research and thinking on the idea that autistic children have difficulty in understanding other people's mental states, by which he means their cognitive states. However, his experiments involve asking autistic children to predict what others have deduced from their observations. To do this successfully there must be some identification with the other person in order to see and think as they do. Autistic children do badly on this task; Baron-Cohen consequently describes them as lacking a 'theory of mind'.

Hobson (1989) has concentrated more on the emotional side and has shown that autistic children have a specific difficulty in reading the emotional expression in people's faces.

There is also evidence which supports the role of genetic factors in some cases, particularly where there is an inherited predisposition to learning or language difficulties (Bolton and Rutter, 1990). It has been found that 15% of autistic children's brothers and sisters have language or learning disabilities.

In order to try to bridge the gap between the organic and psychological understanding of autism it is helpful to bear in mind Alvarez's observation. She writes that although 'autism may start with some form of neurological dysfunction, its subsequent particular form of psychological deficit may need exploration and treatment in terms which take account of the child's capacity for emotional communication' (Alvarez, 1992, p. 185).

In other cases a particular innate vulnerability seems to lead some children to respond to traumatic events with autistic withdrawal. These events include very traumatic births where the life of the baby is at risk and traumatic separations in the early months. Diana seems to come into this category.

> Diana was referred when she was 2 years old for aggressive behaviour, tantrums and language delay. She had no sense of danger and did not feel pain. She would scream in an unbearable way for hours if she could not cope with a situation. She was found to have difficulites in comprehension and tended to treat other people as if they had no feelings.
>
> Diana was felt to have some autistic traits and initially treatment was undertaken by a child psychotherapist working with the mother and child together. In this case there was a history of a very traumatic birth where mother and baby nearly died.
>
> Diana was able to play in a basic way with some toy children and dinosaurs and the therapist gave meaning to her play. At the same time her mother was counselled on how to make Diana feel safe and it was explained that Diana had not been able to internalize a sufficient sense of security. Diana calmed down for the rest of the day after seeing her therapist. Gradually her play changed from the dinosaurs being in control to a series of changing scenes with the good children being kept safe from the frightening dinosaurs. She attended a group for children with language disorders and was referred to an educational psychologist for recommendations as to appropriate schooling.
>
> Diana improved following the individual work;

she started to feel pain, the tantrums stopped and her speech developed at a rapid rate. She was still difficult and demanding but had become more amenable to reason. Diana became more affectionate and responsive towards her parents but one year later she still needed additional supervision and attention and a specialized nursery placement.

TREATMENT

There is a need to try to make contact with autistic children and draw them into the outer world. Child psychotherapists are uniquely placed through their training to reach out to the autistic child and, as already noted, a group at the Tavistock Clinic are achieving some positive and hopeful results.

Special schools are often very sensitive and can be very finely tuned to ways of making contact and building on that. Other special schools use a behavioural approach and for the more severely affected children there may be a focus on teaching in very small steps by repetition and reward.

It seems clear that 'holding' as a treatment method is a forcible attempt to make contact with the child. The experience is often upsetting and exhausting for both parent and child. Child psychotherapists are similarly trying to establish contact but in a more gradual and thoughtful way, both by drawing the child out and following the child's cues.

A treatment programme needs to be established for each child, combining an appropriate educational placement, therapy with the specific aim of reaching out and making contact with the child, and support for the parents. Parents need enormous support and help in finding ways to reach their child and in building on any changes for the better.

OUTCOME

There is the possibility of improvement, particularly for those children with an early diagnosis who are given specialist treatment by a child psychotherapist. As Alvarez (1992) points out, clinicians know that they must work with a deficit which is both emotional and cognitive.

In other cases early placement at a school which specializes in working with autistic children can also lead to improvements in some children. Good services with regard to education, family support and behavioural interventions have been found to make a real although modest difference in social outcome but, according to Howlin and Rutter (1987), the basic handicaps remain.

Some autistic children have a better outlook than others. It is likely that those children with a traumatic history have a better chance of responding to a psychotherapeutic approach.

ASPERGER'S SYNDROME

There seems fairly general agreement that this term is now used to describe a recognizable type of autistic individual who is on the more mildly affected end of the autistic continuum and who does not have obvious language delay. Several authors are suggesting that it would be helpful to differentiate different forms of autism, with Asperger's syndrome being one of these (Frith, 1991). Frith points out that it seems to make most sense to consider Asperger's syndrome as a subcategory of autism. This form is not particularly rare according to Gillberg and Gillberg (1989), who found a prevalence in Swedish children of between 10 and 26 per 10,000.

The same fundamental symptoms are involved. Often the most distressing aspect for the child and parents is the problem with understanding other people. This limits the child in the crucial area of making friends and developing a normal social life.

Frith (1991) postulates that the main feature of children given the diagnosis of Asperger's syndrome is that they are able to speak fluently by the age of 5 years, even if their speech has a few oddities. Some of these children show great improvements with age even though they may have displayed severe autistic symptoms as toddlers. As they grow older the children may show an increasing interest in other people but they tend to remain socially inept. By adolescence they may realize that they are different and have to face a growing awareness that there is a whole range of relationships from which they are excluded.

Children with Asperger's syndrome usually come within the normal range of intelligence and may be able to attend a normal school but it can be a difficult and stressful experience.

Frith (1989) has put forward the hypothesis that an important underlying deficit in autism has to do with a lack of coherence. Autistic people may learn many facts but their knowledge often seems oddly fragmented and they fail to integrate experience and knowledge in a meaningful way. Her theory addresses these difficulties.

Children with Asperger's syndrome may have quite violent outbursts and some can show a very cruel streak (Asperger, 1944).

Outcome

In adult life there may be continuing improvement in that some individuals with Asperger's syndrome show a reasonably good social adaptation and may be very successful, particularly the more able group. However, many remain egocentric, eccentric and isolated (Volkmar, 1987). They may manage routine social interactions but are unable to make close relationships (Frith, 1991).

THE TEACHER'S ROLE

The majority of autistic children will be diagnosed before starting school and are likely to be placed in special schools. It is unlikely that an undiagnosed autistic child will be found within a normal school, although it is possible. One nursery school teacher did approach me for advice as she thought she had such a child and from her description this clearly was the case. The advice is to involve a child psychiatrist and educational psychologist as a matter of urgency.

A mildly autistic child may be able to manage within an ordinary school, as autistic disorders lie on a spectrum with the difficulties in relationships and communication merging into more commonly seen personality traits. The child may well need careful supervision to protect him or her from bullying. Sometimes there is a flexible arrangement with the child being based in a special school but coming into ordinary school for certain lessons.

It is extremely helpful if the teacher can be part of a caring network around the child, together with the rest of the team, which may include the speech therapist, paediatrician, psychiatrist, educational psychologist, social worker and, if possible, child psychotherapist.

Elective mutism (or selective mutism)

Elective mutism is a rare condition where the child is able to speak in certain situations and not in others. A typical picture is of a child who speaks readily at home but who is unable to speak to anyone outside, except to very close relatives. Clearly such a condition gives rise to special problems within a school setting. The children themselves are often very adept at finding ways around the problem by getting other children or brothers or sisters to speak for them.

In fact these children have little control over their ability to speak in more public situations. The term elective mutism does them a disservice by implying a decision or choice when in reality children with this condition are simply unable to speak. In recognition of this the condition has recently been renamed selective mutism (Bishop, 1994).

In some circumstances it is difficult for parents and teachers not to become angry when faced with a child who just cannot speak in school, and there is a temptation to try to force the issue. However, anger is not a helpful approach and only serves to drive children further into themselves.

Fortunately this is a rare condition, with eight children in every 10,000 being affected; girls outnumber boys.

CAUSAL FACTORS

The condition is frequently associated with other speech problems such as a stammer or a difficulty in articulation. There are often family and genetic influences, with one parent being particularly shy and withdrawn. The affected children tend to show abnormal temperamental features (Kolvin and Fundudis, 1981), being quiet, shy and rather withdrawn but also with a stubborn streak.

Elective mutism is also seen more commonly where the parent's first language is different from that of the child's (Bradley and Sloman, 1975; Brown and Lloyd, 1975). Apart from speech and personality factors, a further causative factor is related to trauma. A number of children develop this condition following a traumatic event.

ONSET

In general, the parents first become aware that there is a problem when the child starts at nursery or at infant school. Until that time the child's development has usually been normal apart from perhaps some slight speech difficulty or delay. It is important to distinguish this from transient mutism, which quite commonly occurs when a young child first starts school and lasts for up to six months (Brown and Lloyd, 1975). Transient mutism is the child's way of dealing with severe anxieties about school and separating from mother. Once the child feels more secure and settled he or she will start to talk quite normally whereas the electively mute child will remain silent.

Before making the diagnosis the child's hearing, speech and comprehension need to be confirmed as normal. One way of checking these can be by asking the parents to bring in a recording of the child speaking and engaging in a conversation at home. Sanjay's story illustrates many of the typical features of this condition.

> Sanjay was a 7-year-old who had not spoken since starting infant school. Throughout this time he had communicated by means of his sister, who had spoken for him. He was a quiet, shy, rather withdrawn although stubborn child whose parents came from the Indian subcontinent.
>
> On starting junior school Sanjay was offered weekly psychotherapy sessions with a child psychotherapist. In the first few sessions he conveyed a terrible sense of being stuck. However, in the fourth session he managed to whisper into a toy telephone and this proved to be a turning point. From here Sanjay continued to make gradual progress until six months later he was talking for himself within the classroom and around the school generally.
>
> However, once Sanjay began to speak it became obvious that he had a severe stammer. Fortunately, he was also offered speech therapy and was able to benefit from this although he still stammered when under stress.

OUTCOME

Studies show that elective mutism is difficult to treat (Kolvin and Fundudis, 1981). Behavioural methods have been tried with some success. One 7-year-old girl was enabled to whisper to her teacher using a reward system and much persistence but she did not progress beyond this point. The outlook is known to be poor if the child is not speaking by the age of 10 years (Kolvin and Fundudis, 1981).

Affected children have not been followed systematically into adult life. Some patients have been found to have difficulty making relationships, and were quite solitary and abnormally withdrawn as adults. The outcome was found to be poorer in families where parents had personality problems (Kolvin and Fundudis, 1981). Anecdotally, one woman was still suffering as an adult and was totally unable to speak outside her home; she also had quite a severe personality disorder. There is no doubt that it is potentially a very handicapping condition.

ROLE OF THE TEACHER

Children who cannot speak present great problems for a teacher; they cannot read to the teacher, ask or answer questions. It is difficult to assess their learning or for them to take part in normal classroom activities. One electively mute little girl managed to get a large group of children running around her, which was disruptive to the whole class. It is important to refer the child for specialist help. In these cases a child psychiatric team is the most appropriate agency, as they can offer a range of treatment approaches. A combination of behavioural methods in the classroom, individual psychotherapy and work with the family is most likely to succeed.

Schizophrenia

Schizophrenia is extremely rare in children but the diagnosis can be made using very similar criteria to those used for adults. The usual age of onset is in late adolescence or early adulthood. Some children may experience an acute onset of disturbance but the more typical picture is one of gradual deterioration on the basis of previous long-term impairment.

Children with schizophrenia tend to show difficulties in adjustment before the onset of more acute symptoms; they often have difficulties with relationships, few interests, poor academic achievement and poor adaptation to school.

There is no evidence of an increased risk of schizophrenia in children with autism. Studies have shown that children with schizophrenia often have developmental delays, including language abnormalities and delays, delayed motor development and a lack of social responsiveness in infancy (Asarnow, 1994).

CLINICAL FEATURES

Characteristically, schizophrenia follows a pattern of acute symptoms followed by remission, sometimes with an underlying slow deterioration in thinking and behaviour. The onset may be sudden with overt disturbance, hallucinations and abnormalities in thinking or it may be more gradual. A slow onset manifests with a falling away of interest and of the ability to learn, low mood and anxiety accompanied by social withdrawal.

Either way there tends to be a gradual impoverishment of the personality and increasing isolation. The child or young person's behaviour may be odd, suspicious, disruptive and at times aggressive. There is a particular risk of suicide attempts in young men in the early stages of the illness.

Symptoms are often divided into two groups described as positive and negative.

Positive symptoms
1. Delusions: these are false beliefs such as the conviction that people are spying on the patient (persecutory delusions).
2. Passivity phenomena: these are experiences which convince patients that some outside influence is operating on them, such as the belief that the radio is controlling their thoughts. This may be described as a delusion of control.
3. Hallucinations: these are sensory perceptions with no outside stimulus. Patients may hear voices, for instance, giving a running commentary on what they are doing

when there is no one there. The voices may tell them to carry out specific actions.

4. Abnormal mood states: anxiety and depression are common. More specific symptoms are the blunting of feelings of abnormal mood states.

5. Disorder of movement: odd mannerisms may be present, especially with the chronic form of the disorder.

6. Thought disorder: this is primarily a disorder of language. It may present as a vague way of talking in which the links between different subjects are loosened, making it almost impossible to follow the meaning. In more serious cases there is very fragmented speech with made-up words which is totally incomprehensible.

7. Thought alienation: this refers to the experience of external interference with thinking, such as feeling that outside thoughts have been inserted into one's mind or that thoughts have been taken away or broadcast. The blocking of thoughts may also be experienced or observed.

The above symptoms occur in young people and adults most typically, whereas children may show changeable, impulsive and overactive behaviour or socially inappropriate behaviour such as exposing themselves, shouting and swearing.

The negative syndrome

This can occur in children as well as adults. There is either a gradual onset or it can follow repeated relapses into illness with incomplete recovery. The picture is one of gradual withdrawal, loss of interest and motivation and a progressive blunting of the feelings and emotional responsiveness. Alan and Angela demonstrate two different types of onset.

> Alan was aged 11 when he suddenly began to behave in a bizarre manner, never staying still and talking nonsense. He would rush round the room, stand on his head or try to jump out of the moving car. All investigations were negative and a diagnosis of childhood schizophrenia was made.

Angela was also given the same diagnosis but her illness started when she was about 9. There was a gradual onset over one year with a falling off of her school work and withdrawal from her friends. It was a very difficult diagnosis to make because of the slow deterioration and the teacher's observations were extremely helpful.

Alan, who had more positive symptoms, responded well to phenothiazine medication, whereas Angela, who had an insidious onset with negative symptoms, showed little response.

TREATMENT

In general, the earlier treatment is started, the better the response. Medication is always necessary and usually one of the phenothiazine group of drugs is used in the first instance. Phenothiazines and the other anti-psychotic drugs are thought to have a specific effect on positive symptoms. However, they may not influence negative symptoms or be able to prevent a slow deterioration. There are very few publications on the treatment of childhood schizophrenia, although at present studies are being undertaken on the use of clozapine in these patients.

Admission to hospital is almost always necessary in order to limit the effects of the disturbed behaviour and to initiate treatment. There is evidence that hostility, criticism and over-involvement (expressed emotion) from the family serve to increase the risk of relapse. It has been shown with adult patients that the risk of relapse can be dramatically reduced by social skills training and the reduction of expressed emotion (EE) by the family (Hogarty et al., 1991).

A definite association between high EE and relapse of schizophrenia was demonstrated by Bebbington and Kuipers (1994), who feel that the protective effect of low-EE families is an under-researched area. In any case, work with the family will need to be undertaken in order to support them through the illness and after discharge.

CAUSE

There is a genetic component to schizophrenic illness, with the risk to first-degree relatives being around 5%. It seems likely that many genes are involved and these genes act in an additive way with adverse environmental factors.

Organic factors have been found in some schizophrenics, such as enlarged cerebral ventricles and a reduction in size of the brain. There is an increase in the number of complications at birth in schizophrenics as compared to a normal population.

Biochemical factors have been implicated because of the improvement in symptoms following dopamine-blocking drugs. It is likely that other neurotransmitters also play a part.

OUTCOME

An early onset before 10 years of age usually carries a poor outlook and tends towards a deteriorating course. Almost 70% of affected children show continuing schizophrenia or schizo-affective disorder as they pass through adolescence into adult life.

A good outcome is associated with an older age group, a sudden onset, a stable previous personality and higher intelligence. A better outcome is generally found in the developing world. Approximate outcome rates are as follows: 25% make a full recovery, 50% end up with a chronic fluctuating illness, 15% have continuous symptoms requiring treatment and 10% are left with severe incapacity.

References and further reading

Alvarez, A. (1992) *Live Company*. London: Routledge.
Asarnow, J.R. (1994) Annotation: childhood-onset schizophrenia. *Journal of Child Psychology and Psychiatry*, **35**, 1345–71.

Asperger, H. (1944) Die 'Autistischen Psychopathen' im Kindersalter. *Archive fur Psychiatrie und Nervenkrankheiten*, **117**, 76–136.

Baron-Cohen, S. (1988) Social and pragmatic defects in autism: cognitive or affective? *Journal of Autistic Development and Disorder*, **18**, 3.

Bebbington, P. and Kuipers, L. (1994) The predictive utility of expressed emotion in schizophrenia: an aggregate analysis. *Psychological Medicine*, **24**, 707–18.

Bishop, D. (1994) Developmental disorders of speech and language. In M. Rutter, E. Taylor and L. Hersov (eds) *Child and Adolescent Psychiatry: Modern Approaches*. Oxford: Blackwell Scientific Publications, pp. 546–68.

Bolton, P. and Rutter, M. (1990) Genetic influence in autism. *International Review of Psychiatry*, **2**, 67.

Bradley, S. and Sloman, L. (1975) Elective mutism in immigrant families. *Journal of the American Academy of Child Psychiatry*, **14**, 510–14.

Brown, J.B. and Lloyd, H. (1975) A controlled study of children not speaking at school. *Journal of Association of Workers with Maladjusted Children*, **3**, 49–63.

Bryson, S.E., Clark, B.S. and Smith, T.M. (1988) First report of a Canadian epidemiological study of autistic syndromes. *Journal of Child Psychology and Psychiatry*, **29**, 433–45.

Deykin, E.Y. and MacMahon, B. (1979) The incidence of seizures among children with autistic symptoms. *American Journal of Psychiatry*, **136**, 1310.

Frith, U. (1989) *Autism: Explaining the Enigma*. Oxford: Blackwell.

Frith, U. (1991) *Autism and Asperger Syndrome*. Cambridge: Cambridge University Press.

Gillberg, I.C. and Gillberg, C. (1989) Asperger syndrome – some epidemiological considerations: a research note. *Journal of Child Psychology and Psychiatry*, **30**, 631–8.

Hermelin, B. and O'Connor N. (1970) *Psychological Experiments with Autistic Children*. New York: Pergamon Press.

Hobson, P. (1989) Beyond cognition: a theory of autism. In G. Dawson (ed) *Autism: Nature, Diagnosis and Treatment*. New York: Guilford.

Hobson, P. (1991) What is autism? *Psychiatric Clinics of North America*, **14** (1), 1–17.

Hogarty, G., Anderson, C., Reiss, D. *et al.* (1991) Family psychoeducation, social skills training and maintenance chemotherapy in the aftercare treatment of schizophrenia. II. Two-year effects. *Archives of General Psychiatry*, **48**, 340–7.

Howlin, P. and Rutter, M. (1987) *Treatment of Autistic Children*. Chichester: John Wiley.

Kanner, L. (1943) Autistic disturbances of affective contact. *Nervous Child*, **2**, 217–50.

Kolvin, I. and Fundudis, T. (1981) Elective mute children; psychological development and background factors. *Journal of Child Psychology and Psychiatry*, **22**(1), 219–32.

Kurita, H. (1985) Infantile autism with speech loss before the age of 30 months. *Journal of the American Academy of Child and Adolescent Psychiatry*, **24**, 191–6.

Le Couteur, A., Rutter, M., Lord, C., Rios, P. *et al.* (1989) Autism diagnostic interview: a semi-structural interview for parents and care-givers of autistic persons. *Journal of Autism and Developmental Disorders*, **19**, 363–87.

Meltzer, D. (1975) *Explorations in Autism: A Psycho-Analytic Study*. Strath Tay: Clunie.

Reid, S. (1990) The importance of beauty in the psychoanalytic experience. *Journal of Child Psychotherapy*, **16**, 29–52.

Reid, S. (1995) Frances Tustin Memorial Lecture. Tavistock Clinic, London, 11 February.

Rogers, S. and Pennington, B. (1991) A theoretical approach to the deficits in infantile autism. *Development and Psychopathology*, **3**, 137–62.

Rutter, M. (1978) Language disorder and infantile autism. In M. Rutter and E. Schopler (eds) *Autism: A Reappraisal of Concepts and Treatment*. New York: Plenum Press, pp. 85–104.

Rutter, M. (1983) Cognitive deficits in the pathogenesis of autism. *Journal of Child Psychology and Psychiatry*, **24**, 513–32.

Trevarthan, C. and Marwick, H. (1986) Signs of motivation for speech in infants and the nature of a mother's support for the development of language. In B. Lindblom and R. Zetterstrom (eds) *Precursors of Early Speech*. Basingstoke, Hants: Macmillan, pp. 279–308.

Tustin, F. (1981) *Autistic States in Children*. London: Routledge and Kegan Paul.

Tustin, F. (1986) *Autistic Barriers in Neurotic Patients*. London: Karnac.

Tustin, F. (1990) *The Protective Shell in Children and Adults*. London: Karnac.

Volkmar, F.R. (1987) Social Development. In D.J. Cohen, A.M. Donnellan and R. Paul (eds) *Handbook of Autism and Pervasive Developmental Disorders*. New York: Wiley, pp. 41–61.

Williams, D. (1990) *Nobody Nowhere*. London: Corgi.

Williams, D. (1994) *Somebody Somewhere*. London: Corgi.

CHAPTER 13

Chronic Fatigue Syndrome, Tics, Hairpulling, Sleep Disorders

Chronic fatigue syndrome

Fortunately this is a rare disorder in childhood and adolescence but when it occurs the effects can be devastating for the sufferers and their families. The child may be severely incapacitated for months or even years. An alternative name, which is less favoured by doctors, is myalgic encephalitis (ME).

The cause is not known (Thomas, 1993), which has resulted in considerable misinformation about the disorder. However, it is generally accepted that both physical and psychological factors are involved. The overall prevalence of people who suffer from excessive fatigue is estimated at one in 150,000 (Wallace, 1991).

As the name suggests, the main symptom is an overwhelming and debilitating loss of energy, so much so that every movement becomes a tremendous effort. Children are unable to attend school and adults may be so seriously affected that they are unable to work and are dependent on carers. As Wessely (1994) aptly points out, chronic fatigue syndrome (CFS) is a disorder of our times. It quite frequently starts following a viral illness, and a hypothesis accepted by many British doctors is that the symptoms are due to reactivation of a virus which may then be followed by a secondary dysfunction of the immune system. The range of associated symptoms are varied and include sleep disturbances, muscle pain, depression, emotional lability and gastrointestinal disturbances. All these can be successfully treated despite doubts about influencing the underlying, core problem.

There are psychological components to the syndrome

which need to be identified and treated. These generally respond to a combined approach, taking into account the whole complex of symptoms.

If possible it is most helpful for treatment to be overseen by a doctor with an interest in the disorder. The basic philosophy is that the illness is a real and treatable condition and one from which patients can recover given the right information, management and treatment (Cox and Findley, 1993). The most effective treatment to date consists of graded activity (often with the support of a physiotherapist), cognitive behaviour therapy and drugs. The young person will eventually recover and it is important to provide support which facilitates the appropriate modifications of lifestyle necessary in order to promote recovery. Although fluoxetine (an anti-depressant) seems to be the drug of choice (Goodnick and Klimas, 1993), drugs used alone invariably fail.

> Tracy, a 15-year-old girl, had a mild viral illness which was followed by a sudden major loss of energy. At first she could hardly move at all and was totally unable to attend school. She became depressed and stressed as well as having to suffer forced inactivity.
>
> She was treated by a sympathetic doctor with careful explanation of the disorder, graded exercise, cognitive therapy to counter her negative thinking and fluoxetine medication. Tracy started by attending school on the days when she felt able for one to two hours and gradually built up as her energy improved. The process of recovery took one year.

THE TEACHER'S ROLE

It is important for teachers to realize that this is a recognized condition and that sufferers need every support and encouragement. The affected young person may lose considerable time from school and it is essential that flexible arrangements are made to accommodate to the youngster's limited lifestyle during the process of recovery. It may be necessary to send work home or allow a flexible pattern of attendance.

Tics and Gilles de la Tourette syndrome

TICS

Tics are defined as purposeless, frequently repeated involuntary movements which often affect the upper part of the body, taking the form of repeated blinking, shoulder-shrugging or grimacing. Simple tics are those which are short-lived whereas the more persistent form are known as chronic tics.

Simple tics, like obsessions, may start as ways of coping with anxiety and are similar to the slight twitches many people experience when feeling ill at ease or tense. They are much more common in younger children and tend to improve with age. It is estimated that between 10% and 24% of all children will develop tics at some time in their lives but this is usually a passing phase. In many but not all instances, anxiety will be a factor and it is often most helpful to work on alleviating the anxiety.

Many tics will disappear spontaneously and should be ignored. More disabling or persistent tics will often respond to a combination of behavioural techniques, medication (haloperidol preferably or pimozide in low dosage) together with psychotherapeutic support. Medication should only be used for severe cases when all other methods have failed. The most useful behavioural methods are muscle relaxation training and planned intentional repetition of the tics, which is known as massed practice (Robertson, 1989).

The outlook for simple tics is generally good but there are a few children where the tics become more persistent and widespread at the age of 10 or 11 years. In about 1% of children the tics become persistent and continue into adult life.

GILLES DE LA TOURETTE SYNDROME

Tourette syndrome (TS) is the name given to a hereditary neurological and behavioural disorder which manifests most frequently with motor and vocal tics. The motor tics vary from very rapid jerks to slow stretching movements. The vocal tics may take the form of repeated swear words, but can be any human noise uttered repetitively. These may vary from a sniff or throat clearing to a loud animal noise.

Gilles de la Tourette was a French neurologist who first described the condition. It almost always starts in childhood, with the first movements appearing between the ages of 5 and 9 years. These are sometimes thought to be put on but they are truly beyond voluntary control. The early tics usually involve the face and shoulders and may progress to more complicated arm, leg and body movements. The presence of vocal tics confirms the diagnosis.

Involuntary swearing, known as coprolalia, occurs in about 30% of patients. This is not naughty behaviour and is beyond the child's control. Although the tics are involuntary, sufferers may be able to suppress the symptoms for short periods. This leads to a build-up of internal tension which is then broken by a renewed outburst of tics. Anything which increases the child's anxiety is likely to make the tics worse.

Many young people with TS may have learning difficulties, difficulties in concentration, overactivity or poor memory. Some may also have obsessive or racing thoughts, compulsive behaviour and severe examination anxiety. There is a strong association between TS, obsessive-compulsive states and difficulties with concentration (attention deficit disorders).

Treatment is very similar as that for persistent tics, with medication being an important factor (haloperidol, pimozide or sulpiride). Pimozide has been associated with sudden death, which makes haloperidol the treatment of choice in the first instance. Extrapyramidal side-effects are common with haloperidol and need to be countered with procyclidine. Approximately 70% of TS patients respond well to either haloperidol or pimozide (Shapiro *et al.*, 1989).

Explanation and support for the parents is essential. In addition, children with TS may also have educational and psychological problems which will need addressing.

The outcome for tic disorder is usually good, with the tics at their worst between 9 and 15 years and thereafter improving. The outcome for TS varies, but some young people have their symptoms very well controlled using medication and behavioural methods. Others have more continuing problems and need long-term monitoring and support. Many adults settle into a stable pattern of symptoms which come and go over a milder range of severity (Bruun, 1988).

THE TEACHER'S ROLE

The teacher may be the first to recognize the symptom. Clearly, any suspected case needs a medical referral and the teacher can facilitate this. Once the condition is diagnosed, the teacher's attitude can be very helpful by fostering a sense of acceptance and normality within the school.

It is important to create an atmosphere of understanding within the classroom and to make sure all staff are aware of the condition. The child needs to be treated as normally as possible.

Some children with TS need to let off tension in the form of tics and repressed emotion which may have built up while they were suppressing the symptoms. It is helpful if they can be allowed to leave the class when necessary and have a quiet area for when they are going through a difficult time.

Hair-pulling (trichotillomania)

This is a rare disorder where children persistently pull or twist out their own hair, leaving bald patches, and may also pull out their eyelashes. The cause is not fully understood and it has been suggested that there are links with obsessional disorder. It seems to be a form of self-destructive behaviour and in certain cases is clearly related to stress.

The hair-pulling quickly becomes a habit and the children are often unaware of what they are doing. Once the behaviour becomes established it is often very difficult to treat. Jason's story shows how the hair-pulling can develop as a response to overwhelming stress in an already vulnerable child.

> Jason, a 12-year-old with learning difficulties, was attending a special unit within an ordinary school. He had difficulties with relationships and problems with concentration, and found school stressful. His parents then suddenly separated and he had to leave his home. Jason was more vulnerable because of his learning difficulties and the stress resulted in Jason pulling out his hair to such an extent that there were bald patches.
>
> Fortunately he was referred quite quickly and by relieving the stress at school through liaison with his excellent form teacher and at home through work with mother, Jason was rapidly enabled to stop the hair-pulling.

Treatment is not usually so easy or effective. Behavioural methods have been tried with some success and more recently medication with clomipramine has been described as useful when other methods fail (Swedo *et al.*, 1989; Swedo and Rapoport, 1991). A combination of psychological support, relief of any stress and behavioural methods is the first line of treatment.

Sleep disorders

Common and distressing problems in the toddler years are difficulty in settling and waking in the night or early morning. All these generally respond well to a behavioural approach which aims to help the child develop a more acceptable sleep pattern (Douglas and Richman, 1984).

Psychotherapeutic interventions are also very effective, working with the baby or toddler and the parents together. The work involves taking in the mother's anxieties and understanding how the parents' past experiences may be causing difficulties in the present (Daws, 1989). This approach frequently enables the parents to settle their child.

Medication is generally contraindicated but sometimes short-term medication may be necessary in order to give the parents some relief in a crisis, using a drug such as chloral (Prendergast, 1993). It is important to avoid benzodiazepines, as they can cause behavioural problems in children. Ferber (1989) provides general advice for parents.

Nightmares and night terrors

Nightmares often occur as a response to a frightening event. If they continue, the child willl need further investigation and treat ient, initially via the family doctor. It is well known that nightmares form part of post-traumatic stress disorder and often follow sexual abuse.

Night terrors, sleep-walking and sleep-talking may be related to stress but in many cases there is no obvious cause. Where stress is present, if the source can be removed and the family reassured these sleep disorders frequently resolve (Parkes, 1985).

A child who wakes up frightened after a nightmare needs to be comforted but parents should not waken a child during a sleep terror or during an agitated sleep-walking episode (Stores, 1990). In both these situations the child is deeply asleep and waking may well increase the child's disturbance.

In cases where the sleep disturbance occurs at a reasonably predictable time each night, Lask (1988) suggests waking the child for a few minutes just before the expected time. Medication is not usually necessary or recommended for these conditions.

If the problems persist or if there is evidence of psycho-logical disturbance, further assessment may be necessary. Night-time epileptic attacks are rare but may be suspected if the episode includes stiffening or jerking of the face or limbs or if the child wakes at the start and describes strange sensa-tions (Stores, 1990). In these circumstances a full investigation for epilepsy should be arranged.

Useful addresses

The National Charity for Chronic Fatigue Syndrome
Harold Wood Hospital
Romford
Essex

Tourette Syndrome (UK) Association
169, Wickam Street
Welling
Kent DA16 3BS

References

Bruun, R.D. (1988) The natural history of Tourette's syndrome. In D.J. Dohen, R.D. Bruun and J.F. Leckman (eds) *Tourette's Syndrome and Tic Disorders*. New York: Wiley.
Cox, D. and Findley, L. (1993) Chronic fatigue syndrome. *British Medical Journal*, **307**, 328.
Daws, D. (1989) *Through the Night*. London: Free Association Books.
Douglas, J. and Richman, N. (1984) *My Child Won't Sleep*. Harmondsworth: Penguin.
Ferber, R. (1989) *Solve Your Child's Sleep Problems*. London: Dorling Kindersley.
Goodnick, P. and Klimas, N. (eds) (1993) *Chronic Fatigue and Related Immune Deficiency Syndromes*. Washington DC: American Psychi-atric Press.

Lask. B. (1988) Novel and non-toxic treatment for night terrors. *British Medical Journal*, **297**, 592.

Parkes, J.D. (1985) *Sleep and its Disorders*. London: WG Saunders.

Prendergast, M. (1993) Drug treatment. In M.E. Garralda (ed.) *Managing Children with Psychiatric Problems*. London: BMJ Publishing Group, pp. 85–101.

Robertson, M. (1989) The Gilles de la Tourette syndrome. Current status. *British Journal of Psychiatry*, **154**, 147–70.

Shapiro, E.S., Shapiro, A.K., Fulop, S. *et al.* (1989) Controlled study of haloperidol, pimozide and placebo for the treatment of Gilles de la Tourette syndrome. *Archives of General Psychiatry*, **46**, 722.

Stores, G. (1990) Sleep disorders in children. *British Medical Journal*, **301**, 351–2.

Swedo, S.E. and Rapoport, J.L. (1991) Trichotillomania. *Journal of Child Psychology and Psychiatry*, **32**, 401–9.

Swedo, S., Leonard, H., Rappoport, J. *et al.* (1989) Clomipramine versus desmethylimipramine treatment of trichotillomania: a double-blind crossover comparison. *New England Journal of Medicine*, **321**, 497–501.

Thomas, P.K. (1993) The chronic fatigue syndrome: what do we know? *British Medical Journal*, **306**, 1557–8.

Wallace, P.G. (1991) Epidemiology: a critical review. *British Medical Bulletin*, **47**, 942–51.

Wessely, S. (1994) Review: chronic fatigue and related immune deficiency syndromes. *British Journal of Psychiatry*, **150**, 276.

CHAPTER 14
Conclusion: Hopes for the Future

Children are the country's hope for the future, growing up to form the next generation. We clearly need to invest in our children, and perhaps above all in their emotional and mental health.

Children grow in families and this means supporting parents both financially and emotionally in their difficult task of bringing up children.

Socio-economic factors have a definite effect on children's mental and physical health, with children from the more affluent middle-class backgrounds being much healthier on all parameters. Social and emotional deprivation has a very destructive effect on children and families, often leading to increased levels of aggressiveness. Aggression in childhood has strikingly long-term effects (Goodyer, 1993) in terms of adverse effects on adult social adjustment and relationships.

All adult psychiatric disorders are increased as the number of behavioural symptoms before the age of 15 years rises. There are higher rates of criminality, poorer job histories and more violent deaths (Goodyer, 1993). Conduct disorder is common, is related to disadvantaged families and has pervasive long-term effects. These are important public health problems to which too few resources are given. Apart from government-led strategies to reduce poverty and unemployment, there are well-established preventative measures which could be undertaken given the necessary mental health resources.

The main interventions are related to improving parenting through long-term support, education, increasing parents' responsiveness to their children and offering respite care. Many agencies are involved, including health, education, social services and the voluntary agencies. The knowledge is there but not the necessary resources.

Many schools are making a major contribution to children's mental health by providing a stable, caring and positive environment. However, teachers are under increasing stress and need more support and resources to continue to encourage and work with difficult, vulnerable children.

In 1995 large sums of money are being spent on building more secure units and prisons. This approach to rising crime ignores the sound research evidence which shows that the roots of crime lie in social disadvantage, poor parenting and inequality of opportunity. It would be of greater benefit to society to concentrate these resources through planned multi-disciplinary working on providing enormous support to disadvantaged under-fives and their families.

The state of the child mental health services varies from area to area but there are some worrying trends where well-established and well-functioning teams are being cut or threatened with closure (Hankin, 1993). This does not make sense in terms of effective planning with the aim of improving the mental health of our children. Child and family mental health services play a crucial role in treatment and in preventative services and are relatively inexpensive compared to the cost of new secure units.

The majority of children and young people who do reach children's mental health services can be helped. There are grounds for hope in that at least something can be done to improve the situation.

References

Goodyer, I. (1993) Continuities and discontinuities from childhood to adult life. In D. Black and D. Cottrell (eds) *Seminars in Child and Adolescent Psychiatry*. London: Gaskell, pp. 276–90.

Hankin, J. (1993) Child and family mental health services: the struggle continues. *Young Minds Newsletter*, No. 16, 2–4.

The Children Act 1989

The Children Act 1989 is the most important change of law concerning children in this century. It sets out to simplify the rules in relation to children covering both private and public law. To do this it encompasses private disputes between parents about the future of their children, and public child care law dealing with services to prevent family breakdown and with child protection, and incorporates those children with disabilities previously covered by health and welfare legislation.

Its aims are to strengthen and consolidate the rights of children as well as to increase parental responsibility. For instance, it is now required that medical and nursing staff obtain children's consent before carrying out any examination.

The Act has come about in the context of a government which believes in lessening the state's powers to intervene in and regulate family life. The Act signifies a change from the view that public concern for children requires a legal response. The philosophy behind the Children Act clearly indicates a belief that this is less necessary. Underlying this is the conviction that professionals have to be more explicit about their actions, more accountable to clients and less reliant on legal sanctions (Adcock, 1991).

The assumptions behind the concept of parental responsibility have considerable implications for practice. The Act makes clear that parents have the responsibility for bringing up their children and the state's main role is to help rather than intervene. Changes have already come about as a result of the Act, such as a reduction in the numbers of children being accommodated by the local authority. It has also become more difficult to protect children by removing them permanently from very emotionally damaging homes.

Resources need to be made available to implement the Act and in some areas there is an acute shortage of money which severely limits its usefulness. It is hoped that the Act will be used creatively for the welfare of children. The details are complex and only the main provisions are summarized here.

Appendix 1

Principles guiding the courts

Children come first
The welfare of children must be the overriding consideration in all decisions. To ensure this, the Act lays down a checklist of factors which must be taken into account:

1. the child's own wishes, as far as these are possible to ascertain, taking into account the child's age and understanding;
2. the child's physical, emotional and educational needs;
3. the likely effect of any change;
4. any harm which the child has suffered or might suffer in the future;
5. the capabilities of the parents to meet the child's needs (Department of Health, 1991).

Families matter
A major principle of the Act is that families are the best place for the upbringing of children. This means that the court will only make an order when it is satisfied that to do so is clearly better for the child than making no order.

Delays must be avoided
Children's emotional development is very vulnerable to stress and insecurity. Time is not on their side. The court now has to set a timetable and ensure that the case is heard quickly.

Flexibility
Courts have more flexibility; they do not have to grant the order requested and can now make a different order.

Private law orders

Private law applies to children whose parents are separating or divorcing. When parents cannot agree about the welfare of their children and negotiation has failed, the next step is often to take the matter to court. The court has available a range of specific orders which it can make, depending on the best interests of the child. The type of orders concerning custody and access have been replaced by four new orders, known as Section 8 Orders. These are as follows.

Residence orders
When parents are separating or divorcing and cannot agree, the court can make a residence order stating where the child should live. It may specify how much time the child should spend with each parent.

Contact orders
This order is used when parents cannot agree over contact. This can require the person with whom the child is living to allow contact such as telephone calls, visits and overnight stays with the person named in the order.

Prohibited steps order
If one parent objects to something that the other parent is doing, it is possible to apply for this order, which can prevent the other parent from carrying out the specified action.

Specific issue orders
If parents disagree over one aspect of their child's upbringing, for instance which school the child should attend, the disagreement can be settled by a specific issue order.

Anyone who is concerned about a child's welfare can apply for a Section 8 Order but they need permission from the court to do so. In practice it is usually parents, grandparents, unmarried fathers or the LA who apply for these orders.

Additional private law orders

Parental responsibility orders
This is to cover a situation where an unmarried father cannot agree with the child's mother. He may apply for an order giving him parental responsibility for his child.

Family assistance orders
In specific cases this order may be made, requiring a LA or a court welfare officer to give a family help and support.

Public law

Public law affects children who are in need of help from the local authority (LA). The problem may be one of children becoming beyond parental control and placing themselves or others at risk. In these circumstances a social worker can be appointed to support the child and family. In other cases a child may be in danger of neglect or abuse and here the LA has a duty to protect the child.

The concept of 'significant harm' has been introduced, which suggests a higher threshold for state intervention where harm has been defined as "ill treatment or the impairment of health and development'.

The Children Act clearly expects LAs to promote the welfare of children in need within its area. However, the LA is constrained by the availability of resources and it may recommend that no order be made because the resources are not available.

The new legal concept of children in need includes children with disabilities, abused children and children suffering emotional deprivation (Bennathan, 1990).

The aim is to keep the family together and provide services in partnership with parents such as nursery places, family aides, respite care and family centres. Sometimes there are insufficient resources to provide such support and sometimes these provisions are inadequate to meet the child's need. In the latter case a variety of other public orders are available.

Supervision order

The LA applies for this order, which places the child under the supervision of a social worker. It allows for counselling and a closer monitoring of the child's development.

Education supervision orders
The local education authority (LEA) may apply for such an order when the child is not attending school regularly. An education social worker will be appointed to supervise the child.

Child assessment orders
These can be applied for by the LA if there is a possibility of neglect or abuse and the parents are refusing to co-operate with a medical or psychiatric assessment.

Very serious cases

These are cases where the LA feels that it is no longer safe for the child to remain at home. If the parents will not agree to the suggested course of action, the LA has the power to apply for a care order, an emergency protection order or a secure accommodation order.

Care order
If it is shown that a child is suffering or likely to suffer significant harm through a lack of adequate parental care or control, then the court can make a care order which places the child in the care of the LA.

Emergency protection order
In extremely urgent situations this order allows the court to place the child in the care of the LA for a maximum of eight days, with the possibility of an extension for a further seven days.

Secure accommodation orders
In extreme cases where young people are continually trying to harm themselves or others, the LA may feel that the only way to keep the situation safe is to restrict the youngster's liberty by the use of secure accommodation (Department of Health, 1991).

Gillick competent

The Children Act has established that children and young people need to be consulted over all aspects of their care. The Gillick judgement clarified that children under the age of 16 years were capable of giving full consent to treatment 'if of sufficient understanding to make an informed decision'. In this case they are deemed 'Gillick competent'. In other cases where children are not competent to give consent, the parent or guardian can do so on their behalf.

References

Adcock, M. (1991) The Children Act. *Young Minds Newsletter*, No. 7, 4–5.
Bennathan, M. (1990) The Children Act, 1989. *Young Minds Newsletter*, No. 6, 3–5.
Department of Health (1991) *The Children Act and The Courts*. Heywood, Lancs: Department of Health.

Child Mental Health Services

Many professionals are involved with children with emotional and behavioural problems. These range from highly specialized health services to less specialized health services (such as GPs) to other services (within education, for instance) whose primary purpose is not health (Department of Health, 1995). This model of care suggests that a useful way of describing services for disturbed children is in terms of tiers (Hill, 1994).

A primary level of care would include teachers, social workers, GPs, health visitors and school nurses.

The second tier describes a service provided by a single professional group which then relates to others through a network and would include clinical psychologists, educational psychologists and some child psychiatrists.

The third tier represents a specialist service for more severe, persistent and complex disorders and is usually based in a multi-disciplinary team which is led by a child psychiatrist. The team consists of a variety of professionals, including:

- child and adolescent psychiatrists;
- social workers;
- clinical psychologists;
- community psychiatric nurses;
- child psychotherapists;
- occupational therapists;
- art, music or drama therapists.

The fourth tier is formed of the essential tertiary level services such as inpatient services for children and adolescents who are severely mentally ill or at suicidal risk (Department of Health, 1995).

This is a simplified outline of a complex network of services where there is a dynamic relationship between all the different tiers.

Professionals within children's mental health services

Child and adolescent psychiatrists
Child psychiatrists are fully trained doctors who have had an additional training in both adult and child psychiatry which takes at least

six years. They have a broad training and special expertise in children's development, in understanding the causes of emotional disturbance, and in assessment of the child and family, and are aware of the range of treatment possibilities.

Child psychiatrists are able to take a broad overview of the situation and offer a comprehensive assessment service, a range of treatment approaches and discussion/liaison with other professionals, as well as taking part in training and preventative work. They see themselves as advocates for children and are able to speak out for the individual child's needs and best interests.

Child psychotherapists

Child psychotherapists are usually experienced professionals in social work, teaching or psychology before undertaking a five- to six-year additional training in child psychotherapy. They are required to go into analysis in order to understand their own unconscious processes as well as to increase their openness to others and their capacity to take in emotional pain.

In particular, child psychotherapists are trained in understanding how children feel, think and behave. This includes understanding children's non-verbal communications and unconscious motivation.

Child psychotherapists are involved in working in multi-disciplinary teams in order to assess and help children and adolescents who are distressed, disturbed and deprived at all levels of severity, and are particularly able to help the more emotionally disturbed children (Boston and Szur, 1983). They help professionals in health, education and social services to understand difficult and worrying young people, and through this understanding these other professionals are enabled to work more effectively within their own settings.

Specialist social workers

There is a long tradition of specialist social workers working within child psychiatric settings. These social workers have developed expertise in understanding and treating disturbed and dysfunctional families and in working as part of a multi-disciplinary team. They are based in a clinic but are able to undertake work in the community such as visiting families at home and liaising with other agencies.

The major part of their work is direct therapeutic and supportive work with parents and families but they are also involved in liaison with schools, social services, housing departments and mental health services as well as in welfare rights work.

Community psychiatric nurses (CPNs)
Child and adolescent CPNs provide an invaluable link between the clinic and the community. They are trained psychiatric nurses with special experience of children, normally having completed the ENB 603 course in Child, Adolescent and Family Mental Health.

CPNs are based in the clinic but have the flexibility to work in people's homes, schools and other centres in the community as the situation requires.

CPNs offer experience of child psychiatry together with a knowledge of the local community and its resources. Increasingly, children are being referred with complex emotional, health, educational and social problems, with many agencies being involved. By working closely with the various agencies, the CPN is in a position to co-ordinate a network of care, which is a prerequisite for successful therapy.

Clinical psychologists
Clinical psychologists have a degree in psychology followed by a further training in clinical psychology. Many tend to specialize in behavioural methods of treatment. Some work within a single-speciality psychology service and this is an increasing trend. Others still work in psychiatric clinics as part of the team.

Occupational therapists
Occupational therapists are often integral members of the multidisciplinary team. The range of work they offer includes individual counselling, therapeutic work with children with physical difficulties, family work, group work and support and counselling to parents and carers.

Educational services

Educational psychologists
Educational psychologists have a first degree in psychology, a teaching qualification and experience. They are required to assess children with special educational needs and advise parents and teachers as to the best way of meeting those needs. Sadly, the necessary resources are not always available.

Educational psychologists also consult with teachers to help them with the therapeutic work they undertake within the classroom as well as advising on referrals to other agencies.

The educational welfare service

Education welfare workers or, as they are now more commonly called, education social workers have no formal arrangements for training, although this may soon change. The main focus of their work is with school non-attenders and their families but they may also work with families under stress, often in a liaison capacity.

References

Boston, M. and Szur, R. (eds) (1983) *Psychotherapy with Severely Deprived Children*. London: Routledge.

Department of Health (1995) *A Handbook on Child and Adolescent Mental Health*. Oldham, Lancs: HMSO Manchester Print.

Hill, P. (1994) *Purchasing Psychiatric Care: Contribution of the Child and Adolescent Psychiatry Section*. London: Royal College of Psychiatrists.

Name Index

Name Index

Subject Index